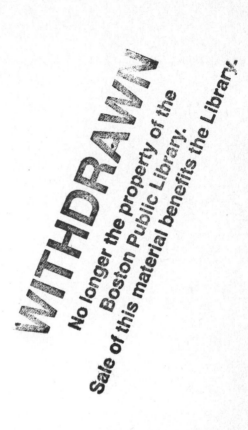

The People of England

The People of England

A Short Social and Economic History

Maurice Ashley

Louisiana State University Press
Baton Rouge

Contents

Notes are grouped at the end of each chapter

Illustrations

ILLUSTRATIONS

Norwich Market Place, 1806, by John Sell Cotman (Tate Gallery)

Boulton's and Watt's factory at Soho (British Museum)

Coalbrookdale c. 1788 (Mansell Collection)

The opening of the Liverpool to Manchester railway, 1830 (Science Museum)

The viaduct over the Sankey Canal, 1831 (Weidenfeld & Nicolson Archives)

Cartoon showing the bread riots of 1830, from Looking Glass No. 12 (Weidenfeld & Nicolson Archives)

Ascot races, from the Illustrated London News, 1844 (Weidenfeld & Nicolson Archives)

Over London by Rail, 1871, by Gustave Doré (Mansell Collection)

The Dinner Hour, Wigan, 1874, by Eyre Crowe (City Art Gallery, Manchester)

Rowntree employees playing tennis in the factory grounds (Rowntree Mackintosh plc)

Edwardians relaxing on the river, by Bernard Partridge for Punch (Weidenfeld & Nicolson Archives)

Emmeline Pankhurst being arrested outside Buckingham Palace, 1914 (Museum of London)

Bank holiday outing by car at Easter, 1923 (BBC Hulton Picture Library)

Unemployed ex-servicemen in London, 1925 (Mansell Collection)

Sheltering in the London Underground during the Second World War (Popperfoto)

Riot in Brixton, April 1981 (Camera Press)

Preface

I wish to express my deep gratitude for the help and advice that have been given me in writing this book to Professor Christopher Hawkes and Mrs Sonia Chadwick Hawkes, Dr J.N.L. Myres, Professor H.R. Loyn, Professor Frank Barlow, Professor F.R.H. Du Boulay, Dr Joan Thirsk, Dr George D. Ramsay, Sir Henry Phelps Brown, Sir Harry Campion, Sir Norman Chester and Lord Stewart of Fulham. I need hardly say that they are in no way responsible for my opinions.

In a book of this general nature I have limited my employment of the three musketeers of historical writing: Perhaps, Possibly and Probably; but I am fully aware that Truth frequently walks on a knife edge. I have also confined my references chiefly to direct quotations from the works of expert modern historians, which are proper for me to acknowledge.

In giving monetary figures I have not tried to evaluate them in present-day terms because such an attempt is full of snags: for example, the price of a motor car today may be ten times what it was fifty years ago, but it will not be the same car. I must however remind readers that before 1971 the pound sterling was equivalent to 20 shillings and a shilling was equal to 12 pennies. Thus when I refer to pennies (240 to the pound) they are not equivalent to modern 'pence' (100 to the pound).

I dedicate the book to the memory of my uncle, Sir William Ashley, one of the pioneers of English economic history, whose work first aroused my interest in the subject. His shade will, I hope, forgive me if my approach is not completely academic since half my adult life has been spent as a journalist and an element of autobiography has crept into my last chapters.

Maurice Ashley

ONE

The Impact of Civilization: Life in Celtic and Roman Britain

'Who the original inhabitants of Britain were, indigenous or foreign,' wrote the Roman historian Tacitus, 'is, as is usual among barbarians, little known.' But one fact is certain: 500 years before the birth of Christ most of the people in what we now know as England were 'Celts' or, more accurately, Celtic-speaking tribesmen.

Who were these Celts? They were communities speaking a language ancestral to modern Welsh. In prehistoric times their forbears had spread from the steppes of southern Russia right across the face of central Europe north of the Alps. They must have been prolific: unable to find sufficient food to maintain themselves they searched for richer soil. In early classical times they had been warlike, for in 390 BC they sacked Rome and in 279 BC they devastated Delphi. But by 200 BC they were decisively defeated by the Romans and submitted to their rule.

During the first millennium BC the Celts occupied much of what is now Austria from the upper reaches of the Danube as far as Czechoslovakia, Bavaria and Switzerland. Still seeking new lands to conquer or in which to settle, they expanded into Belgium and France, giving them the name of Gaul, and parts of Spain and Portugal. Coming from the European mainland they crossed the straits of Dover (narrower then than they are today) or even ventured from the Low Countries in their coracles or wooden boats across the North Sea.

Basically the Celts were colonists in the same sense as the Pilgrim Fathers. For although they had at times to fight for what they needed, they were hardly warriors like the Romans, the Franks, the Germans, the Visigoths and the Vandals of their age, at any rate once they had settled. The Welsh monk Gildas, himself a Celt, was to write much later that they were 'unwarlike' and 'completely ignorant of the practice of war'.[1] It is true that they possessed two-wheeled chariots drawn by ponies, which in battle they drove up and down to frighten their enemy before they dismounted and wielded their daggers, lances and slings. Though they fought their way into maritime regions such as east Yorkshire and parts of Wales, their settlement was always a cumulative process, mingling with the native population. In the course of colonizing much of what was to become England (they called it Albion) they built hill forts, no doubt effective enough against cattle raiders, but useless to fend off trained soldiers. The Roman commander-in-chief, Julius Caesar, who was to defeat the Celts both in Gaul and in the country he named Britannia, noted that 'the Britons call it a fort [*oppidum*] when they have defended a tract of dense woodland with a rampart and a ditch'.[2]

The Celtic forts were not planned systematically to withstand an invading army. Even Maiden Castle in Dorset, which has been described as 'a stupendous fortress' (its outlines may still be seen today), presented little difficulty to the Roman army. By the time the Celts had found their way by sea to the island that was thought to be the last outpost of the western world and settled down with their wives and families either upon the light upland and forest-free soils such as constituted Salisbury Plain, or upon the gravel of river banks, they behaved as peasants peacefully cultivating their fields, not seriously organized for war. The Celtic aristocrats – that is to say, the tribal chieftains and their relatives and companions (*equites*) – sublimated their martial instincts into hunting; it has been said that for them 'fighting was a sport rather than a necessity'.[3] Though in the last millennium before Christ swords and spears were being manufactured by bronze founders and iron forgers, what the mass of the Celts appreciated most were the axes and sickles, buckets and cauldrons which helped them to sustain their modest agricultural life.

Undoubtedly the country was populated many thousands of years before the Celts arrived: first with the inhabitants of what is called the Old Stone Age, who fed themselves by hunting or grubbing up wild fruit and vegetables and dwelt in caves that were warm in winter and cool in summer. Later came the pastoralists who kept their own flocks and herds and also cultivated grain crops. After that a succession of immigrants appeared who knew first of copper, then of bronze (copper with the addition of tin) and finally of iron. It was during the Iron Age (600–500 BC) that Britain became a largely Celtic country.

The Celts practised mixed farming, which well before their time had been the basis of subsistence. Their settlements were single farms or hamlets of round wooden houses. Land for cultivation was parcelled into squarish small fields, divided by banks, which can still be observed through the magic eyes of air photography. They used foot ploughs or light ploughs drawn by a couple of oxen, which did little more than scratch the surface of the soil without turning the sod. Their food was supplemented by hunting and fishing. No towns in the modern sense of the word existed, though some of the hill forts served as tribal centres.

The Celtic settlements had spinning and weaving, basketry and carpentry. Pots could be made at home, but pottery manufacturing centres existed, whose goods were distributed by pack-horse. Bronze, which was normally cast, was again the work of specialists. Bronze and iron utensils were manufactured and sold by travelling metalsmiths, except that in the case of tribal chieftains a workshop would have been maintained for the production of weapons as well as other high-class goods. Lead was mined, notably in the Mendip hills, its exploitation being first seriously undertaken by the Romans; from it silver was produced by the method called cupellation, the cupel being a small flat circular vessel employed for assaying and refining.

When in the second half of the fourth century BC a Greek explorer, Pytheas by name, who had been commissioned to discover new trade routes, reached present-day Cornwall from Marseilles, he noted that tin was mined there and also in the Isle of Wight. Forty years later another Greek traveller reported that ingots of tin, smelted in Cornwall and intended for export, were sent to St Michael's Mount (near Penzance) where they were bartered for goods coming from the Roman world. Three centuries after this the Greek geographer Strabo noted that wheat, cattle, minerals (gold, silver, iron), hides, slaves and hunting dogs were exported, while imports included bracelets and necklaces, amber, glassware and 'suchlike trifles'; wine was largely imported from Italy. Thus the land which later came to be known as England was an early example of an underdeveloped country exporting raw materials to pay for manufactured goods, mostly of a luxury class.

We may therefore picture the Celtic-speaking peasant farmers - the first inhabitants of England about whom we know anything much - working, sleeping and eating in round huts of timber and cob (that is, clay-coated wattle work) with just one largish living-room and under it a number of cells or pits for store rooms, kilns and privies. The roofs were thatched; and since drier soil of chalk or gravel or limestone was preferred for building-sites, floors and pits were less liable to damp than if they stood on clay. Around the huts would be found pasture for livestock, except where the farmsteads were situated on high ground whence the cattle could be driven down the valleys to graze. These early settlers avoided the forests that covered much of the country, growing especially on the clays between the rivers and their gravels, for example in most of London and the Home Counties.

After a purely pastoral life receded and the hoe gradually gave way to the plough, women who might previously have worked alongside their menfolk in the fields would spend more time indoors weaving or making pottery. The kinds of grain that were grown have been discovered: oats and rye most often in the north, but a great deal of barley and also wheat. The finding of brooches, bracelets, golden neck rings and other jewellery that can be dated from pre-Roman times suggests that a number of wealthy people existed – presumably chieftains, their women and their retinue. On festive occasions wines were drunk as well as mead, an alcoholic beverage made from fermented honey and water, which has been called hyperbolically the Celtic champagne. Much later the Venerable Bede was to write in his celebrated *History of the English Church and People* that vines were cultivated in various parts of the country; Verica, one of the Celtic tribal chieftains, displayed upon his coinage a vine leaf as his emblem. Since Verica ruled over modern Sussex perhaps the medium-sweet wine produced there today was anticipated by the Celts. As to industry, iron was mined in Sussex and elsewhere, while copper had been known from at least 2000 BC. By Roman standards, however, Celtic Britain was far from rich. Disparagingly Cicero was to assert – wrongly – that neither silver nor gold came from Britain and that its slaves were uneducated. By and large it was a self-sufficient economy, though the export of corn suggests that a surplus was available in a good season.

Nevertheless it is easy to exaggerate the primitiveness and poverty of Britain as compared with the material strength of republican Rome. Julius Caesar remarked on the temperate climate, warmer than that in Gaul. Tacitus, writing during the early Roman Empire, noted that severity of cold was unknown. Consequently with the exception of olives and other trees and plants that flourished in hotter climates the soil yielded 'and even abundantly all ordinary produce'. The numerous rivers were full of edible fish including salmon; oysters might harbour pearls, and from cockles a red dye was extracted. Caesar, who collected this part of his information at second hand, wrote that the population was remarkably big and the ground thickly covered with homesteads. Other foreigners who visited the country in Celtic times described the male inhabitants as tall and fair with blue eyes, tall at any rate in comparison with the darker Mediterranean peoples. They were clean-shaven, but kept their hair long and had graceful flowing moustaches. They did not wear hats or caps; they dressed in brightly coloured clothes and leather shoes or sandals.

While the men ploughed the land or looked after their flocks the women spun and wove woollen cloth or linen fabrics out of which to make clothes, and converted into bread the corn, which was harvested before it was ripe and dried in kilns and ovens; for this purpose they used small hand-mills or querns and cooked hot food for their menfolk on tripods, pyrites being sparked off by flint or tinder. Such evidence as we have suggests that the Celtic women were treated as equals in a way not followed until recent times. It is true that in the notes collected by Caesar he recorded that wives were shared between ten or twelve men, but it is more likely that the Celts had at any rate principal wives. In aristocratic society archaeology appears to show that women were accorded parity with men. When the Romans finally conquered the country and transformed it into an imperial province, two of the biggest tribes were ruled by queens who fought from their chariots just as the kings did. One of them, Queen Boudicca of the Iceni, had a huge frame, a terrifying aspect, a harsh voice and red hair that reached to her knees – formidable indeed.[4]

Comparatively little is positively known about the tribal life of the Celts. But it is likely that the land belonged to the tribe as a whole rather than to individuals, although cattle were private property. Serfdom and slavery existed, chiefly of men who had been captured in war and degraded. Each tribe had its gods, whose assistance was invoked in moments of crisis. The Celts believed in an afterlife; the soul, they thought, was immortal and would be transferred to the bodies of living men after death. According to Diodorus, a Sicilian historian who wrote during the first century after Christ, this doctrine of the transmigration of souls was a tenet of the Druids, a privileged priestly caste, whose headquarters lay in the island of Anglesey. In the memories of the Druids were stored the customary laws of the Celts, although the tribal chieftains also had a part to play. The Druids were not priests in temples (the idea that they were connected with Stonehenge has long been exploded) but are recorded as worshipping in groves; their ceremonies, which included the sacrifice of human lives as well as those of animals, were intended to placate their various gods and goddesses. Their influence on the Celts was profound and they must have been the best-educated men in Britain.

5

During the centuries before the birth of Christ the Belgic immigrants crossed into Britain from western Gaul. These, the only Celts whose invasion is recorded in Greek or Latin documents, came over from the nearest position in the Belgic territories, that lying to the north-west of the lower river Seine. In his book on the conquest of Gaul Julius Caesar stated that they were the bravest of the Celts because 'they were the least often visited by merchants with enervating luxuries for sale'. He also tells us in the notes he collected before his expedition there that the coast of Britain was inhabited by Belgic immigrants 'who came to plunder and make war . . . and later settled down to till the soil'. (Caesar was concerned with them because it was from the Belgic areas of Britain that the main resistance to his forces came.) They colonized modern Kent and also the drift soils north of the Thames. They dominated much of the south-east, but avoided the difficult country in the Sussex Weald. Others were in Hampshire and Wiltshire; the Parisi, neighbours of the Belgae from the Seine valley, had earlier occupied eastern parts of Yorkshire.

These tribes made a remarkable contribution to economic and cultural progress in their new homes. They introduced a gold coinage (later silver and also copper) from Gaulish models based on Greek or Macedonian; they made pottery on the true potter's wheel; they had longer and wider ploughs with shares (cutting blades) constructed of iron which could exploit heavier soils than before; and their blacksmiths produced stronger iron axes with which forests could be cleared. Also like the earlier Celtic settlers, they practised what is known to archaeologists as the La Tène art style (La Tène was a Celtic lake-side site in Switzerland) with abstract patterns, freely flowing curves and fantastic or humorous reliefs of animals and human faces.

Of course the Romans regarded the Celts as barbarians, as they did everyone but themselves. But in fact, as Dr John Corcoran wrote, 'in general, the technological level of the La Tène Celts, with very few exceptions was equal to, and in some matters surpassed, that of the Romans'.[5] The Belgic settlements were never true towns, but they certainly had rural markets and in good years the export of wheat enabled them to pay for imported luxuries.

The Celts, it is clear, were virtually illiterate, but otherwise they certainly should not be described as barbarians. Their art was vigorous and of a higher quality than much that the Romans could produce. They owned strong ploughs, four-wheeled carts and beautifully shaped pots. Their men shaved with razors, using oil instead of soap. Their women had bronze dress-fasteners to hold together their colourful clothes, dyed purple, green or crimson, and they had polished metal mirrors in which to contemplate their looks. The men exercised with long swords, played a kind of hockey and amused themselves with fighting cocks and dice. They were also musical, possessing flutes, horns and trumpets. They drank wine, cooked with olive oil, used knives and spoons (but not forks) to eat with at meals, and owned table lamps. Thus the standards and culture among the Celts who settled in the area that was to become England were far from contemptible. In spite of the short lives they must have lived, they enjoyed an equable climate, a cultivable soil and varied recreations.

In the Roman republic little was known about the offshore island. It was partly for this reason that Julius Caesar, whose information was sparse and largely inaccurate, carried out a reconnaissance in force during 55 BC. On the basis of what he learned and because he believed that a full-scale military operation would strengthen his hold on Gaul, he organized a much bigger expedition in the following year to which he committed 5 legions, 2,000 cavalry and over 800 ships: his aim surely was conquest. But the Belgic charioteers resisted him as far as they could; though they were beaten, Caesar decided to withdraw after imposing the best terms obtainable. His conclusion was that the island was valuable for its corn and slaves. Hearing after his victories there that trouble was brewing in Gaul, from which he had launched his invasion, and since, as he wrote, when the summer was over 'the Britons could easily hold out for the short time that remained', he recrossed the Channel with his ships crowded full of hostages and prisoners intended as slaves, and relied on promises given him by the kings of the Celtic tribes that they would pay an annual tribute to Rome. His great-nephew and successor, Octavius, who assumed the title of Emperor Augustus, preferred to reinforce the army in Gaul rather than bother with the Britons. So it was not until nearly a century later that Britain became a province of the Roman Empire.

During the interval, however, commercial relations between Britain and the European mainland grew closer; Strabo's list of exports and imports applies to this period. Merchants visited Britain from the Rhineland and Spain as well as from Gaul and Italy. Wine, pottery, glassware and metalwork were brought there in considerable quantities, while the Roman authorities must have received intelligence that the output of food in the island was sufficient to maintain a permanent garrison and that its military needs could be supplemented by the exploitation of local resources. So it was resolved that it would be cheaper to defend the western

7

extremity of the Roman Empire by stationing a garrison in Britain than by strengthening the forces occupying Gaul, which had been required to provide food for the Rhineland as well as the Roman army there and its own inhabitants. It was also hoped that gold and silver would be discovered in the new province. Thus it was partly for economic reasons that the Romans were induced to subdue Britain by conquest in AD 43, as Julius Caesar had intended.

The subjugation of Britain had been on the agenda of the Roman emperors for nearly a century when Claudius determined to put it into effect. He dispatched four legions and auxiliary troops amounting to about 40,000 men, who rapidly overcame the Celts because they were disunited. Now the mists began to lift from the history of the country that Caesar had named Britain. It was found to be divided into fifteen principal Celtic kingdoms: they lay thicker in the south than in the north and it was in the south-east, where the Belgic tribes had chiefly settled, that the people were most cultured and civilized and agriculture farthest advanced. Verulamium (near modern St Albans) was the capital of the most powerful Belgic tribe, the Catuvellauni, who unsuccessfully battled against the Roman army. After the conquest the Romans garrisoned the north with bases at Chester and York, also at Lincoln in the Midlands and Caerleon in south Wales. The victors left the rest of the country in the hands of the Celtic or British tribal communities (*civitates*) who had to pay taxes and obey the orders of the Roman Governor and Procurator. During the first century after the conquest, chiefly because of Celtic rebellions, the romanization of Britain proceeded slowly.

Rome's most significant contributions to the social and economic development of the country were the building of towns and the introduction of 'villas', that is to say, landed estates. It has been a matter for argument how far towns can be said to have existed before the coming of the Romans. Undoubtedly the Celtic kings possessed fortified wooden strongholds, which were called in Latin *oppida*, but these were nothing like the Roman towns or cities, where sophisticated centrally-heated buildings, markets, streets and shops were to be found. Sometimes, however, Romano-British towns were constructed on or near the sites of these *oppida*, though generally the new towns were erected in valleys and not on hill tops. The Romans first built four towns or *coloniae* specifically for the benefit of their retired legionaries: they were Colchester, Lincoln, Gloucester and later York. The only town which is known to have been given a municipal status was Verulamium; that is to say, it was provided with a charter conferring Latin citizenship on its inhabitants. All the rest of the towns in Roman Britain were built with the help of Roman technology but at the expense of the Britons. Twelve of them were capital cities, the cantonal centres of tribal areas with specific rights and duties.

What were these towns like and how many of them were there? About fifty towns are known to have been distributed in Kent, in southern England (as it was to become), around the mouth of the river Severn and a few, such as Leicester and Aldborough, in the Midlands and north. They were laid out in a chequer-board pattern surrounded, though seldom at the start, by walls and excellently served by road. Each town had a city hall (*basilica*) and a forum, which was used as a civic assembly and a market-place. The houses, rectangular in shape, were ordinarily built of local materials such as stone or timber, with the rooms grouped round a court or corridor, with thatched roofs, painted plaster walls and in some cases tiled mosaic floors. Shops were normally the quarters of craftsmen who made goods to order and lived either above the premises or at the back. The houses rarely contained bathrooms, but invariably a bath house was built in each town with an aqueduct, drains and sewers: there women bathed in the mornings and men in the afternoons and evenings. The sort of shops that were established along the main streets were butchers, blacksmiths, tanners, dyers, shoe-makers, potters, glass-makers and wine shops. A number of towns had amphitheatres large enough to hold their whole population. They also contained temples, where the gods worshipped included Roman emperors, who were chief priests when they were alive and deified after they were dead; sometimes Celtic and Roman deities were fused, such as Minerva, the versatile Roman goddess, and Sul, the Celtic sun god.

Most of these towns were quite small: in the forums all the citizens could gather, as they had done in the famous Greek city-states. In fact most Romano-British towns were in size and population what would be regarded today as modest villages. It has been estimated that Silchester in Hampshire, capital of the Atrebates tribe, the town which has been most thoroughly examined by archaeologists, contained some 150 buildings and a population of only about 1,200 people. A modern geographer has suggested that all the Romano-British towns, if put together, would have covered but four square miles.[6]

One town about which we know less than we should like is London. Although the word itself is Celtic and a trading settlement on the north bank of the Thames may have existed before the arrival of Claudius, as a city it was a Roman foundation. Tacitus wrote that by the middle of the first century AD it was crowded with merchants and a great centre of commerce: evidently it had become a busy entrepôt at the lowest point where the Thames could be bridged. Fifteen years after the Roman conquest it was destroyed by Queen Boudicca when she and her tribe rose against the Romans in AD 60. After her defeat London was rebuilt as a more civilized city, with an efficient draining system, an adequate water supply and buildings of timber, stone and brick. A meeting-place of no fewer than six main roads, London grew to be an active trading port, importing oil and wine and exporting corn and slaves. Its estimated population of 20,000 or 30,000 would have made it the fifth largest town in the northern provinces of the Roman Empire. It contained the first and only mint known to have been established by the Romans in Britain. The Procurator or Finance Officer, Gaius Julius Alpinus Classicanus, who was sent to Britain by the Emperor Nero after Boudicca had been defeated, lived in London and was buried there; but what the precise legal status of the city was has not yet been resolved. In the fifth century, after the Romans had left, London was for a time a derelict port inhabited by squatters.

So much has been written about the Roman towns of Britain that one is liable to have an exaggerated impression of their economic importance. Apart from the mining of minerals, the manufacture of glass and the making of pottery, industry, as it is now known, scarcely existed: Britain was almost entirely an agricultural country. Although a good deal of small-scale manufacture took place in urban workshops, such as the making of tools, agricultural implements and some textiles, many of the people who lived in the towns (which were, as has already been indicated, the size of small modern villages) went out from them each day to work in neighbouring fields and came back to the protection of the town walls at night. The bulk of the population was engaged in farming: the production of food was stimulated by the constant demands of the Roman garrison. Taxes were chiefly paid in corn (*annona*). The well-to-do spent more of their time and money on landed estates than in the cities. And one may hazard the guess that most towns were much like, say, Welshpool today, though with a population half its size, where farmers gather on market days to sell their produce, wholesale or retail, to do some shopping and to quench their thirsts in inns which stay open all the afternoon for their benefit.

Whereas the towns may be dated back to an early stage of the Roman occupation, the 'villas', focal points of landed estates of 1,000 to 2,000 acres belonging to men of wealth and enterprise, evolved more slowly and were mostly confined to lowland areas with rich and ample arable land. The highlands were largely, but not entirely, pastoral. A few villas developed out of the isolated farmsteads that were characteristic of the pre-Roman Celtic period. The owners would also have town houses and could afford to employ a bailiff, servants, labourers and domestic slaves. The villa or main house on the estate usually had six to nine rooms distributed around a courtyard with no upper storey, though some smaller farmhouses were also called villas. The family and its serfs or slaves lived in the villa, while farm buildings and huts accommodated numerous agricultural labourers nearby. Villas have been identified chiefly in Kent and south-eastern England; few have been located in Devonshire or Cornwall, on Salisbury Plain or in the fenlands, which the Romans started to drain. Normally villas were clustered in the neighbourhood of towns where their surplus produce could be sold. These country estates were not as delectable as in other parts of the Roman Empire. Only at Fishbourne in Sussex has a palace or 'classical luxury villa' been found: that no doubt was owned either by a high Roman official or a client king.

On the open fields belonging to these large estates a fair-sized plough with a coulter and a mould-board to throw the soil into ridges and furrows would have been used. The bulk of the population, however, who were either smallholders, tenant farmers or villagers, lived in round or square cottages built with wood or stone and had pits for storage. They occupied only a few acres and cultivated the less promising ground on chalk or gravel, employing the light wheel-less scratch plough, its wooden shares tipped with iron, that had been employed by their ancestors. Furthermore, by contrast with the large open fields on the villa estates the arable land cultivated by the poorer classes was still divided into enclosed rectangular plots, an acre or two in extent, which yielded barely enough food to live on.

It was once thought that the Romans, being essentially town dwellers, brought no agricultural improvements to Celtic Britain. But now ploughs with large coulters and mould-boards, reliable axes, iron-tipped spades, rakes, balanced sickles and two-handed scythes are all attributed to them,[7] though the new type of plough which needed eight oxen to draw it may have been used only on villa estates. A disadvantage to agriculture, however, were the towns and roads the Romans built, which introduced numerous kinds of common weeds. On the other hand, the systems of roads and the enforcement of peace made the land more accessible and allowed it to be more intensively worked.

Although Britain was essentially an agricultural province capable of supplying enough food for their army, the Romans also encouraged the development of mining and industry, minerals being by law government property. The hoped-for precious metals were discovered, but only on a limited scale. At Dolaucauthi in Carmarthenshire were, as far as is known, the only gold mines. Whether they were worked by slaves under the direct supervision of the Roman army or handed over to concessionaires under an imperial licence is uncertain, but plainly the technical expertise must have been provided by Roman engineers and most of the profits went to the Roman emperors, even if some of the gold was handled and sold by goldsmiths in British towns. The mining and cupellation of silver from lead was, to begin with, carried out under military management in the Mendip hills, Derbyshire and elsewhere, but later was leased out to concessionaires. Lead was also alloyed with tin to produce pewter mugs and dishes during the last two centuries of the Roman occupation. Some coal was mined. Tin, for which Britain had been known from earlier times, was not in great demand until the Spanish industry dried up in the course of the third century. Though domestic consumption increased, tin was not to any large extent exported.

The one manufacturing industry that developed on a widening scale was pottery, made by wheel out of the clay to be found in many parts of Britain. The industry was stimulated by the fact that cheap Samian ware, imported in quantity from Gaul and elsewhere in Europe, ceased for various reasons to be available towards the end of the second century. The best-known British pottery came from Castor on Nene (near Peterborough) and from the New Forest. The Castor pottery, which consisted chiefly of drinking cups, was highly decorative, often painted with scenes of hunts, gladiatorial combats and chariot races, while the New Forest pottery was simpler and utilitarian since it was largely intended as kitchenware, although it also furnished flagons, goblets and vases. Whereas the manufacture in the Castor district was organized on a big scale, the New Forest potters were independent craftsmen who can be pictured as carrying their wares on the backs of donkeys and selling them directly in neighbouring villages. It is known that the potteries in Dorset, Shropshire and Yorkshire served the needs of the Roman army under contract as well as supplying civilian markets. Some of the so-called villas also had small pottery works.

12

The character of Roman Britain was by no means uniform. The lowland zone was comparatively densely populated and was inhabited principally by peaceful farmers or wealthy landowners looking after the cultivation of their estates or dwelling in neighbouring towns. The west Midlands and Wales were also fairly thickly populated, but the east Midlands and East Anglia were less so. The highland zone, that is to say, the area lying to the north of a line stretching from the mouth of the Severn to the Humber or Tees, lacked both towns and villas: the inhabitants were mainly shepherds, who lived in hill-top villages; they tended their flocks in the valleys and were little affected by Roman civilization or culture. On the whole, the north-west and Wales were less romanized than the east and the north-east, and the extreme north was under direct military control. What the total population of the country was is a question of inspired guesswork: recent research suggests that in the second century it might have been as high as five million.[8] The evidence of air photography indicates that more people lived in the south than in the north.

What was consolidated during nearly 400 years of Roman occupation was a class society. In the cantonal capitals the administrative class would have spoken Latin, which was the language of the army, commerce and, in its later stages, Christianity. For all official purposes, too, Latin must have been used because Celtic had virtually no script. The upper and middle classes were for the most part bilingual, but the villagers in the lowlands knew little or no Latin and in the highlands none at all. It has been estimated that some 800 Latin words were borrowed by the Celtic language, such as *brassica, fibula* and *papyrus*, a fact which has been held to prove that the language differed importantly from that of the western Empire in general and Gaul in particular. The notion that in Roman Britain the common people all spoke Latin and lived comfortably in centrally-heated houses has long been discarded. In fact the distinguished historian R.G. Collingwood suggested that 'as in northern Gaul and Germany the economic development of Britain may have been towards converting free peasants into coloni of great proprietors'. The gap between the rich with their 'villas' and town houses and the poor living on a subsistence level in small villages or hamlets was vast. As to slaves, it is known that their children were exposed to die.

For many years the British people lived and worked securely enough under the protective screen of the Roman army. According to Tacitus, they were reconciled to paying their taxes and bore other burdens imposed on them without flinching. For food they had sufficient corn to make

13

bread, meat from farm animals, fish – chiefly shellfish but also river fish such as pike, perch, dace and eels; their fruit included apples, plums, wild strawberries, raspberries and blackberries; and cultivated vegetables, notably peas, parsnips, radishes, carrots and celery, all introduced by the Romans. Salt, obtained either by being boiled from the sea or dug from salt springs at places like modern Droitwich, was plentiful and essential for preserving food during the autumn and winter. About the only kind of sweetening was procured from honey; as sugar was unknown, British teeth were relatively free from caries. Cooking was done on a charcoal fire raised on a stone hearth.

Men wore tunics and breeches, but not long trousers, although these had been worn by earlier Celts. Tacitus tells us that the loose-flowing Roman robe known as the *toga*, made of white wool, became fashionable. Shaving was done with bronze or iron razors and must have been a slow and painful process, out of which barbers could earn a regular living. It was not until the second quarter of the second century that beards were commonly worn. Women had all or most of the aids to beauty familiar to them in recent times: mirrors, face powder, rouge, tweezers, combs and perfumes. Wealthy ladies had slave girls to look after them. If they needed to recuperate from the duty of supervising the housework they and their husbands could visit and enjoy the hot springs at Bath and Buxton, celebrated holiday resorts then and of the future. At home dogs and cats were kept, but not as pets. Dogs were indigenous and, being needed for hunting, were valuable exports; cats were introduced by the Romans to cope with mice. Early Welsh laws speak of 'a perfect cat, perfect of ear, eye, teeth, claw, without marks of fire, and it should kill mice and not devour its kittens, and should not go caterwauling every new moon', while big dogs were told to catch and fetch.[9]

For the well-to-do at any rate plenty of entertainment was available. Pantomimes were performed in the theatres and bull-baiting, cock-fighting and gladiatorial displays in the amphitheatres. Dinner parties were given at home and restaurants could be patronized in the towns. But most of these leisure activities did not stretch far downwards. The agricultural labourer earned extremely modest wages, though his food was provided for him: he had to work for five days to buy a pair of boots.

Life was short, for medical knowledge was limited. The average expectation of life at birth was thirty years at the most; so consoling superstitions abounded. The Romans were relatively tolerant about them, though they insisted on the worship of dead emperors and wiped out the Druids, not because they disapproved of their human sacrifices but because they were thought to have provoked Celtic opposition to rule by their conquerors. Christianity penetrated into the country during the fourth century – a small church of that date was discovered at Silchester – but took hold slowly. It boasted its martyrs, including St Alban, who was put to death at the beginning of the fourth century. A notable heretic in Roman Britain was Pelagius, who was accused of questioning the omnipotence of God by propagating the doctrine of free will. Mithraism, which pictured life as an unending struggle between good and evil, was also imported from the east and was a cult that appealed particularly to soldiers and the merchant class. Whether in pagan or in Christian terms, the belief in an afterlife was general; grave goods, which included both food and ornaments, have been discovered in cemeteries and crematoriums: they bear witness to the conviction that the dead needed provisions to carry with them on their journey to the other side.

Naturally, generalizations about Roman Britain are not all valid at the same time. It has to be remembered that the military occupation lasted for nearly 400 years, as long a period as that from the accession of Queen Elizabeth I to the accession of Queen Elizabeth II. Roman economic and social practices took hold of the Celts slowly and in some cases hardly at all. For instance, it was not until the third century that British pottery and pewter came into big demand. After an era of general prosperity in the second century inflation and the depreciation of the currency caused a severe depression, which Diocletian vainly tried to remedy by publishing an edict in 301, freezing prices and wages throughout his empire. The rebuilding and enlargement of 'villas' which took place in the fourth century can be interpreted as showing a fairly rapid recovery in Britain. By the middle of that century a flight both of capital and labour is believed to have taken place from Gaul, which was then being attacked both by the Franks and the Teutons, into what was thought to be the safer shelter of Britain. Thus from the point of view of the national economy the fourth century was a flourishing age, though the chief beneficiaries were the upper classes.

Notes

1 Gildas, *de excidio Britanniae*, ed. Hugh Williams (1901), p. 33
2 R.G. Collingwood, *Roman Britain* (1937), p. 81
3 Nora Chadwick, *The Celts* (1970), p. 136
4 Cit. Dio Cassius, ibid., p. 50
5 Introduction to Chadwick, op. cit., p. 38
6 George C. Boon, *Silchester: the Roman Town of Calleva* (1974), p. 53 etc; E.W. Gilbert, 'The Human Geography of Roman Britain', in H.C. Darby, *Historical Geography of England before 1800* (1969), p. 65
7 Sheppard Frere, *Britannia* (1978), p. 317; cf. Shiman Applebaum, 'Agriculture in Roman Britain', *Agricultural History Review*, VI (1958), p. 73
8 Peter Salway, *Roman Britain* (1981), p. 544
9 Nora Chadwick, *Celtic Britain* (1963), pp. 88, 91

TWO

The Anglo-Saxons
and the Vikings

The relative prosperity of Britain during the fourth century became known throughout Europe and excited the cupidity of barbaric peoples, including the Scots in Ireland, the Picts in Scotland and the Saxons in northern Germany. Even earlier, in the third century, they had aimed by sudden raids to seize cattle, capture slaves and carry off such wealth as could be found by way of jewellery and silver vessels. Of their depredations Edward Gibbon wrote: 'a philosopher ... will confess that the desire of spoil is a more rational provocation than the vanity of conquest'.

By now the huge Roman Empire was not only menaced by invasion on all sides, but was disrupted because its rulers – named Augustuses and Caesars – were constantly plotting against and quarrelling with one another. Yet a large garrison still remained in Britain, which was also guarded by a Roman fleet. Towards the end of the third century one of Diocletian's Caesars, Constantius Chlorus (Constantine I), overthrew a usurper, re-organized the defences of the province and drove back the Picts and Scots, two 'savage alien tribes' as Bede called them, although they continued to harass the country throughout the following century. Constantius I died at York in 306 and his son, Constantine the Great, temporarily reunited the Empire. In 343 the Emperor Constans, a son of Constantine the Great, came to Britain in person, treated with its assailants and allowed some of them to settle, employing them as mercenaries or *foederati*, like poachers turned gamekeepers, to ward off other barbarians.

Eighteen years later the future Emperor Julian dispatched one of his best generals with a field army to cope with the Picts and Scots. It cannot have been a successful mission, for eight years afterwards the future Emperor Valentinian I had to order Count Theodosius to suppress freebooters and pirates 'intimidating Britain as never before'. In 367 the Picts, Scots and

Saxons banded together, overran the wall first built by the Emperor Hadrian, which stretched from the Solway Firth to the south of the river Tyne, and scattered in plundering hordes throughout the lowlands. The soldiers who manned the wall were corrupted; Roman military deserters and escaped slaves roamed and ravaged the country, so that anarchy prevailed. Though Theodosius succeeded in restoring order and organizing the rebuilding of the defences, fifteen years later an ambitious Roman commander named Magnus Maximus, stationed in Britain and disappointed at being promoted too slowly, headed a revolt against the Emperor Theodosius (father of Count Theodosius), denuded the province of most of its troops, and, taking British volunteers along with him, attempted to carve out an empire for himself in the west, but was defeated and killed in Italy in 388.

It is not possible to date precisely the end of the Roman occupation of Britain, but during the first decade of the fifth century the whole of the Roman Empire was breaking up. In 409 the Emperor Honorius notified the cities of Britain in response to an appeal for help that they must undertake their own salvation,[1] since the Romans themselves were then being overwhelmed by Vandals, Huns and Goths thrusting across the Rhine and the Danube. A year later Rome was sacked. When in the middle of the fifth century the Britons once more appealed for assistance against the barbarians who, they said, were driving them into the sea, no answer was received.

At one time it was thought that after Britain had been abandoned by the Romans the country was rapidly devastated and its inhabitants crushed by the invasion of Angles, Saxons, Jutes and Frisians, who were impelled to find new homes because of the pressure upon their means of subsistence, brought about by overpopulation, scarcity of food and flooding from the sea. But in fact for much of the fifth century the Britons managed to maintain a civilized life and to cope with such immigrants. In 429 Germanus Bishop of Auxerre, who had once served in the Roman army, arrived in south-western Britain accompanied by the Bishop of Troyes with the purpose of overthrowing the Pelagian heretics and found it a reasonably placid land. He then taught the Britons how to defeat the forces of Picts and Scots by shouting 'Alleluia!' three times before they closed with their foes. Some twenty years later when he was an old man Germanus again visited the island with another bishop and he still found it to be wealthy and not yet subjected by pagans. The Welsh monk Gildas, who wrote his admonitory tract entitled *The Ruin of Britain* in about the middle of the sixth century, was able to record that after the pillaging of the Picts and Scots the country had quietened down and 'was becoming rich with many sources of affluence that no age remembered the possession of such afterwards'. The departure of the Romans also brought about a revival of Celtic art, as is testified by pottery, jewellery, metalwork, enamelwork and sculpture belonging to the period. The late Sir Ian Richmond wrote about two Celtic stone heads discovered in Northumbria, saying that they represented 'with sad and awesome clarity the standards of a world which Rome had neither extinguished nor submerged'.[2]

Although, as has been noticed, Gildas, almost the only contemporary authority for this century, had deprecated the military qualities of his fellow Celts (who he believed were being punished by the barbarians because of their sinfulness), he admitted that some of them at least 'came out of the mountains, from caves and thickets ... and carried on war unceasingly'. For the first time, he added, they inflicted slaughter upon their enemies because their trust was not in man but in God. Writing some fifty years later than Gildas, the Byzantine historian Zosimus described how after the Romans left 'the people of Britain took up arms and braving every danger freed their cities from the barbarians threatening them', and observed that the Gaulish tribes followed the British example. Thus the Britons offered prolonged, skilful and at times successful resistance to the Anglo-Saxon invaders as they turned from sporadic raids to deliberate colonization. In some areas trading relations developed between the settlers and the romanized Celts, over whom they were eventually victorious. Indeed many of these colonists may well have been simply refugees anxious to find good land on which to settle.

Who were the Anglo-Saxons and what was their early history? Remarkably little is known about them before they invaded Britain. The literary evidence is mostly derived from a short essay written by Tacitus about Germany in which he mentions the Angles but not the Saxons. The men, he thought, were about five and a half feet tall, all with 'fierce blue eyes, red hair, huge frames, fit only for sudden exertion'. They had no cities, which they regarded as 'the work of giants', no commerce and no coinage. They lived in scattered villages and single farms, in houses built of timber or lath or plaster but never wholly of stone: the wealthy had long houses with steep roofs, while their servants lived and sometimes worked in small outhouses. All of them were inured to cold forests and swamps. The agriculture they practised was on a small scale; they were chiefly stock-raisers and their arable farming was extensive, that is to say,

they tilled fresh fields every year, which explains their migration south-
wards and westwards. Thus they lived by keeping sheep and cattle, pigs
and goats, growing barley, oats, rye and wheat, and by hunting. At feasts
they drank a kind of ale made from barley. Essentially they were a fighting
people who enslaved their captives. As soldiers their weapons were swords,
javelins and shields, and they were intrepid sailors who treated 'the dangers
of the deep' as 'their intimate friends'. When not fighting, Tacitus
observed, they spent their time in idleness. Their kings were chosen by
birth and their generals by merit. Their loyalty to their kings or chieftains
was direct and personal; when they went into battle (according to Tacitus)
it was considered a disgrace if they did not show bravery equal to that of
their leaders.

The Anglo-Saxons worshipped a variety of gods and goddesses of
whom the commonest was Mother Earth. Although they believed in an
afterlife, they were more concerned about their mundane reputation for
courage and endurance. Favours were expected from their gods in return
for the observance of religious rites; when they went to war they carried
images of Mercury or Mars. Socially, kinship was all-important. When a
crime was committed, the blood price (*wergild*) that had to be paid was the
responsibility of the whole kindred. The entire tribe took part in deliber-
ations, but it was deferential to monarchy as forming part of the natural
order of the world. It has been said that they were 'pagans . . . whose vision
of life in peace time was limited to the bare satisfaction of physical needs
by the cultivation of land, and whose primitive notions of social and
domestic comfort left no room for the economic and architectural com-
plexities of town life'.[3] Monogamy was strictly practised and adultery
severely punished. The Anglo-Saxons could neither read nor write. Compared with them, the Romano-Celts were a cultured and civilized people.

As with the Celts, the Anglo-Saxons' invasions and colonization began
as trickles and ended in floods of free peasants searching for richer land to
cultivate. It used to be thought that the destruction and desolation in
Britain caused by 'those wild Saxons of accursed name, hated by God and
man', as Gildas described them, must have been achieved by highly-
organized united armies. In fact, however, as is shown by the *Anglo-Saxon
Chronicle* (written admittedly many years after the events), the kings or
chieftains of the Angles and Saxons, the Jutes and Frisians first came over
in only a few ships at a time; and they occupied small districts near the
coast before they gradually penetrated along river valleys and tracks (but
rarely the Roman roads) into the heart of the country. Thus it was a

colonizing movement carried out initially in the face of considerable opposition from the Britons.

Scattered settlements began to be made in the east and south-east of the country. Following the example set by the Romans of hiring mercenaries (*foederati*), one of the British tribal rulers or overlords or 'tyrants' invited a body of Jutes to come to Kent so as to lend their support in warding off other looters and freebooters. This particular effort failed to pay off, but the Britons, when they were not fighting one another, managed to confront the invaders of their kingdoms on equal terms. Around the beginning of the sixth century a notable victory was won over the Anglo-Saxons at Mount Badon, probably somewhere in the west, and for another forty years after the battle the Britons maintained their independence in the west and south-west as well as in enclaves in Cambridgeshire and the fens and on the Chiltern hills in Buckinghamshire. But slowly and steadily the Anglo-Saxons defeated, thrust back and absorbed the Britons, occupying Sussex, Surrey, Middlesex, Suffolk and Norfolk, Essex and Wessex, east Yorkshire, Oxfordshire and Bedfordshire – in fact much of the most fertile arable land in the country. By the seventh century the Britons were confined to three detached regions: Wales, the west and the south-west – Exeter was still in their hands at the end of the century – and also to the area west of the Pennines and north of the Yorkshire Wolds, which were wetter and better suited to pasturage. The evidence of intermarriage between Anglo-Saxon men and British women is extremely slight and sporadic, for example in Northumberland and Staffordshire. Most of the Britons who survived in English settlements must have become the slaves of their conquerors. Practically the whole stamping ground of Romano-Celtic civilization was wrested from them.

What were the consequences of the overrunning of Britain by the Angles, Saxons, Jutes and Frisians? The two characteristic Roman institutions, the towns and the villa estates, disappeared. The colonists knew nothing of town life and were not converted to it. Although a few towns were sacked and burnt most of them decayed very gradually and were evacuated because of disease, famine or lack of trade. Writing in about the middle of the sixth century, Gildas said that they were no longer inhabited as before, but 'being abandoned and overthrown, still lie desolate'. Life in the towns, it has been observed, continued, but not town life: for example, early Anglo-Saxon settlements of a sort have been discovered inside the walls of Canterbury, Winchester and York.[4] London was indestructible and revived because it was the centre of the whole communication system of the country and a trading port through which such imports as Rhineland glass and Egyptian bronze could reach Anglo-Saxon men of wealth: it was, wrote Bede, 'a mart of many people coming by land and sea'. The villas disappeared speedily, partly because they were militarily insecure but mainly for economic reasons. They are not mentioned by Gildas and no evidence has been found to show that the Anglo-Saxons occupied former Romano-Celtic villas, though in time new villages were to be built on the sites of villa estates.

At the peak of English society stood the king. Kings who were overlords (*bretwaldas*), kings of wide areas and petty kings were all to be found. Was English kingship an institution which grew up when tribal chieftains and their retinues settled in the land they had conquered, or was kingship imported from their birthplaces? Kingship, we are told, was almost universal in the Heroic Age, when even the heathen high priests were subordinate to secular monarchs. The epic poem *Beowulf*, though written in the seventh or eighth century, embodied traditions of Anglo-Saxon kingship before the conquest of Britain. Whether Cerdic, believed to be the first King of Wessex, who claimed descent from the war god, Woden, was already a king before he arrived in Britain, and whether Hengest, the Jutish chieftain who was invited by a British ruler to settle in Kent and repel the Picts, was in fact the same as the king of that name who came from Denmark and wintered in Frisia, are mysteries never likely to be solved. What is fairly certain, however, is that kings in England were chosen from members of a kin endowed with the blood royal but not by laws of heredity or primogeniture. For example, Alfred, the famous King of Wessex, was preferred to his nephews, the sons of his elder brother.

Anglo-Saxon kings had councils of wise men (the *witan*) whom they consulted but whose advice they did not necessarily take. Their income was derived from royal estates and from food rents (*feorm*) paid by their subjects as they travelled round their kingdoms. A typical *feorm* might consist of barrels of ale, loads of cheese, several oxen, fish and geese, honey, butter and loaves. The royal palace would originally have been a large wooden hall where nobles and courtiers gathered and justice was done according to the customary laws of the country from which the king's subjects came. Fines for crimes against the royal family or trespasses on royal estates were at least six times as heavy as those levied on noblemen. A royal ship, discovered at Sutton Hoo in Suffolk, revealed that English kings lived in style, with silver bowls and spoons, magnificent swords and golden helmets. Whether, as is most likely, it was an imported institution or not, kingship soon became a recognized part of the English way of life; and although the kings were obliged to acknowledge the force of kinship in the social system, they tried to adapt it to the good of the community as a whole and did so successfully in the long run.

After the kings in the social scale came the nobility or thanes (*thegns*), as they were called, who were of two kinds: those directly under the king's orders, who were periodically on duty at his court, first known as his companions (*gesiths*); and others who were hereditary landowners, their standing being measured by the fact that they possessed a minimum of five 'hides' of land, a church and a kitchen, a bell and a castle gate, and a seat in the king's hall. From the king's thanes were selected *ealdormen* – royal officials put in charge of specific districts and given responsibilities as the direct representatives of the king. The thanes as a class were men who did not work with their hands and spent much of their time hunting. But they stood ready to serve the king in war, were leaders in the local folk moots or law courts, and were in duty bound to supervise the repair of fortifications.

Next to the thanes in the social hierarchy were their companions (*geneatas*), generally mounted men who acted from time to time as ostlers, grooms, huntsmen and bodyguards to their masters. They paid little or no rent and were free from regular agricultural work, but were required to mow and reap at harvest time and to maintain the hedge around their master's house. These *geneatas* have been called the peasant aristocracy.

Below the lord's companions were the churls (*ceorls*) or husbandmen. It used to be thought that, to begin with at any rate, the churl had always been a free peasant proprietor, not the subject of any lord except the king; but at least by the time of Alfred the Great the churl was clearly only half free, since he had become a tenant, and besides having to pay rent in kind – ewes, lambs, hens, cheese, honey, barley, hay, timber, malt – he might further be required to work two days a week for his landlord and three days at harvest time, if he were ordered to do so, and also to take part in ploughing his landlord's fields. The average landholding of a churl is uncertain: in one context it is described as a 'hide', which may simply have been a term for an area of cultivated soil sufficient to support a single household: in that case it could have been about thirty or forty acres or even more, varying from place to place. The churls also had to contribute to the king's food rent and serve when called upon in the militia or *fyrd* and perform other public duties if required. A husbandman might originally have been a freeman who had inherited his land but because of bad

23

harvests, illness or other misfortunes was compelled in order to ensure his survival to become a leaseholder and undertake services for his landlord, who in return would provide him with corn stored in his barns and afford him protection by able-bodied armed servants against rogues and ruffians. Alternatively, the churl could have been a slave freed by his master (a freedman or *libertinus*) and provided with cattle and sheep, farming tools and household utensils, which would be repossessed after the tenant's death.

Finally came the cottagers, who paid no rent but were required to work long hours in return for a few acres of land which they could call their own, but which were insufficient to feed their families. To obtain the means of livelihood they hired out their labour to those who were better off than themselves. Besides such agricultural labourers the large land-holder needed full-time shepherds, swineherds, bee-keepers, smiths and dairymaids. Most Anglo-Saxon thanes and well-to-do churls with large acreages owned slaves: they were either Britons who had been taken prisoner or voluntarily surrendered on account of hunger in the course of the invasions, or ex-criminals, or sometimes even peasants who had committed minor offences and could not afford to pay their fines. These slaves were valued at the price of eight oxen and were given rations of meat and corn enough to last them a year. A slave who worked on Sunday at his master's orders had to be set free and his master fined. Modest fines were also exacted if women slaves were raped. Slaves could be bought, sold or exported.

The countrymen's wives and daughters made their contribution to the work of the household by baking, cooking and looking after beer barrels and the tubs used as baths. They also sheared the sheep, milked the goats and ewes, made clothes at home and embroidered them. Women's rights were even greater than those of Celtic women. Brides received gifts after the consummation of marriage, which they were allowed to keep provided they bore children, and wives retained a third or a half of the family wealth when their husbands died. A suitor paid a bride price to the father of the girl he wished to marry, which was returnable if the marriage did not take place. He was also required to make a further gift on the morning of his wedding as a return for his wife's virginity. But he would get it back if she failed to produce a child. Women could not be compelled to marry a man they disliked, even if he were approved of by their kin, and divorce was easy to obtain by mutual consent. If a woman became a widow, she could decide whether she wanted to marry again or whether she preferred to remain single and enjoy her own property. Upper-class women might own land and have personal property ranging from furniture to horses. At the foot of the social ladder were women slaves, who could be ill-treated and even put to death and received less food than the men slaves.

The English lived either on farms in landed estates or in villages, preferring valleys, clearings from the forests or river banks to the hilltops and chalk uplands favoured by the Celts. The village was the heart of social and economic life throughout the early part of English history. Villages varied in size and were assessed in multiples of five 'hides' when it came to the question of deciding how much the king's food rent, measured in oxen, cheese and the like, ought to be. The king might also require the building or repair of bridges by the village community. The villagers occupied wooden huts covered by thatched roofs and usually with sunken floors, one all-purpose living-room and outhouses. Fires were lit on open hearths, the smoke going up through a hole in the roof. Generally an ale-house was to be found, and a building large enough to hold the moot or village council when it met to take decisions on matters of local importance. The villages would usually be protected by a stockade, a ditch or a bank to discourage marauders, human or animal.

The countryman worked from morning until sunset ploughing, reaping with scythes, planting, digging, mowing, weeding, spreading dung and sometimes bringing forest or waste under cultivation. In a colloquy written by Aelfric, Abbot of Eynsham, in about the year 1000 a ploughman is made to say:

> I work very hard. At daybreak I drive the team out to the field. No winter weather is so bitter that I dare stay at home for fear of my lord; but when the oxen are yoked and the share and coulter fixed to the plough I must plough every day a full acre or more . . .

An acre was in fact the normal day's ploughing expected of villagers. The ploughman had also to look after the oxen he drove, feed them with hay, give them water and dispose of their dung. And since it was such demanding work to extract a livelihood from the soil if the weather was bad or a pestilence prevailed or murrain decimated their cattle, many free peasants were compelled as the years passed on to accept obligations to wealthy and powerful landlords. As Dorothy Whitelocke wrote, 'the impression of late Anglo-Saxon society given by Domesday Book is that the lesser freemen depended more on the lord to whom they commended themselves than on their kinsmen'.[5]

Parts of England were cultivated in open fields, that is to say, large arable fields where farmers had strips on which they could grow what they liked. The fields were called 'open' because they were big enough to contain land cultivated by all the villagers and because they had no fences or hedges between the strips, though hurdles were in fact essential for keeping out wild or straying animals. The strips were separated from each other by furrows. The reasons for having strips were various, but the most important was that the ploughs drawn as a rule by eight oxen or six oxen and two horses needed to be turned as little as possible. In addition to the open fields for growing crops, villagers might have hay meadows, grazing land, woodland, which offered fodder for swine, and sometimes marshes and ponds. Woodland was particularly valuable because pigs were the commonest kind of meat eaten by Anglo-Saxons.

Air photography has revealed that the Celtic square or rectangular fields disappeared almost completely from the Midlands and were replaced by strips. Such strips have been discovered in many parts of England, except where pastoral farming predominated. The north and north-west, the highlands, the fenlands, Wales, the Welsh border country, East Anglia, the Weald, the New Forest and stretches of Devonshire and Cornwall never had strip fields. Although it has been said that 'the plough was king in the eleventh century', it must never be forgotten that sheep farming was nearly as necessary to the Anglo-Saxon peasants as the growing of corn. The shepherd, like the ploughman, lived a full life, as he had not only to take his flock backwards and forwards to the pasture land but also to guard them with dogs against wolves and thieves. It has been estimated that by the time the Normans came there were about three or four sheep to every man, woman and child in the country.[6]

Nevertheless arable farming was essential to the community, because not only did it produce grain for bread, the staple diet of the poor, but also fodder needed by farm animals. Wheat and rye were sown in the autumn and barley and oats in the spring. As the supply of manure was generally insufficient farmers must have learnt by experience that it was wise to leave part of their land fallow so as to recover fertility every year or every other year. Where mixed farming was practised the cattle, sheep and goats would graze on commons or meadow and pigs munch acorns or mast in the woodland; but meadowland was not extensive so it is likely enough that use was made of the stubble, left in the fields lying fallow, for grazing. The laws of Ine and Alfred show that the Anglo-Saxon rulers were much concerned about the protection of the arable fields against the incursions of wild animals such as wolves, bears and wild cats and about preserving timber needed as building material or firewood, and therefore laid down penalties for the unleashing of swine in the woods without permission and the unauthorized felling and burning of trees. Gradually questions of common interest to smallholders and tenant farmers, such as the rotation of crops, the joint ploughing necessary owing to the scarcity of draught animals, the clearing of forests, the sharing of meadows and the cultivation of woodland, must have led to the taking of decisions by the village assembly or (later) the manorial courts. But it was not until the twelfth and thirteenth centuries, when the growth of population and the need to plough up fresh land by a united effort became paramount, that they caused much of the country to be subject to what is called by historians 'the common-field system'.

Surprisingly little industry is associated with the coming of the Anglo-Saxons. Evidence exists of soap-making, the production of leather goods, woodwork and metalwork and the manufacture of glassware, which had to be laid sideways on tables because it would not stand upright. Textiles were home-made. The wealthy could buy gold jewellery, including beautiful brooches, and silver spoons, but no jewellers' shops have yet been discovered. Pottery was less distinguished than it had been among the Celts. Stamped pots have been found chiefly in East Anglia, the stamps being symbolic and representing the pagan gods after whom our days of the week are named – Tig (Tuesday), Woden (Wednesday), Thor (Thursday) and Frey (Friday). Frey was the fertility god; the symbol of Thor, the thunderer, was a swastika. Some potters worked for specific cemeteries; others made household goods, which were sold by barter, since initially no coins were minted.

Silver and copper coins have been found which date from the seventh and eighth centuries and were issued by individual moneyers. The penny is believed to have been named after Penda (632–54), ruler of the Anglo-Saxon kingdom of Mercia. One of his successors, Offa (757–96), introduced a heavier silver penny bearing his name, which was to remain the basis of English currency until the time of King Henry III. Offa is also credited with promoting commerce through his relatively friendly relations with the Emperor Charlemagne, whose dominion covered much of western Europe. English merchants visited France and the Baltic countries to display and sell their wares. Exports included woollen cloaks, cheese, hunting dogs, pottery and metal goods as well as slaves, not quite such an extensive list as that of the earlier Celtic exports outlined by Strabo. Imports included wine, fish, pepper, jewellery and wheel-made pottery, luxury goods for the most part. But clearly the introduction of a generally accepted silver coinage was evidence of the growth of trade.

Undoubtedly the English people who replaced the Celts throughout much of the land in the late sixth century were primitive, illiterate and violent, with no coinage, little trade, no towns or stone buildings and small-scale agriculture. The nobility fought, hunted, drank and feasted. They lived in large halls built of wood and containing stone floors with a screened-off service area, the walls hung with arms, warmed by log fires, where 'they sat long at supper and drank hard', surrounded by their armed retainers seated on built-in wooden benches. In the evenings the hall was lit by candles, rush lights or oil lamps. If the sparks flew upwards from the central hearth and caught the thatched roof and the timber walls, these buildings were quickly set on fire. Often late-night parties in the noblemen's halls ended in flames, drunkenness and confusion. Men wore their hair long, grew moustaches and dressed in knee-length tunics and cloaks buckled at the right shoulder and long trousers. The women wore linen undergarments and full-length tunics with tight sleeves, and the well-to-do sported girdles, brooches and necklaces of garnet or amber, crystal or amethyst. Outdoors the nobility entertained themselves by hunting wolves and other prey, indoors by singing and listening to music from harps, lyres and drums, or by playing a kind of draughts. They drank wine and mead, ate quantities of meat and river fish and were partial to herrings: they prized a wheaten loaf (though rye was the ingredient of most bread – the month of August is named after the Anglo-Saxon word for rye). Besides cereals, fruit and vegetables were plentiful and the best people ate butter. Men carried knives with which to cut their food, but seldom forks or spoons. As with the Celts, they rarely suffered from bad teeth as the only sweetening was still honey. On the other hand, arthritis was common, plagues frequent and medical treatment confined chiefly to herbal remedies and magical cures aimed at the credulous: for example, an elaborate charm comprising gibberish was incanted to prevent dysentery and amulet rings were worn to staunch bleeding. By the time of King Alfred, a devout Christian, in the ninth century his laws laid down that 'the women who are in the habit of receiving wizards and sorcerers and magicians shall not be suffered to live'.

In contrast with the men of substance who fought, hunted and drank but did not toil, the lot of the ordinary villager consisted chiefly of work. He had either to plough, plant and reap or look after herds by day and by night. The only treats he could look forward to were drinking parties at harvest time and dead men's wakes. In the long run his struggle to prise a sufficient living from the soil was liable to be defeated by the weather or illness or fire and sword. When his kindred could no longer help him he was obliged to turn for security, if not comfort, to the service of greater men.

Remarkably little is known about how the Anglo-Saxons divided up and organized the cultivation of the lands they had acquired when they settled in their new homes. Theirs was an aristocratic society, so it is reasonable to assume that the kings or chieftains had the pick of the best lands and that they in turn endowed their thanes with some of them. On the other hand, the rank and file as pioneer farmers sought for lighter and more easily worked soil in which to grow their crops. After all, once the Celts had been thrust back, assimilated or enslaved, plenty of good land was to be found in the east or south of the country with access to the fresh water so necessary to rural life. Anglo-Saxon settlements were particularly thick along the Thames valley. Vast tracts of wasteland and scrub could be used to pasture animals and of woodland to feed pigs. Anglo-Saxon laws insisted that landlords must not encroach on such areas to the extent of denying to their tenants the enjoyment of customary rights in them.

The village community was the basic social unit in Anglo-Saxon England, though many hamlets and single farms are also known to have existed. A village consisted of small wooden huts clustered round a church, a pond or a green, or alternatively of huts spaced out along a lane or a street. In one of the few villages that have been excavated well over a hundred such huts were discovered, but no larger building; the guess has been hazarded that if the village was controlled by a nobleman his residence or hall might have lain at some distance from the agricultural settlement. The usual position, as has been noticed, was that villagers required about thirty acres of arable land to support themselves and their families. They were expected to obey customary laws relating to their holdings, to find their taxes to the king and later to the Church, and meet their debts promptly. They paid for the tenancy of their land by producing rents in kind and also might provide specific services for their landlords; thus they were only half free, but they were not serfs. They seldom left their villages, except to attend their lord's courts ('hall moots', where rights known as 'sake and soke' were exercised). Town dwellers were few. Big landlords often employed their own craftsmen, such as goldsmiths, blacksmiths and carpenters.

In some cases where a landlord furnished working capital and tools for leaseholders, it was laid down that if he attempted to increase their rents by demanding additional services, the tenant need not agree to them unless he were given a free dwelling. If any villages existed without landlords or with several landlords (as in a few cases that were later recorded in *Domesday Book*), they must have been exceptional.

During the last quarter of the sixth century the Anglo-Saxons inflicted a series of defeats on the Britons, who were driven back into the south-west and into Wales. The principal kingdoms that were then set up by the Angles, Saxons and Jutes consisted of Bernicia, Deira, and Lindsay in the north and Kent, Sussex and Wessex in the south. Five remaining British kingdoms were noted during that century by Gildas, who castigated their rulers for fighting among themselves and leading unchristian lives. Bede added to 'the unspeakable crimes' recorded by Gildas the failure of the Britons to 'preach the Faith to the Saxons who dwelt among them'. How far Roman civilization and culture survived the settlement of the Anglo-Saxons is still disputed. Gildas himself knew Latin and read Virgil, and it is reasonable to suppose that in the Welsh monasteries other monks knew of Latin literature. On the whole, however, it is safer to suppose that what English society was to acquire by way of Roman law and Roman culture owed most to the conversion of the new inhabitants by the Roman Catholic Church, which was begun at the end of the sixth century and completed by the close of the seventh century, when fifteen bishoprics had been set up and the parish system introduced.

By then England was moving towards political unity. Three principal kingdoms covered the land: Northumbria in the north, Mercia in the Midlands and Wessex in the south: mighty kings emerged, such as Offa in Mercia, who built a dike stretching from north Wales to the Bristol Channel, which marked the frontier with the surviving Celts, and Alfred the Great, educationist and law-maker; both laid claims to be overlords or even 'kings of the whole land of the English'. By the reign of Alfred (871–99) the Anglo-Saxons were becoming literate, and the beginnings of English history were marked by the foundation of the *Anglo-Saxon Chronicle*, which unfortunately confined its attention to political and religious events and throws little light on social and economic history. But Bede, whose *History of the English Church and People* was translated into English at this time, possibly by Alfred himself, is a little less specialized and reminds his readers at the outset that Britain was 'rich in grain and timber; had good pasturage for cattle and draught animals, and vines cultivated in various places ... well known also for its plentiful springs and rivers abounding in fish'. It was a tragedy that just as King Alfred was beginning to fashion a world of the mind and the spirit, the country should have once more been torn apart by invaders who, tempted by a land of milk and honey, loaves and fishes, started, as the Anglo-Saxons had done before them, first to loot and then in the last third of the ninth century to colonize.

In some ways the assault of the Vikings – a word that meant pirates, who came from Denmark, Norway and Sweden – can be compared to that of the Anglo-Saxons themselves, who had peopled a fruitful country five centuries earlier. Like them they were pagans, like them they were seafarers and like them they began by raiding and afterwards turned to settlement. Furthermore their malignity was exaggerated, since the impression conveyed by documentary evidence derives from the writings of Christian monks, who found all heathens obnoxious. Indeed when Alcuin, a Yorkshireman who entered the service of Charlemagne, learned about the first Viking ravages, which destroyed the church at Lindisfarne in Bernicia, the northernmost English kingdom, he wrote a letter to the Christian people living in Kent advising them to read Gildas, the monk who had described the devastation by the Anglo-Saxons, and added 'you will find that you are almost in the same case'. Finally, just as the term Anglo-Saxon was used to cover a variety of European peoples, so the word Viking was employed as a generic phrase embracing all Danes, Norwegians and Swedes.

However, differences can also be discerned. For example, the Norsemen were familiar with Christianity, which held sway in much of southern and western Europe; they were not merely farmers but active tradesmen too, accumulating considerable wealth in silver through commerce with the east; they were also fishermen and as boat-builders were infinitely superior to the Anglo-Saxons. Moreover the English raiders, to begin with at any rate, had been confronted with the sophisticated Roman system of defences, whereas the Vikings discovered, no doubt to their surprise, that the English had neither a fleet nor coastal fortifications. That was why the new assailants were able with impunity to sack churches and monasteries that had been built near the sea.

The exact motive force of the Viking attacks, which covered much of Europe during the ninth century, has been disputed. It is sometimes argued that the Viking expeditions were not caused by overpopulation but were launched for social and political reasons: youthful kings or war-lords with splendid sailing ships and skilled seamen at their command realized their ambition to find fame and fortune overseas. Nonetheless much of north-west Scandinavia was infertile and the climate unfriendly; if it had to support some 500,000 Danes and 200,000 Norwegians, then hunger for land surely played its part. Some of the Vikings raided not England but Ireland and the outlying Scottish islands, such as the Orkneys and the Shetlands. Once they consolidated their positions, they managed to live fairly harmoniously with the existing inhabitants. After all, they had much the same social system as the English, who, like themselves, came from the north of Europe, based on ties of kinship and obedience to their chieftains. Although at home the Vikings were mainly stock-breeders, in their new colonies they practised a similar kind of agriculture to that of the Anglo-Saxon farmers, with the distribution and organization of the arable fields determined by the need for co-operative ploughing, the ploughland rather than the hide becoming the basis of rural arrangements. They were tolerant of religions other than their own; and they were rapidly Christianized.

Consequently although the Scandinavians maintained their own customs and were socially dominant in the areas which they conquered and settled, they did not disturb the established population by massacre or eviction. Indeed, they opened up fresh land to cultivation: this was definitely the case in north-eastern England and also in Leicestershire, Nottinghamshire and Derbyshire. The fenlands and the swamps in East Anglia had not been attractive to invaders, but valuable land was available for colonization once it had been cleared. The Romans had pioneered with drainage. In some places the Vikings are known to have bought and sold estates. How precisely the land they obtained was divided is not known, but it was done, so the *Anglo-Saxon Chronicle* records, by their armies. Either the warriors were given shares according to seniority, or they acquired the overlordship of Anglo-Saxon villages which they enlarged. Certainly an element of military compulsion can be seen in the establishment of the Viking settlements throughout eastern England, which nearly a century later was to be known as the Danelaw, an area positively defined in a treaty concluded in 886 between Alfred the Great and one of the Danish kings, Guthrum: it stretched in effect from Northumberland to Buckinghamshire.

In contrast the Norwegians, who mostly reached north-western England indirectly from Ireland, were purely colonists, who settled in Lancashire, Cheshire and Cumberland, particularly in the coastal districts. Here again the local population was not displaced. In the Danelaw neither the institutions nor the methods of farming and trade of the settlers differed materially from those of the English except in two respects. The first was that a large proportion of the Danish settlers were freemen, not bound by obligations to any particular landlord. Many of them were known as 'sokemen', of whom no fewer than 11,000 were listed in Lincolnshire alone. The precise meaning of a soke is uncertain; literally a sokeman was a man who owed suit at a court of law: it is likely therefore that he was required to attend a lord's court and pay him in occasional labour or money as recognition of his superior personal status, but did not need his lord's permission to alienate his land and was himself responsible for payment of his taxes (*geld*). A large number of freemen were also recorded in parts of the Danelaw. Neither the sokeman nor the freeman necessarily owned many acres of land or more than one or two oxen. They did, however, represent the rank and file of the Viking armies that settled in England (particularly in the north-east and in East Anglia) and enjoyed a degree of personal liberty superior to that of the average Anglo-Saxon villager.

Secondly the Vikings proved to be litigious people. Heavier fines were levied by their codes of law for breaches of the peace than by such Anglo-Saxon codes as those of the Kings of Wessex, Ine and Alfred. Possibly that was because they were less, not more, law-abiding than the English. But in any case it came to be recognized that in the Danelaw a different customary law was administered in the *wapentakes*, a Danish word equivalent to the 'hundreds' into which the Anglo-Saxon shires were subdivided. The Danes introduced the first juries – juries of presentment – consisting of twelve thanes, who swore to accuse no innocent person and to protect no guilty one. When those accused were presented at the *wapentake* courts they were tried by ordeal, a rough-and-ready method, which meant in effect that they were likely to be judged guilty.

Broadly then it can be said that the Viking colonists proved good farmers, adventurous sailors, tradesmen who opened up commerce across the North Sea, sticklers for the letter of the law and people capable of living peaceably with their neighbours, while a large number of them were freemen who possessed their own property, with which they could do as they pleased. Many Scandinavian words were absorbed into the English language, notably the word law itself and also husband, happy, wind and sky. 'An Englishman', it has been said, 'cannot thrive or be ill or die without involving the use of a Scandinavian word.'[7] The Vikings had a distinctive hairstyle, with 'bared necks' and 'blinded eyes', meaning fringed hair. They were hard workers and heavy drinkers, took baths regularly and contributed to the growth of commerce and the development of market towns. They helped to transform the social and economic life of England.

In so far as the historical impact of the Vikings on English life was novel it was, however, partly brought about by reactions against them. King Alfred and his successors, who fought them and ultimately subdued them, did so both by building a navy and by establishing fortified *burhs*, which in time attracted markets that in the long run transmuted them into country towns. Ports too were fortified, as in Southampton and London. These *burhs* and ports (a port originally implied a town with a market) were protected by stonework, earthen mounds and reconstructed Roman walls. At the same time the Vikings themselves built new towns: they enlarged York and for a while occupied London. The Danish armies set up military bases known as the Five Boroughs – Lincoln, Nottingham, Derby, Leicester and Stamford – all of them on rivers, behind which their colonists, having divided out the land under military supervision, were able to practise peaceful and profitable arable farming and stock-breeding.

Experts have disputed whether the Vikings had been commercially minded in the lands from which they first migrated. They had no coinage of their own and the evidence of mercantile activity is derived largely from the excavation of vanished towns. On the other hand, the treasure that they accumulated from raiding other countries and from piracy must have been partly spent on buying foreign goods, which would, after all, have been a form of trade. These contacts and their skill as sailors would have stimulated foreign trade after they settled in England. The newcomers were also proficient at woodwork and ironwork and in building ships. It is not surprising, therefore, that the area of the Five Boroughs and much of East Anglia, which were largely peopled by Vikings, were reckoned before the time of the next invasion, that of the Normans, to be the wealthiest, most populous and busiest regions in England.

By the tenth century, having fought victoriously against the Vikings, the Anglo-Saxon kings achieved a measure of political unity throughout the land. The Vikings were Christianized and the Church was powerful. It was in this century that a monastic revival took hold, so extensive that it is estimated to have absorbed a sixth of the wealth of the kingdom. The idea of 'tithe' – that is to say, the idea that a Christian should contribute a tenth of his income to religious purposes – dated from the seventh century. However, it was not until the reign of King Athelstan (925–39) that payments to the Church such as plough alms (a penny from each plough team), burial fees, Peter's Pence (paid to the Papacy) and church scot – a tribute in kind due at Martinmas for the support of the clergy and based on a man's landholding – were enforced by secular penalties. The reign of King Edgar (959-73), which was also known as the Age of Dunstan, after the pious and influential prelate who became Archbishop of Canterbury, saw not only the building of monasteries but also the introduction of severe punishments for failure to pay tithe, which became reserved entirely for the upkeep of parish churches, though some of it found its way into the pockets of the landlords who built them in the first place. Obviously, tithes paid on crops ('the great tithe') and on farm produce of all sorts, and the various church dues demanded by law, constituted a heavy burden on the free or semi-free peasants which, when added to the exaction of *geld* and *feorm*, must (especially in bad times) have been a threat to the independence of smallholders, who relied simply on the cultivation of their own land to maintain themselves and their families.

Later in the tenth century, too, the Viking invasions were renewed and the vigour of the royal Anglo-Saxon dynasty undermined. King Ethelred (978-1016) vainly attempted to buy off the new invaders by levying a tax called *Danegeld* (usually but not always at the rate of 2 shillings per hide), but finally gave up the struggle and fled to Normandy. From 1016 to 1035 England was ruled by a Danish king, Canute (Cnut), the 'first Viking leader to be admitted into the civilized fraternity of Christian kings'.[8]

During Canute's reign (he was also King of Denmark and Norway) commerce flourished. It was protected by a sizeable navy, which was paid for by the renewal of *Danegeld*. Merchants were active both in London (with an estimated population of over 10,000) and in York; Norwich, Winchester and Southampton were fair-sized towns. It was believed that 10 per cent of the total population lived in towns during the early eleventh century. Besides trade with the Baltic countries and France, close relations with the Papacy (Canute himself visited Rome in 1027) opened up business with Italy. Continuing commercial relations with France and Flanders at about this date are witnessed by elaborate treaty arrangements over tolls and the safety of ships' cargoes. As in Celtic times, imports consisted chiefly of luxury goods, jewellery, silks, furs and wines, but oil, pepper and fish (from Normandy) were also purchased. Exports from England still included slaves and hunting dogs, metalwork, textiles and embroidery, but cheese and butter also appeared among them. Precise figures do not of course exist, but various scattered pieces of evidence suggest that English commerce expanded significantly in the years that preceded the kingdom's conquest by Duke William of Normandy.

At the same time taxation was high. In 1018, the year Canute was acclaimed king, he levied a tribute of *geld* amounting to £72,000 plus £11,000 from the citizens of London. The collection was so unpopular that rioting took place. Not only did King Canute collect *geld* to pay for his navy but he also instituted an annual tax known as *heregeld* to meet the cost of his army. Furthermore he maintained the stringent penalties imposed by his Anglo-Saxon predecessors for failure to pay dues to the Church and gave orders that tithe from arable and sheep farmers must be punctually collected. Because of these secular and ecclesiastical taxes the lot of the peasant, whether Anglo-Saxon or Scandinavian, must have become harder during his reign.

Heavy taxation continued to be levied by Canute's Danish successors. In 1041 King Harthacnut ordered the whole of Worcestershire to be punished because two of his thanes had been murdered in Worcester Cathedral when they were collecting taxes. Fiscal grievances were supplemented by difficulties due to natural causes. In the year when Harthacnut died, 1042, 'as he stood in his drink and fell on the ground with horrible convulsions', the *Anglo-Saxon Chronicle* also recorded that the weather was severe and the crops suffered and 'during the same year more cattle died than anyone remembered either by reason of disease or inclement weather'. Thus Anglo-Saxon England entered its last quarter century subjected to high taxation and economic depression. Both have been experienced since.

Notes

1 It has been suggested that this rescript of the Emperor Honorius was addressed not to the British cities but to Bruttium in Italy, but this argument has not been generally accepted. John Matthews, *Western Aristocracies and the Imperial Court A.D. 364–425* (1975), p. 320

2 D.B. Horden (ed.), *Dark Age Britain* (1956), p. 15

3 J.N.L. Myres, *Roman Britain and the English Settlements* (1937), p. 436

4 John Wacher, *The Towns of Roman Britain* (1966), p. 422; S.S. Frere, 'The End of Towns in Roman Britain', in John Wacher, *The Civitas Capitals of Roman Britain* (1966), p. 85

5 *English Historical Documents c. 500–1042* (1955), p. 58

6 W.G. Hoskins, *Provincial England: essays in social and economic history* (1963), p. 6

7 O. Jespersen, *Growth and Structure of the English Language*, cit. in H.P.R. Finberg and J. Thirsk (eds), *The Agrarian History of England and Wales A.D. 43–1042* (1972), p. 473

8 F.M. Stenton, *Anglo-Saxon England* (1943), p. 391

THREE

Early Medieval England

During the reign of Edward 'the Confessor' (1042–66), the last Anglo-Saxon king of England but one, the country was prosperous, even wealthy. It has been described as one of the richest countries in Europe, with a population that has been estimated at about two and a half million including the Celts, Anglo-Saxons and Scandinavians. That was smaller than the supposed population of Roman Britain and may be presumed to reflect a decline in the amenities of civilization. But it was a comparatively large population, as so much of the land was still forest and waste; certainly in a bad year, such as 1044, when a terrible famine is recorded, corn was so scarce that the price rose to unparalleled heights. In general, however, the weather was temperate, with warm summers and dry winters, and famines were rare.

English society was then dominated by a small group of leading land-owners plus a much bigger group who had only one or two smaller estates. Within these estates tenant farmers and agricultural labourers lived together as neighbours and often as fellow members of the same village church. Most of the villages that existed before the eighteenth century were already to be found on the map. Thus England could be considered as an old country fairly fully settled. As Professor Postan put it, 'the occupation of England by the English had gone far enough to have brought into cultivation and covered with agricultural settlement most of the area known to have been occupied in later stages of English history'.

The kingdom could afford to pay out substantial sums of *geld* to maintain armies and fleets and to buy off the Vikings. Seventy mints were at work in the country and the English silver coinage was the wonder of the world. In 1051 the country was sufficiently flourishing for the collection of *geld* to be temporarily suspended and the weight of the coins to be increased from eighteen to twenty-seven grains. Besides the coinage, hoards of unminted silver were accumulated during the eleventh century. King Edward had spent his youth in Normandy and while it is an exaggeration to say that during his reign the 'normanization' of England had already begun, he had many friends and acquaintances, including the German Emperor and the King of France, a fact which helped to stimulate international trade, bringing the offshore island into a closer relationship with the rest of Europe.

Although in the main England was a country of large estates, clustered villages and small hamlets, it was also starting to be urbanized again for the first time since the Romans left. One-tenth of its people now lived in towns. The population of London rose to about 30,000 by the eleventh century. Other sizeable towns included York, Oxford and Lincoln. The affluence of East Anglia and the commercial contacts of the Danish settlers there were reflected in the fact that both Norwich and Ipswich were particularly busy towns. In East Anglia sheep farming as well as arable was becoming important. Already wool was beginning to be a valuable export, especially to Flanders, where cloth was manufactured. The sale of raw wool to Flanders and elsewhere helps to explain the growing wealth of silver in England during the eleventh century. Most English towns depended on commerce and internal trade rather than industry for their development. The only industry of any significance was the mining of minerals such as tin and iron ore.

During this century the village rather than the shire remained the centre of social and economic life. Villagers (*villani*) might be freeholders or tenants of a landlord to whom they paid rents or for whom they provided services. In addition were cottagers (*bordarii* or *cottarii*), who did not have enough land to feed their families and had to work for others. The average villager, however, possessed a holding large enough for his essential needs (fifteen to thirty acres) and could grow rye or wheat for bread and barley and oats to make ale and porridge and to provide fodder for his sheep, goats and cows, though the cows were few in number, much milk and cheese coming from ewes and goats.

Partly because of the disruption of country life brought about by the redistribution of estates after the Norman Conquest and partly owing to bad harvests, epidemics or other periodic misfortunes, the ordinary villager became increasingly dependent on his landlord for help and protection. Consequently, as the years rolled by, the medieval 'villein', as he was known, developed into a kind of serf, while slaves, previously the lowest class in the community, numbering at least 5,000 in the middle of the eleventh century, disappeared, chiefly because their economic value was considered doubtful. In much of the country small farmers worked in their own fields and also had to provide labour for their landlords if asked. They could not leave the landlord's estate or manor, as it came to be called, without his permission and then might have to pay him a fine (*chevage*) for receiving it. They also had to accept financial obligations, such as payments at the time of their sons' marriages (*merchets*), at deaths (*heriots*), when their daughters misbehaved (*leyrwite*) and on other occasions in accordance with the custom of the manor (*tallage*).

In the uplands – in Northumbria, for example – where husbandmen were principally shepherds, hamlets or isolated farms were the centres of life: here the landlord was a chieftain to whom the hamlets paid food rents, but their inhabitants rarely had to work on his home farm, for where it existed it was devoted to animal husbandry. In Wales village lands were divided into 'in-fields', intensely cultivated, and 'out-fields', used to feed cattle or on which to grow occasional crops. Kent was an exceptional shire, for here too were hamlets, but the arable land consisted of single fields where groups of kinsmen worked together, and parts of the shire were purely pastoral. East Anglia was also unusual, for it was dominated by mixed farming without any regular rotation of crops, and the villagers tried to concentrate their arable strips in one corner of the open fields.

Other parts of England contained no lord's land at all, or no freeholds or no serfs; but the Midlands came to consist chiefly of manors, which included a lord's home farm or 'demesne' and a large amount of land ploughed and tilled by villagers who were at best half free. In eastern England more free tenants were to be found. The unfree villager's obligations were determined by the customs of the manor where he happened to be. In a good season he might manage to subsist in reasonable comfort. In many areas the food and drink that he obtained from grain was supplemented by fish and eggs. Flour was ground in local water-mills, belonging not to the community but to the landlord, who had to be paid for their use. The villages and hamlets were surrounded by huge amounts of wasteland and woodland. This was a kind of bonus for husbandmen, since it provided them with game, food for their sheep and pigs and also with firewood. Even marshes could be utilized as sheep walks.

As Edward the Confessor had no son Duke William of Normandy, an ambitious and masterful man in the prime of life, who doubtfully claimed that the succession to the throne of England had been promised him, invaded the country, tempted, like the Anglo-Saxons, the Danes and the Vikings before him, by the wealth of a land five times the size of Normandy. Whether he really hoped to subdue it or not, his crushing victory over his rival claimant, Harold Godwineson, at the battle of Hastings enabled him to be crowned at Westminster. The Normans introduced not only a new dynasty but a new aristocracy, a new language, French, and a reorganized Church. Unlike previous conquerors, the Normans did not consist of a horde of hungry peasants eager to colonize a land with an agreeable climate and a fertile soil. The Conquest was 'the establishment of foreign landlords over an indigenous population'.[1]

A typical family that came over with the Conqueror were the fitz Gilberts, cousins of Duke William. Richard fitz Gilbert was granted the lordship of Clare in Suffolk, which gave its name to the English branch of the family; but Richard also obtained holdings of land in various shires and by marrying into another wealthy family acquired further estates. By the thirteenth century the Clares were Earls of Hereford and Gloucester and Lords of Glamorgan and Gwynlewg and reputedly the second richest peers in the realm.[2] The destruction of King Harold's army along with his brothers and kinsfolk, together with the defeat later of rebel English nobles, gave the new King the opportunity to confiscate large English estates and transfer them to his followers. By the end of his reign in 1087 King William himself held one-fifth of the cultivated land in the country, his earls and lay tenants-in-chief one-half and the Church one-quarter. By that time also only two English barons (south of the Tees) were tenants-in-chief, that is to say, held their lands directly of the King. All other lay tenants-in-chief, fewer than 300 in number, were Normans, Frenchmen, Bretons or Flemings. Only two bishops were Englishmen.

Apart from the transformation of the tenants-in-chief the most significant change introduced by the Normans was the concept of the manor. That is not to say that manorial estates and routine labour services had not existed before. But the Normans assumed that the whole country was divided into landed estates, each containing lords of the manor, with tenants under an obligation to pay their *geld* or taxes at the lord's hall of residence (*mansio, manerium* or *manoir*). These manorial estates varied considerably in extent: sometimes they might cover several villages; at other times they could be coincidental with only one village community; and a number of villages were shared between more than one manorial lord. Broadly, manors were composed of peasant communities with the lord's rights superimposed. On the whole, the trend was for the manor and village to grow together. The concept of a landed estate, owned by a powerful lord and consisting of free tenants, half-free husbandmen, cottagers and serfs or slaves was characteristic of England in the tenth and eleventh centuries, but as an institution with manorial courts, where local questions of a civil and criminal nature could be settled, it was established and made uniform in the reign of William I.

The Norman concept of the manor was part and parcel of a legal view of landholding. What the Normans insisted upon was that all land was owned by the king and that landlords held their properties directly or indirectly from him. In Frank Barlow's words, 'every holder of land was a link in a chain which led ultimately to the king and the links were forged as finely as medieval man could contrive'.[3] At the top of the social pyramid the king enfeoffed, that is to say, vested control of estates in, his Norman baronage, while at the base the villagers commended themselves to the protection of barons and knights who, in return for rent paid in money, kind or services on their demesne land, undertook to care for their dependants against all comers. The act of commendation was common throughout Europe in the tenth and eleventh centuries and the process had begun in England well before the arrival of the Normans. The accumulation of estates by comparatively small numbers of landlords had indeed been characteristic of the reign of Edward the Confessor. Most of the really large estates or 'honors', as they were called, were scattered throughout different parts of England. Whether this was because similar patterns had existed in Normandy, or whether Norman tenants-in-chief were vested with estates that had already been dispersed by their previous Anglo-Saxon owners, is not clear; but what is known is that King William enfeoffed the men whom he trusted most with the lands that lay on the borders of Wales and Scotland and on the eastern and western coastlines, because he relied on them to secure peace on the frontiers.

All the king's tenants-in-chief were required to maintain forts and bridges, to provide castle guards and to perform other military services if called upon to do so. The tenants-in-chief in turn vested household knights with land and used them to maintain law and order in their honors; they also relied on them as escorts when they made their progresses through their estates. But the Norman kings retained the Anglo-Saxon militia or *fyrd* and normally employed professional soldiers or mercenaries, who were hired for prolonged campaigns in England or France. The idea that mounted and armoured knights were essential to warfare in the early Middle Ages is mistaken. Horses were expensive and therefore not to be put at risk if avoidable. Moreover most military operations consisted of sieges, where cavalry was not needed. Gradually the baronage was allowed to pay money to the monarchy instead of providing military services; this was known as shield money or 'scutage' and was employed by the king to hire mercenaries. Both William I's sons raised scutage and by the time the Angevin dynasty ruled it was done regularly, notably during the reign of King John (1199–1216). The host of knights and horses, familiar to later generations from the pictures in the Bayeux tapestry, that William I carried over as his army to win England by the battle of Hastings, soon became obsolete.

In essence the Norman regime was administratively tidy. That is why British historians used to write of 'the manorial system', 'the feudal system', the 'open-field system' and so on, even though these systems have at times been too precisely defined. The greatest triumph of William I's reign was not the introduction of these systems, but the official record compiled by a fact-finding inquiry into the lands and wealth to be found in the royal domain and in the hands of the tenants-in-chief. The survey was carried out hundred by hundred. Twelve questions were asked in each case so as to elucidate in every manor or estate the names of the landholders at the time of Edward the Confessor and in the reign of William I, the size of the holdings, their present and potential value, their liability for taxation, the number of their inhabitants – freemen, sokemen, villagers, cottagers, slaves – and the amount of woods, meadows, pasture, mills and fisheries. The exact purpose of the inquiry has been the subject of debate, but broadly the aim was to ascertain the real wealth of the country the Norman Duke had conquered. The survey is of fundamental importance to the economic historian, because the information was supplied either by the tenants-in-chief themselves or by local juries summoned from the hundreds to the shire courts. The compilation of the King's Book (it was not until ninety years afterwards that it received the name of *Domesday Book*, 'because its decisions, like those of the Last Judgement, were unalterable')[4] was a unique achievement, for it painted a convincing picture of how men lived in a land ruled chiefly by the plough.

The economic structure of England set out in *Domesday Book* is of manorial estates consisting of fiefs. The king enfeoffed his honorial barons, the barons enfeoffed their knights and so on along the feudal chain. But the landholders developed their properties in different ways. First, they might cultivate their own home farms or demesnes through stewards and bailiffs, who reported to them regularly on the value of the crops and herds, which could either be assigned to their own use or be sold at fairs and markets. Secondly, they could, and generally did, lease most of their land to tenants, who paid rent in money, kind or services. Thirdly, the landholder could let his land to a middle man or 'farmer' (*firmarius*) for a fixed sum over a fixed period of time during which the farmer would enjoy all the rights belonging to the lord, including, for instance, the profits of jurisdiction and the customary services of the sub-tenants in return for agreed annual payments. The disadvantage of such contracts from the landholder's point of view was that the farmer naturally exploited the estate to its maximum yield and thereby impoverished it. Nonetheless the latest view is that almost all the Domesday estates were 'farmed'.

The Norman Conquest made a bigger impact on the social than on the economic character of the community. In the first place, French became the spoken language of the ruling classes and the Normans, by bridging the Channel to the European mainland, opened the way to the acquisition of French culture. By the twelfth century heraldry became fashionable and tournaments were introduced into England – five tilting grounds were to be licensed by King Richard I (1189-99). The castle was a Norman innovation, although with the exception of the Tower of London, reconstructed during William I's reign, castles were initially built of wood rather than stone. To begin with, castles were erected chiefly in towns, but by 1100 thousands of them had sprung up throughout the country, being intended as baronial strongholds. In many places houses were knocked down to make room for them. Chain mail was worn by knights and expensive breeds of horses were ridden by them.

Not only did the newcomers control the shire courts, but they also had honorial courts over which their sway was almost as absolute as was the king's in his own peripatetic court (the *curia regis*). The manorial courts (*halimotes* or courts leet) also reflected the authority, sometimes exercised with mercy and sometimes with harshness, of the lord's representatives, usually his stewards, who presided over them. Often these courts ordered the hanging of thieves, whether they were caught in the act and whether they were arrested in the manor or in its neighbourhood. But by and large rough justice was done, and the average peasant could understand clearly enough what was reckoned fair and lawful, especially as he was often called upon to perform as judge or juryman in determining the minor affairs of the manor.

In England hunting was of course no novelty, but it was a passion with William the Conqueror, who introduced the idea of royal chases protected by special laws. The most unpopular of these hunting preserves was the New Forest in Hampshire; by widening the boundaries of the forest several villages and hamlets on the outskirts were completely destroyed. Heraldry, 'courtly love' and chivalry, which have been called the ethics of a military aristocracy or a closed caste of knights, can all be assigned to Norman times. King Henry I hung a shield painted with golden lions – precursor of the royal arms – around the neck of his son-in-law, Geoffrey Plantagenet, upon his marriage in 1127. But these ceremonial aspects of the life of the ruling classes did not attain their apogee until the reign of Richard I. None of it can have meant much to ordinary Englishmen, for whom the manorial court, the baronial castle and the village church were the symbols of authority they had to respect. Otherwise they were set apart from their Norman conquerors, who, in Professor Barlow's words, represented 'a restless, drunken and emotional society gorged after 1066 with unaccustomed wealth'.

From Norman times onwards the village church was the hub of social life. Over 8,000 churches were to be found in England by the end of the thirteenth century. The bells rang out to remind the people not only that it was a holy day or that Mass was being celebrated, as it was every day, that a wedding was in progress, or a funeral service was being conducted, but even to tell them that it was the right time of year to plant peas and beans. The congregations of parishioners were made more conscious of the character of Christian beliefs through staring at mural paintings and sculptured images of saints than by listening to prayers recited in Latin. But, as in Anglo-Saxon times, the church was also employed as a market-place or as the scene of dancing and merry-making, though such uses were deprecated by the bishops. The churchyard, too, was often the habitation of the living as well as of the dead: there fairs were held and sporting events took place and some priests kept their cattle.

But the Normans, though they reorganized the bishoprics, were more concerned with promoting monasticism than with the duties and behaviour of the village clergy. Hitherto only Benedictine monasteries had been established in England. In 1077 the first priory belonging to the celebrated reformist order of Cluny was set up at Lewes in Sussex and in the twelfth century the Cistercian and Carthusian orders, both promising austerity and simplicity, began opening houses in different parts of the country. The late Professor David Knowles entitled the century and a half that lasted from 1070 to 1216 'the monastic period of English spirituality'. In 1100 over half the seventeen cathedrals were monastic. Generous gifts of land were conferred on these new orders by kings and noblemen for the salvation of their own and their wives' souls. Whole churches were granted to foreign monks, who not only kept their endowments but also the tithes and merely paid vicars a pittance. The rectories, which received church dues in full, were usually in the hands of junior members of wealthy families, who might or might not attend to their ecclesiastical duties; their earnings amounted to about twice those of a tenant farmer and they were supplemented by charges for baptisms, marriages and funerals.

The gulf between foreign monks and the native clergy grew wide. The principal way in which the monks benefited the kingdom was by setting up hospitals and expanding the wool industry with large flocks of sheep kept in their fields. But the monks led a life apart, dedicating their souls to the service of the Almighty, while the ordinary English parochial clergy were for the most part simply leading members of the village community, who cultivated their glebe (the land belonging to the local church) like any other villagers owning a few acres. Although during the twelfth century Church Councils forbade the marriage of the clergy (except those in minor orders), the majority had wives and families. Gerald of Wales (Giraldus Cambrensis) wrote of a typical clergyman who 'kept a hearth girl in his house who kindled his fire, but extinguished his virtue'. Life was short. Fathers often handed over their tenements to their sons before they died, since without the possession of land a man could not marry. If the father died young his widow might be allotted a third of his goods and chattels, but his eldest son could inherit the tenement when he became fifteen. Because they had to wait for a home of their own, men and women generally plighted their troth and were bedded long before they married, even though fines could be imposed by the manorial courts for acts of fornication. As was usual in later English history, once a woman was with child, a wedding followed with all due ceremony.

So naturally the village clergy must have known what was going on, and can scarcely have been strict about the sexual behaviour of their parishioners. Few of these clergy were educated men; in origin they might have been bright village children who were apprenticed, as it were, to the vicar of the parish. If they were the sons of villeins, their fathers had as a rule to buy permission from their landlords to send their children to school, for some slight knowledge of Latin was the stock-in-trade of the village clergy. John Pecham, Archbishop of Canterbury, asserted in 1281 that 'the ignorance of the priests casts the people into the ditch of error'. Generally speaking, they contented themselves with the familiar ritual of the church

45

services, which except on Sundays were little attended by ordinary folk; for the landlord and his henchmen preferred them to get on with their work in the fields. It was not until the Franciscan greyfriars and the Dominican blackfriars came to England in the first half of the thirteenth century that eloquent and persuasive preaching reached the mass of the people.

Strangely enough (to quote the words of Professor Carus Wilson), 'the widespread establishment of monasteries' was 'a potent influence on the growth of English towns and trade'.[5] For the monks bought food, drink, clothing and building materials for themselves and their servants and sold the produce of their estates to raise ready money with which to pay their papal taxes. The towns of St Albans and Bury St Edmunds, both containing shrines, were visited by pilgrims who needed to be entertained and looked after as in a hotel, and developed in that way. New towns, as has been noted, grew up during the reign of Alfred the Great and his successors, partly at least out of the defensive *burhs* built to resist the Danish invasions. But the coming of the Vikings in the tenth century had destroyed a number of infant English towns (such as Ely), while the Norman Conquest initially proved a setback to town life because King William I laid waste and depopulated many of them when he devastated the Midlands and northern England in the process of suppressing rebellions against his government during the early part of his reign. Furthermore, in a number of towns houses were demolished to make room for the Norman castles.

It was only a temporary setback, however. In the long run the presence of Frenchmen in England opened up trade with the European mainland and induced foreign merchants to settle in London and elsewhere. One of the leading characteristics of town life was the holding in them of weekly or twice-weekly markets, a practice widely carried on until the present day. Even before 1066 it has been said that 'every borough had a market and every borough had a port, a place of trade,'[6] where fishermen sold their herrings, butchers their meat and countrywomen their eggs and cheese.

In the early Middle Ages towns were built or rebuilt on the sites of former Roman cities (*civitates*); their walls and gates were repaired and the main roads to and from them reopened. The building of towns required a royal licence or 'charter of liberties', but this was freely granted because in return for a variety of privileges, such as the right to levy tolls and establish a municipal court, the burgesses undertook to pay a regular fixed sum into the royal treasury: this was known as the *firma burgi* or, if granted in perpetuity, the fee farm rent. King Richard I founded Portsmouth and King John founded Liverpool. Sometimes the right to build towns was delegated by the king to secular and ecclesiastical magnates. By the thirteenth century examples of town planning were to be found at St Albans, Bury St Edmunds, Salisbury and Oxford, but most new towns were expanded villages or reconstructed Roman cities, dominated by cathedrals or castles and often centring on market-places. Town houses were built of timber and merchants lived over them behind their shops. It is an oversimplification to attribute the growth of towns to any one cause. For example, cities that were capitals of shires had often been deliberately fortified centres of local government. But, in general, new medieval towns owed their existence to economic reasons. The wealth of many of them derived from the wool trade.

A good part of the Italian cloth industry and almost the whole of the cloth industry of Flanders became dependent in the early Middle Ages on the export of English wool. The bulk of the wool obtained from the sheep of western England, the Midlands and Yorkshire was exported. Flocks of twenty to thirty thousand sheep were not uncommon on a number of estates. The shepherd was a valuable and busy man. He was advised to 'provide himself with a barkable dog' and lie nightly with his sheep. During the lambing season he would arm himself with a stock of candles because he had to sit up with the sheep all night. The shepherd who owned his own sheep was generally excused from labour duties exacted from other villagers by their landlords. If, however, the shepherd was working for a manorial estate, he received perquisites such as a bowl of whey, the right to keep a number of his own sheep with his landlord's flock, and to take some of the sheep's urine as manure.

Though much of the English wool was bought by foreign merchants, coarser wool, such as that obtained in Devonshire and Cornwall, was prepared by carding, spinning, weaving, fulling, dyeing and finishing to make native cloth. English cloth was purchased by the royal household, but the export of such cloth was relatively small, though some coloured cloths found their way to Venice and Spain. In spite of attempts by the government to prohibit the export of wool during the thirteenth century so as to give encouragement to the manufacture of cloth at home, foreign sales continued virtually uninterrupted. Thus the export trade remained the most profitable side of the wool industry. Large landowners would make contracts with export merchants; middle men – sometimes burgesses in the towns – would move around collecting wool from local peasants and then sell it to big exporters.

The first assembly of wool merchants met in 1275 and granted the proceeds of an export tax on wool to King Edward I (1272-1307). Richard I's ransom had been paid for largely in wool; and it was to prove a diplomatic weapon of high value to Edward III (1327-77) when he embarked on what was to be the Hundred Years War against France. The wool tax varied from 7 shillings to 40 shillings a sack (364 pounds in weight); forced loans were raised on wool from time to time, which came to be known as the 'maltote'. To simplify the collection of wool taxes the staple system was introduced by the government. Staples – official markets – were set up in places abroad and at home where a monopoly of selling wool was imposed. The first compulsory foreign staple was created in 1313 and the first home staple in 1326. The English merchants who paid taxes on their sales were not unduly concerned because they could recoup themselves by raising the price or paying the growers less. Wool, it has well been said, 'entered into every phase of English life in the Middle Ages'. By the first decade of the fourteenth century over 32,000 sacks were exported annually. The average price per sack was 10 marks or about £7. The wool dealers or 'woolmen' were 'financial capitalists in a pre-capitalistic age'.[7]

Besides the foreign merchants who came to England to buy wool, Jews had likewise arrived at about the time of the Norman Conquest, but do not appear to have had much to do with commerce in the Middle Ages. They were chiefly financiers – or money-lenders – many of whose loans are known to have been to landowners, including one archbishop of Canterbury. They were confined to ghettos and were under the special protection of the king, who could tallage them, that is to say, tax them, as he wished. Edward I expelled them from his kingdom in 1290.

The wool industry and the domestic cloth industry were not the only factors in promoting town life. Commerce, which had been stimulated by the settlement of the Vikings in eastern England and had transformed such towns as York, Lincoln and, above all, Norwich, expanded rapidly in the twelfth and thirteenth centuries. Tin, lead and coal were exported as well as corn, butter, cheese and hides. In return wine was imported from France, fruit from Spain, Portugal and Italy and fish and whale oil from Scandinavia, which also supplied pitch and tar. Currants came from Greece, sweet wines from the Levant, and dyes, such as woad, were also brought from France. Foreign merchants, notably Germans and Italians, settled not only in London but also in a number of east-coast ports. Newcastle upon Tyne was founded by Henry I and exported coal and lead. Other east-coast towns which thrived on commerce were Ely, Yarmouth and Ipswich. In the west overseas trade, particularly with Norway, made Bristol into a growing port.

Domestic industry also thrived. As early as the twelfth century the establishment of craft gilds of weavers and fullers bore witness to the development of the cloth industry. It suffered a setback in the thirteenth century, when increased exports from Flanders swamped much of the home market, but recovered by the middle of the fourteenth century, when some 50,000 cloths were exported. The processing of salt for preserving meat gave employment in a large number of towns and ports. Iron was fashioned into spades, sickles and other agricultural tools. Lead was needed for plumbing and silver was extracted from mines in Derbyshire and sent to the mints.

Besides the regular town markets were fairs, which also required a royal licence. Annual fairs, some of them lasting as long as a fortnight, were generally associated with religious festivals: for example, that of St Giles at Winchester and that of St Ives in Huntingdonshire. They were often patronized by foreign as well as English buyers. Care was taken to prevent both markets and fairs clashing with one another. It is fascinating to realize how much religion impinged on trade and industry. Markets were held in churches and graveyards. Until the reign of Henry III (1216-72) Sundays were the most popular days for town markets, because it was only then that working men and women found time to do their shopping.

Craft gilds, though they were comparatively few in number during the early Middle Ages, had religious functions and often religious origins. They selected a patron saint and made themselves responsible for maintaining lights on his altars. They also performed Mystery Plays. 'It is easy to understand', it has been observed, 'how a religious fraternity when composed of most of the men of the town following a particular trade would come to interest themselves in purely trade affairs.'[8] But the gilds that flourished most in the era after the Norman Conquest were merchant gilds, which conferred on their members the exclusive right to buy and sell at the town markets without having to pay tolls. Normally the right to form a merchant gild was granted in town charters, and the town government often coincided with membership of the merchant gilds, of which at least a hundred are known to have existed in the thirteenth century. They had social as well as economic purposes, but these were less significant.

Although commerce and industry progressed, agriculture remained the occupation of most Englishmen. Even townsmen might own land outside the city walls which they paid to have cultivated. Whatever the size of the population was in 1066, it is believed to have more than doubled between the end of the eleventh and the end of the thirteenth centuries. Because of the need for bread and ale, villagers on the whole preferred arable farming to keeping sheep and cattle in the early Middle Ages. The number of sheep kept then is unknown. Obviously some parts of the country, such as Lincolnshire and the Cotswolds, which had rich grasslands, produced large sheep with long wool, while the chalk uplands in the south-east contained only small sheep with short wool which was not exported but made into native cloth. Although, unquestionably, large abbeys (particularly in the eastern counties) had impressively big flocks, it has been estimated that the number of sheep in the thirteenth century was no higher than in the eleventh century and the average villager is said to have kept only two cows and five or six sheep. It was the fourteenth century that witnessed the greatest period of sheep farming. Sheep were valued for their wool rather than for their mutton. Pressure of population on the supply of food became intense. Prices rose by as much as 50 per cent or more in the first half of the thirteenth century and real wages fell. The productivity of the land declined because of the constant scarcity of manure. When bad weather ruined the crops people actually starved.

The acute need for land which thus arose meant that an impulse was given to agricultural improvement and the taking of fresh soil into cultivation. Landlords either expanded the area of the home farm – the thirteenth century has been described as 'the golden age of English demesne farming'[9] – or aimed at increasing their output by a three-field instead of a two-field rotation of crops. They did not 'farm' their land so much because, as has been noticed, the 'farmers' were liable to reduce the value of their holdings through losses of stock or equipment. Moreover as prices rose, the value of fixed rents declined. So it became more profitable for landowners to recruit agricultural labourers to work for them full-time at a relatively modest cost. These estate labourers were known as *famuli*; they were often recruited from cottagers and received yearly wages. Undoubtedly the direct employment of labour was more productive than relying on customary services, which were reluctantly given in lieu of rent. Nevertheless several landlords reimposed labour services, which had been conditionally suspended earlier, as they were entitled to do. Thus the commutation of services into money rents slowed down, though villagers might only be required to undertake light seasonal work, such as mowing and haymaking in their landlord's meadows. But by the end of the thirteenth century village society was certainly moving away from full-scale villeinage and money rents were becoming commoner.

Husbandmen, who had thus been relieved of excessive obligations to their landlords, now finding their existing acreage insufficient to feed themselves and their families, began wherever they could to obtain new land by clearing waste of scrub and timber. For the villages of England that were built in Norman times or earlier were mostly surrounded by wasteland, woods, marshes and fens. As has been noticed, from Anglo-Saxon days onwards many village fields were divided into strips of various sizes, and it has been inferred that in some cases at least agreement must have been reached among the villagers about how their fields were ploughed, about the rotation of crops and about the grazing of animals when the fields lay fallow. What is certain is that with the growth of population in the twelfth and thirteenth centuries village after village began carving out fresh ploughland from the neighbouring wastes. This process, known as 'assarting', was arduous. It necessitated the sharing of plough teams (since the provision of eight oxen to draw a heavy plough was beyond the reach of most husbandmen) and led easily to co-operation in other matters. We know, for example, that in some Yorkshire villages at this time a group of farmers worked together in breaking the sod of a fresh tract of land year by year. A strip of ploughland, the work of a day, was allotted to each farmer in turn in proportion to the land he already held in the village fields.

Clearly the rotation of crops in such newly acquired land had to be agreed upon. Other decisions that were required to be made concerned gleaning, the division of hay meadows, the pasturing of sheep and goats, the provision of mast with which to feed pigs and the maintenance of rights of way to the strip fields. Decisions on these important questions were reached either in the manor court when the estate coincided with the village, or else at a village assembly meeting in the church or the ale-house. This common-field system, which lasted until the eighteenth century, evolved gradually and was by no means rigid or universal, since much depended on the nature of the soil in each area; nor did it apply where sheep farming was the principal occupation. But unquestionably it reached maturity in the thirteenth century when the search for more land was imperative, prompted by a growing population and rising prices, and it became necessary to make the best possible use of the strip fields.

Nevertheless the problem that remains is whether Englishmen were better or worse off in the thirteenth century than they had been before. From 1180 to 1220 England suffered from a period of inflation which has even been compared with that of the sixteenth and twentieth centuries:[10] but a boom undoubtedly followed, as was shown by the rise of prices, higher capital investment, expanding markets and the building of Gothic churches. Commerce prospered. Besides raw wool and metals, corn was exported, notably to Norway, whence the well-to-do acquired among other things falcons in return. Wines from Bordeaux and Gascony were also luxury imports (English vineyards were already being abandoned during the previous century); fine coloured cloth was brought from Flanders and Italy and silks and spices from the Near East. Domestic demand was considerable. The towns needed food and pottery off which to eat it. Timber and stone were required for building, wood or coal for lighting fires, metals for plumbing.

As usually happens, it was the rich who profited most from this increasing economic demand. The estates of the bishops of Winchester, the bishops of Ely and the abbots of Peterborough all rose in value in the thirteenth century. Taxation was not excessive. Some monastic estates, particularly those of the Cistercians, became in effect great capitalist ventures, earning huge incomes from their sheep runs. Thus it is beyond doubt that the large landowners, lay as well as ecclesiastical, flourished during the thirteenth century. According to the anonymous author of a life of King Edward II (1307–27), 'the earls and other magnates of the land, who could live according to their station or their inheritance, regard all their time as wasted unless they double or treble their patrimony'. They did so by exploiting their resources to the full, using manure and marl to augment their arable yields, improving their drainage, employing capable managers and full-time labourers such as ploughmen and dairymaids and by buying up the land of their poorer neighbours. The higher clergy all benefited from gifts, generously bestowed on them for pious purposes. The gentry or 'knightly class', who helped to run the country by serving as keepers or justices of the peace, as jurors or coroners or forest officials and by taking an active part in local government – heads of families who might have owned several manors or at least estates of 500 to 600 profitable acres – generally succeeded in maintaining, though not necessarily bettering, their material position; some of them in fact had to borrow or alienate part of their heritage and were reluctant actually to become belted knights, as this was proving expensive. Yet they liked to emulate the standard of living of the baronage and sometimes this cost them dearly.

But what of the bulk of the peasantry, who earned their living by working in the fields all day in order to feed and clothe themselves and their families, besides often having to help on their landlord's farm and pay him rent or customary dues? They surely were no better off. Professor Edward Miller has written: 'Wherever we look, the immediate impression conveyed by the records is that villages were very full of people, so full that the expansion of cultivation was failing to keep pace with the multiplication of mouths to be fed.'[11]

A contrast can then be drawn between landowners great and small, who prospered because of their ability to sell corn and wool, and ordinary modest farmers, the yield from whose soil might have been deteriorating owing to the impoverishment of well worked fields caused by lack of fertilizers. Indeed, they may have been ignorant of the value of enriching their soil, for dung was used as fuel and straw was burnt. The increase in population, which dates from the eleven-eighties, was reflected in rising rents and prices, though wage rates remained fairly stable and thus real wages fell. This can be considered one of the greatest inflationary periods in the history of England, which reached its peak at the end of the twelfth century.

The second half of the thirteenth century has been described as a period 'when the steady worsening of the ordinary peasants' conditions of life was so widespread as to imply a general failure of agricultural and industrial development to keep pace with mounting numbers'. On the other hand, the fact that, owing in part to the steep rise in the price of corn, which doubled between the beginning and end of the thirteenth century, new land was being brought into cultivation and with it a fully matured common-field system, ensuring an agreed rotation of crops, meant that some real benefits were gained by tenant farmers. Not only were wasteland, woodland, moorland and marsh ploughed up, particularly in Cheshire and Warwickshire, but a hundred square miles of fenland were reclaimed in Lincolnshire. The overpopulation of the villages may also have been checked by driving some countrymen into the neighbouring towns. Fifty-two new towns were built in the twelfth and fifty-seven in the thirteenth century. Cloth manufacture came to villages, especially in Gloucestershire, Somerset and Hampshire. Fulling mills were erected throughout the country; weaving at any rate was not confined to the towns.

In spite of mitigating factors, however, the standard of life of the ordinary villagers, whether they were ploughmen or shepherds, appears to have declined to mere subsistence level before the Black Death, the plague which shattered the whole country in 1348. Even the villager who kept sheep was hit by scarcity of pasture, which landlords tried (usually with success) to retain for their own use. The condition of the peasantry in general during the thirteenth and early fourteenth centuries has been pictured as 'one of growing impoverishment'.[12]

What did Englishmen and women look like at this time and how did they occupy themselves when they were not working? Well-to-do landlords did not of course toil in the fields: they left the running of their estates to their stewards and bailiffs. The Normans who settled in England, according to William of Malmesbury, were 'so elegantly attired as to arouse envy'. At the table they were epicures, 'but not to excess'.[13] They wore tunics with short sleeves, fastened by a belt, and mantles secured to their throats and shoulders, banded stockings and low shoes. Their ladies wore long gowns of dull hues with jewelled belts. By the thirteenth century brighter-coloured dresses, made from imported cloth, became fashionable. Peasants wore breeches with their shirts tucked into the waistbands. They wore no hat or cap and generally worked bare-legged. Peasants' coats were worn to the knee, those of the knightly class to the calf, and the nobility's to the ankle. Norman residences, often built of stone, were more sophisticated than the glorified barns of the Anglo-Saxons. They had upper floors with a vaulted undercroft and stairs leading to the halls, which were arched, tiled and ornamented and furnished with trestle tables and benches.

Villagers continued to live in wooden cottages with thatched roofs and usually two rooms, one of them a kitchen, where food was boiled or baked and served on spits. Chimneys were uncommon and windows had shutters but no glass. Stone castles and houses began to be built in larger numbers in the twelfth century. Carpets and baths were introduced by Henry II's queen, a Frenchwoman from Aquitaine. Manor houses might have walled-in gardens and fish ponds, nut trees, flower beds and, above all, fruit trees and vegetable patches. The typical pleasure garden was an orchard. Entertainment was sometimes provided by wandering minstrels and jugglers, but villagers amused themselves with country songs and danced in the ale-house or churchyard. The famous song 'Sumer Is Icumen In' dates from the thirteenth century. Violent sports, such as wrestling, cock-fighting and bull-baiting, took place on village greens. No taverns were yet in existence, but there were cook-shops as well as ale-houses, where the ale cost a halfpenny a gallon. Besides hunting, the wealthy played chess and backgammon, ladies did needlework, and jousting tournaments were arranged, which ladies enjoyed as spectators.

Norman patronage of monasteries brought with it the establishment of song schools and grammar schools. Great cathedrals were built which required the services of choirboys. The universities of Oxford and Cambridge, which were principally concerned with instructing future clerics in Latin grammar and theology and where the teachers were chiefly foreign scholars, came into being in the thirteenth century, and since Latin was a universal language, education and learning were international. The distinguished English scholar, John of Salisbury, who was a master of logical and scientific methods, became Bishop of Chartres.

The so-called twelfth-century Renaissance occurred during a period in English history that was relatively prosperous and peaceful. The thirteenth century witnessed political struggles throughout the British Isles, beginning with the rebellion against King John, which resulted in the sealing of Magna Carta, and culminating at the end of the long reign of Henry III in the first meetings of parliaments. But it was practically free of foreign wars, since King John had lost most of his ancestors' conquered territories in France.

In sum, during these centuries (at any rate up to the last quarter of the thirteenth century) the population of England was certainly increasing, town life was being extended, London was growing fast – it received its first charter from William I and the right to appoint its own sheriff and justiciar from Henry I – agriculture and industrial production were growing, hitherto uncultivated land was being farmed, prices were rising, as was capital investment, new markets were opening, particularly for the sale of wool, and a native textile industry had its beginnings. Even those historians who assert that these changes did not amount to a 'boom' but 'an impending doom' do not deny that the overall picture was one of social and economic progress.[14] That was to be temporarily halted by plague and famine during the first half of the fourteenth century.

Notes

1 Frank Barlow, *William I and the Norman Conquest* (1965), p. 100
2 See Michael Altschul, *A Baronial Family in Medieval England: The Clares 1217–1314* (1965)

3 Frank Barlow, *The Feudal Kingdom of England 1042–1216* (1972), p. 109

4 V.H. Galbraith, *The Making of Domesday* (1961), p. 200

5 *Medieval England*, 1 (1958), p. 212

6 J. Tait, *The Medieval English Borough* (1936), p. 130

7 Eileen Power, *The Wool Trade in English Medieval History* (1955), *passim*

8 Sir William Ashley, *The Economic Organization of England* (1939), p. 30

9 Cf. J.Z. Titow, *English Rural Society 1200–1350* (1969), pp. 44 seq.

10 P.D.A. Harvey, 'The English Inflation of 1180–1220', *Past and Present*, 61 (1973), p. 30

11 *Past and Present*, 28 (1964), p. 33

12 See the introduction to H. Rothwell (ed.), *English Historical Documents 1189–1327* (1975)

13 Cit. Barlow, *William I and the Norman Conquest*, p. 194

14 H. Rothwell, loc. cit. Whereas Professor Postan, Dr J.Z. Titow and Ian Kershaw have taken a pessimistic view of English economic life before 1348, Professor J.C. Russell has maintained that England was a prosperous country in all but the worst years of the fourteenth century.

FOUR

The Late Middle Ages

Although the population of England had been increasing rapidly during the thirteenth century, reaching a level of over three and a half million, by the middle of the fourteenth century it was slowing down or even diminishing. At that time most English peasants were living a meagre existence, often cultivating an acreage which yielded insufficient grain to feed their families satisfactorily. This was partly because the land had been over-cropped or even exhausted in consequence of the scarcity of manure needed to restore its fecundity. Owing to the growing demand for food and drink from a larger population and the decline in fertility of much of the soil, agricultural prices were rising and so were rents. Thus the wealthier landowners benefited. So did such peasants as were able to feed their families on rye, barley, oats and beans, supplemented by cheese from their ewes and cows, while growing enough wheat for sale to pay their rents to their landlords. But many smallholders and customary tenants, who lived on the margin of subsistence, were severely hit, especially in a bad year. Those who had no surplus of corn to take to the market found it difficult to pay their rents or buy the smallest luxuries. It is generally accepted that rural tenants needed to cultivate at least fifteen acres to support a family of five, but it has been estimated that fewer than half the population had fifteen acres in the early years of the fourteenth century: the majority of the tenants on the manor of Taunton, for example, had under fifteen acres on which to grow their crops.[1]

The cottagers, who constituted the lowest level of agricultural society, also had their difficulties. They relied for their livelihood on being hired out as farm labourers; but once the big landlords gave up cultivating their own demesnes, as they were already beginning to do towards the end of the thirteenth century, it was less easy for such labourers to obtain regular remunerative work. Moreover while the wealthy were content to let their land to tenants, the position of the smaller farmers, who also normally hired labour, deteriorated, many of them having to borrow at a high rate of interest or selling out to survive. Another factor that must have injured the corn-growing peasant was that a halt to the reclamation of arable land took place because of the profitability of wool; nearly 30,000 sacks of wool were being exported annually: thus sheep, it could be said, were already devouring men. Farming methods were relatively primitive. Rents were steep and real wages low. One piece of evidence that has been discovered, showing that the economic position of the peasantry was worsening towards the end of the thirteenth century, is that in many instances fines imposed in the manorial courts were being waived because of the abject poverty of the persons involved.

If then, as seems clear, most peasants were hard pressed to maintain themselves and their families whenever the crops were poor, as was the case in 1290, 1314, 1315, 1316 and 1321, they faced a real danger of starvation. The harvest of 1315 was particularly disastrous. Not only was grain scarce, but the resulting search for food of every sort, whether poultry, meat, game or eggs, sent prices rocketing and a terrible famine set in. Moreover the crisis was not confined to England, so relief was hard to procure by importing food. During the famine, according to a contemporary chronicler, the lay and ecclesiastical magnates both cut down the alms they customarily gave to the deserving poor and vagabondage multiplied. The famine was accompanied by the spread of epidemics and a great murrain (or scab) among sheep; it also extended to cattle, causing in some places horses, which were immune to such disease, to be substituted for oxen to draw the ploughs.

The mortality engendered by the famine was underlined by a subsequent rise in agricultural wages, though the famine created poverty and stress for many farmers whether they were free or unfree. Taxation levied on the population and the requisitioning of food to meet the cost of the unsuccessful wars of King Edward II (1307-27) in Scotland were last straws. The English people as a whole were outgrowing their resources, a situation that was to recur in the twentieth century.

A generation after these famines, which killed about a tenth of the population, the plague, which came to be known as the Black Death, reached England in the summer of 1348. It was a bubonic pestilence, coming from the Near East and Middle East, and was spread by black rats. It was also pneumonic and transmitted by direct contagion. Its violence varied from place to place. All English towns were injured by it, but some villages escaped. A conservative estimate that has been generally accepted is that it wiped out a third of the population. The clergy, both monks and parish priests, were the worst sufferers: half of them died in some parts of the land.

It is a mistake to underestimate the effects of the Black Death, even though it came upon a rural society that was already changing its character. During the first half of the fourteenth century the era of 'high farming' or 'demesne farming' by manorial landlords was, as has been observed, nearing its end. The commutation of labour services for money rents had been taking place in much of the north and west of the country, though it had still not happened everywhere in the south and east except in Kent. It has been calculated that in the second half of the thirteenth century money rents represented a higher proportion of rents than did labour services. For the conclusion had been reached by many landowners that it was more profitable to hire agricultural labourers by the week to till their fields for them, or to employ *famuli*, than to depend on customary labour, demanded from tenants, which was resented, scamped and therefore uneconomic. Lastly, other landlords had by then abandoned the cultivation of their home farms, preferring to let their land to free tenants, thus becoming *rentiers* instead of large-scale farmers.

All these trends were accentuated by the Black Death, which unquestionably benefited such smallholders and labourers as survived it. First, the peasantry who could afford it were able to buy land cheaply; secondly, labour could exact higher wages; thirdly, villeins could commute their labour services for modest rents. Free tenants could also obtain longer leases. The rise in wages was prohibited by a royal ordinance of Edward III in June 1349 ordering that both wages and prices must be stabilized. The ordinance was later confirmed by Parliament, which passed a Statute of Labourers in 1351. Similar attempts to hold down prices and wages have been made by twentieth-century governments, hitherto without conspicuous success.

In the Middle Ages these restrictions had to be administered by justices of labourers (afterwards by justices of the peace) who in the long run found themselves thwarted by the laws of supply and demand. Few landlords were able to avoid the payment of higher wages by requiring services from their manorial tenants which had already been wholly or partly commuted, but where they had not been commuted before the plague they did attempt to exercise their rights. When they did so, it was common for villeins to flee from their homes either to another manor or into towns where labour was greatly needed. The fugitives were welcomed and had little difficulty in finding work. It was in fact not the magnates but the smaller farmers, the men who owned a hundred acres or so and employed half a dozen men, who were most eager to prevent wage increases;[2] for they could not transform themselves into *rentiers* as the wealthy were doing. Rises in wages (some were doubled), stable prices, lower rents and the opportunity to buy land cheaply meant that the second half of the fourteenth century was a marvellous time for the mass of the English people who had stayed alive. Furthermore the abolition of week work and even of boon work in their landlords' fields enabled peasants, hitherto only half free, to devote themselves entirely to cultivating their own farmland or to tending their own flocks, actually increasing productivity. The magic of property turned sand into gold.[3]

The commutation of labour services for money rents, as has been noticed, had gone a long way before the Black Death. Landlords were aware, as Walter of Henley observed in his book on husbandry (a treatise written in the thirteenth century), that 'customary servants neglect their work', and that hiring full-time labour from men who had no fields of their own was more satisfactory. But the situation was still fluid after the Black Death. Since the recession continued for many years with prices stationary and wages high, the impulse for landowners to break up and sell or rent their home farms was accentuated. At the same time customary tenants, finding land cheap and wages rising, became increasingly discontented over the remaining feudal obligations and ready to abandon their homes if such obligations continued to be exacted. But it was another hundred years or more before the manorial system completely disappeared.

Meanwhile social unrest gathered momentum. To start with, the justices of the peace did succeed for a time in checking the rise in wages by imposing penalties, though occasionally they met with forcible resistance. On manors where commutation had not yet taken place the tenants often failed to do the work that was demanded of them, even at harvest time, when they were normally feasted by their masters as a reward for their efforts. Cases are known where bailiffs were defied or a manorial lord's hay crops were damaged by sabotage. Repair work was neglected, trespassing became common, rents were withheld, and jealousy was expressed of the well-to-do who sat back to indulge themselves on ample food and wine while serfdom lingered on. William Langland, a minor cleric, was to write during the thirteen-sixties in his celebrated poem *Piers Plowman* of how men 'laboured at ploughing and sowing with no time for pleasures, sweating to produce food for the glutton to waste'. The Black Death was succeeded by further, if less virulent, epidemics in 1361 and 1369, the first becoming known as 'the mortality of children'; gales ruined harvests and frequent pestilences struck the growing city of London.

But possibly the heaviest burden that was felt among the mass of the people was the taxation levied on everyone in the kingdom to pay for the interminable war against France after King Edward III laid claim to be the rightful heir to the throne in Paris. His income from taxation and his estates amounted to about £30,000 a year, and this was supplemented by subsidies voted by Parliament and a tax on wool granted by the leading wool merchants. On the security of such taxes the King was able to borrow from Italian bankers. But while Edward was away fighting in France there was a general refusal to pay taxes, as a result of which the King dismissed his Lord Treasurer, ordered the arrest of merchants and defaulted on his loans from the Italians. 'The Song against the King's Taxes', dating from before his return to England, averred that 'people are reduced to such ill plight they can give no more. I fear if they had a leader they would rebel.' Later the 'Song of the Husbandman' attacked oppression both by tax gatherers and manorial officials.[4] However, a series of victories over the French excited national pride and the Treaty of Brétigny, ratified at Calais in October 1360, gained Edward III a large sum as the ransom of the titular King of France, whom he had captured in battle.

After the war was resumed later in the thirteen-sixties, the English army was less successful. The duchy of Gascony, which the English monarchs had inherited from Henry II, was reoccupied by French forces. Thus the profitable wine trade was lost. Only Calais, captured in 1347, was retained, where the wool staple was established to the advantage of exporters. Edward III's death in 1377 and the succession of his grandson, Richard II, who was a minor, was a grave blow, for once a strong hand was withdrawn the French started raiding the English coasts and attacking the herring fisheries.

Though individual noblemen benefited from the war, no one else did. At the outset of the new reign the regency obtained from Parliament the right to levy a poll tax of a groat (fourpence) from the whole population over the age of twelve and another one, this time graded according to rank, was imposed in 1379, the yield from which proved disappointing. In 1381 a poll tax of 3 groats (1 shilling), which was equivalent to a normal week's wages, was demanded of every person over the age of fifteen; so that a man and his wife, however poor, might be mulcted, provided no wealthy households were to be found in a village or a district willing to contribute generously to the assessment.

This, the third such tax in four years, transformed grumbling into wrath and sparked off a rebellion, generally known as the Peasants' Revolt, though others than peasants took part in it, including some knights, minor clergy and London artisans. The rebellion broke out in Essex during May 1381, when tax collectors provoked the outburst by their intrusions into everyone's affairs: it quickly spread to Kent and East Anglia and culminated in an assault on London by a mob armed with knives, cudgels and axes. Savoy Palace, the home of the King's uncle, John of Gaunt, was burnt to the ground, prisons were broken open and the Archbishop of Canterbury and the King's Treasurer were dragged from the Tower of London to be hacked to death. The underlying discontents of the mass of the people were thus brought to light. What happened was that the comparative well-being that villagers and agricultural labourers had begun to enjoy when, after the Black Death, land grew cheaper and real wages rose higher made men and women the more conscious of lingering grievances. The revolt was a demonstration that they were now so advanced on the roads to freedom and prosperity as to feel rancour at even the vestiges of past oppressions.[5] The main centres of the revolt were in fact the most affluent and flourishing parts of the kingdom. The complete abolition of serfdom was demanded by the leaders of the rebels, together with the ending of poll taxes and the institution of a statutory limitation on rents.

Another deeply felt vexation was over the Statute of Labourers, even though it had by then become a dead letter. Anger with the justices who had tried to enforce it was coupled with hatred of the collectors of the poll tax. Abbeys and priories were attacked and court rolls, which specified the rights of manorial lords over villeins, were set aflame. A withered old woman in Cambridge cried 'Down with the learning of clerks!'[6] Monasteries and churches were broken into because the imposition on villeins by the ecclesiastical hierarchy both of customary services and tithes was particularly detested. Lawyers, Members of Parliament and foreigners (such as Flemings) were also the targets of the insurgents' indignation. The King's Ministers were thought to be corrupt, but not the young King himself, whose sympathies were wrongly believed to lie with the rebels.

Though for a time the upper classes were paralysed by the unexpectedness and ferocity of the revolt, the rising was repressed within a month. It did not, in fact, contribute much to the final abolition of serfdom, but it was the first time that the common people of England had spoken and expounded their grievances. What was even more significant was the resentment shown over restraints on wages and over the burdens of direct taxation, a resentment that has been manifested throughout modern as well as medieval history.

The rise in wages, the fall in land values and the reduced prices of grain that induced big landlords to give up arable farming during the fourteenth century are known to have stimulated sheep farming. Sheep were immune from plague, the labour needed to look after them was comparatively small and the demand for wool from export merchants considerable. Seven years after the Black Death 40,000 sacks of wool were exported annually, and the average output in the middle of the fourteenth century was 18 per cent higher than it had been at the beginning. It is impossible to estimate with any assurance what the total production of wool amounted to yearly, or how large the flocks of sheep in the country were, because of the difficulty of measuring the domestic demand for wool to make clothes; but it must have been growing fast, because between the end of the eleventh century, when fulling was introduced, and the year 1300 landlords had been building fulling mills all over the country since they thought that they would prove extremely profitable. Many cloth-workers were outraged at having to pay for the use of these mills, believing, as has invariably happened with all mechanical inventions throughout English history, that they were robbing men who worked with their hands of their rightful employment.

In fact the proliferation of these mills, which were operated by water power, signalled a change in the cloth-making process so important that it has been called an industrial revolution. Before these mills became available the fulling procedure, that is the beating and compressing of the woven cloth to clean it and thicken it, had been done by craftsmen and 'trodden under foot in water', as Langland wrote. This simple mechanization of fulling saved time and money. Now it was reckoned that a mill could full as much cloth in a day as eighty men. Before it was introduced fullers were usually townsmen. At first the merchant and craft gilds forbade taking unfinished cloth away from urban areas, such as Bristol and Leicester, to fulling mills outside. The mills required access to swiftly running water and were therefore usually to be found in the countryside. Consequently the cloth-making industry became dispersed. Instead of carding, combing, spinning and weaving being done in the big clothiers' premises in towns, much of it was put out to craftsmen working in their own

63

homes. Spinning was frequently done by women (hence the word 'spinster') working in their cottages, and weavers often combined their craft with agricultural work. Cloth for export needed the finest wool. So during the fourteenth century the export of wool declined and that of cloth increased. Whereas in the first half of the century wool exports averaged 30,000 sacks, in the second half they fell to 8,000 to 9,000 sacks. On the other hand, while in the middle of the fourteenth century only 8,000 cloths were exported, from 1366 to 1368 an average of 16,000 were exported; by 1392 the figure was 43,000 and in the first half of the fifteenth century it rose to 56,000.[7]

The reasons for this remarkable growth of the cloth industry and the reduction in the export of wool were various. First, the demand for cloth to be made into soldiers' uniforms was considerable, as it was also for civilian clothing in the colder parts of northern Europe, such as Scandinavia. Secondly, it was cheaper to buy wool in England than abroad for manufacture into cloth because of the heavy export duties levied on raw wool, particularly by the Government of Edward III when he was at war with France. The recovery of Gascony after the war receded from southern France meant that cloth could be exported there and wine brought back. A new group of English merchants, known as the Merchant Adventurers, specialized in the cloth export trade, sometimes employing their own ships of 100 to 200 tonnage. But it was not only Englishmen who sold cloth abroad. Italian merchants, notably Genoese, exported cloth from London and Southampton, partly in exchange for luxury goods such as silks, sweet wines, spice and jewellery. German merchants belonging to the Hanseatic League, who had their own headquarters known as the Steelyard or Teutonic guildhall in London, doubled their exports of English cloth during the fifteenth century, though in return for their privileges they were ultimately compelled to agree to the right of English merchants to trade in their territories in northern Germany and in Danzig. Thirdly, the frequent changes in the location of the wool staples confused the export trade: at one time the only staple was at Antwerp, then at Bruges and then at Middelburg; finally it was at Calais, which remained in English hands until the middle of the sixteenth century. The Merchants of the Staple had a quasi-monopoly (except that the Italian merchants were allowed to carry the wool they bought directly to the Mediterranean and merchants in northern ports, such as Newcastle, were permitted to ship directly to the Netherlands). As the price for their exclusive rights the Merchants of the Staple had in effect ensured the pay of the garrison and the upkeep of the fortifications at Calais, usually by loans to the Crown secured by the Customs on wool. While the Merchants of the Staple and the Merchant Adventurers dominated the export trade, they were not monopolies: any merchant might join them provided he abided by their regulations

The consumption of cloth at home must also certainly have risen. The guess is that at the end of the fourteenth century it might have amounted to about 10,000 cloths a year,[8] the domestic manufacturers gaining at the expense of cloth imported from Flanders that had been valued so highly by well-dressed Englishmen in the early Middle Ages. As cloth was comparatively dear, half the cost of production consisting of the quantity of labour put into it, the larger market which opened up for it at home suggests that the smaller population was reasonably prosperous. In the fifteenth century the industry had its ups and downs. During the first quarter a depression prevailed, but in the second quarter cloth exports, mainly undyed and unfinished, reached their peak; the third quarter saw a decline, partly because the Hundred Years War with France was renewed during the turbulent reign of King Henry vi (1422–61) and partly on account of the long-drawn-out quarrel between English merchants and the Hanseatic League. After Edward iv became King he reached an agreement with the King of France in 1475 and in the same year concluded a treaty with the Hanseatic League. Consequently the export of cloths attained the level of 50,000 a year, which furnished employment for at least 20,000 men and women.

Besides cloth and a diminished trade in wool, chiefly bought and sold in Calais, English exports in the fifteenth century included corn (whenever a surplus arose), metals, especially tin and lead, some coal and hides. Wine was one of the principal imports, coming not only from France, but also from Germany, Italy and the Near East. Twelve thousand tuns (casks) of wine came from the Bordeaux area (the number was much higher before the war, when Gascony belonged to the English Crown), being paid for in grain, fish, cheese and cloth. Wine was cheap, though the cost of carriage was considerable and heavy duties were levied upon it dating back to the middle of the twelfth century. Millions of gallons were drunk by the better off, including gentry and townsmen. It was also sold in taverns, Langland writing of how innkeepers bawled out 'White wine! Red wine! Gascon and Spanish! Wash down your meat with the finest Rhenish!' One fancies however that, as today, labourers stuck to ale, which cost about 3 shillings a barrel, while a bottle of wine could cost eightpence.

During the fifteenth century the population, which had been declining or static since the plagues of the previous century, began slowly to rise again. Young men married earlier and wages were higher. With the abandonment of their home farms by the big landowners, serfdom was vanishing. Arable land was cultivated by smallholders, and free tenants and cottagers were employed as agricultural labourers. Declining productivity of the soil, brought about by the intense needs of the population in the thirteenth century and a shortage of manure, meant that many fields relapsed into waste and hundreds of villages disappeared completely. But because of the amount of land that came on to the market land values still fell and vacant holdings existed. Much arable land was turned over to sheep farming. The bishops of Winchester, for instance, reduced their acreage under the plough and increased their flocks and herds, and several landlords directly managed their pastureland instead of being content with their income as *rentiers*. A few landlords experimented with new crops and others were able to benefit from industry, notably cloth manufacture, but also from minerals such as coal outcrops in Yorkshire and the tin mines in Cornwall.

The structure of society remained hierarchic, as it had been in Anglo-Saxon times. At the top were the ruling classes, dukes, earls and barons. Dukes' incomes averaged £4,000 a year and those of the other nobility around £3,000. Their landed properties assured them such comfortable incomes, even if the services of their retinues and employees became more expensive because of staff shortages after the pestilences of the fourteenth century. For a time the demand for land slackened; it became more difficult to exact manorial dues, such as heriots; the profits from arable farming were hit by rising wages and falling or stagnant prices. But, as at later stages of English history, the aristocracy could stand a great deal of ruin. They could obtain money rents by commuting the remaining labour services; they could raise entry fines; they could turn over to sheep farming; they could profit from ransoms when fighting under Edward III; they could invest in wardships; they could exploit their judicial rights at courts leet; they could let out their meadows; they could marry their children advantageously into the mercantile class; they could even sell fruit grown in their orchards. It has been estimated that the higher nobility was not materially worse off in the later part of the fourteenth century. In fact the ostentatious living and lavish hospitality of fourteenth-century magnates has been seen 'not to suggest straitened resources'.[9] The class below the higher nobility, the bannerets, knights, esquires and vavassors, though sometimes falling into the hands of money-lenders, were able to profit, if on a smaller scale, from the same means as were open to the nobility. They could invest shrewdly in land, obtain profitable windfalls in war time, acquire offices and fees. They could marry advantageously.

Knights varied in character: few of them were any longer the heavily mounted, armed cavalrymen who fought for the Norman kings. The number of such high-class knights had fallen by the reign of Edward I from 5,000 to 500. The knight described in Chaucer's *Canterbury Tales* is 'a true, perfect gentleman' who had fought in the Crusades, possessed fine horses, whose bearing was modest and 'never a boorish thing he said in all his life to any, come what might'. Such knights were men of good families who had served as professional soldiers and were known as knights banneret. In addition there were household knights, who were retainers either of the king or the nobility and acted as courtiers or soldiers as required. Their fortunes were bound up with those of their masters. Some knights were functionaries of abbots, others were petty followers of magnates, a few were lawyers or had been educated in baronial households and then became merchants. By a proclamation of 1278 Edward I laid down that all freeholders with an estate worth £20 a year must accept knighthoods, but the expense involved in becoming a belted knight meant that the honour was often evaded, as it was to be when King Charles I's Ministers revived the distraint of knighthood in the seventeenth century. Some merchants and lawyers welcomed the chance of becoming knights, for they could afford it. Thus wealthy men were able to climb the social ladder. But equally, as Professor Postan wrote, 'the income of the average knight who stayed on his land and did not hire himself out as a soldier did not rise to anything like the same extent as professional officers and may not have risen at all'. The 'knights of the shire', who were first summoned to Parliament at the end of the thirteenth century, were in fact sometimes not knights at all. Whether Edward I by creating an enlarged knightly class and introducing its representatives into Parliament did so because they were a rising class or a falling class has been a matter for argument.

Below the rank of knights came the squires or esquires (often sons of knights), who when serving in the army were paid 1 shilling a day compared with the 2 shillings received by the knights. In peace time this group of knights and esquires comprised the gentry, who managed their own estates, acted as justices of the peace, occupied manor houses or built themselves houses of stone, lived amicably with their neighbours and employed servants and labourers whom they generally, but not always, treated well. Some of the gentry emerged from the yeoman class. The

67

word 'yeoman' is confusing: it has been employed to describe both farmers who owned sixty to a hundred acres of land which they cultivated themselves with the aid of their families and one or two servants; and also 'journeymen' (literally day workers), who hired themselves out to master craftsmen in the towns, qualified men usually hoping to become masters themselves. Such yeomen often had gilds or fraternities of their own which negotiated with the craftsmen's gilds. This was the case, for instance, with the weavers in Coventry and the saddlers in London.

Outside the hierarchy of the landed classes stood the freemen or burgesses of the towns that had proliferated during the early Middle Ages. They were often monopolists laying down strict rules about buying and selling and about who had the right to be elected to the town councils. Such freemen had to fulfil qualifications and pay entrance fees before they were enfranchised. Villeins who had fled from their manors to the towns in the fourteenth century might find work and receive protection from their former masters, but were merely lesser members of the urban communities. Normally an apprenticeship in trade lasting seven years was required before a journeyman could become a full citizen, though this rule might be waived for the sons of existing burgesses. During the fifteenth century more freemen were admitted in most towns, yet the population as a whole remained lower than it had been in the thirteenth century when many towns were growing up. Fullers and weavers, who had in some towns been barred from becoming freemen, were now allowed to do so, understandably enough, as the clothing industry had come to be the most important in the kingdom.

Coventry, Exeter and York were examples of cloth-making towns where burgesses were frequently fullers or weavers. York had a mayor who was a weaver as early as 1424. 'Generally speaking,' it has been said, 'urban life was much easier in the late Middle Ages than it had been in earlier times.'[10] Towns like London and Bristol, whose populations increased little during the later Middle Ages, nevertheless grew more prosperous, chiefly through foreign trade. Thus they contained a distinctive mercantile class which included wealthy citizens like Sir Richard Whittington (though without his famous cat) – he was described by an Italian contemporary as 'that loadstar and chief chosen flower among English merchants' – who could not only afford to be knighted but could aim to marry into the landed gentry. Bristol engaged in much overseas commerce, particularly with Spain and Portugal, exporting the cloth of the Cotswolds and west Midlands. London was the biggest port in the kingdom, had a population of about 40,000 and was rich enough to lend money to English kings.

The mayors and aldermen of the larger towns often had to resolve disputes between the numerous craft gilds, which fixed prices, wages and standards of workmanship, but which were often accused of charging too much for their work. The larger gilds were incorporated as livery companies, though only the older and more prominent members were allowed to wear liveries. In London the Mercers, Grocers, Drapers, Fishmongers, Goldsmiths, Skinners, Merchant Taylors, Haberdashers and Salters were the earliest companies to receive charters. Similar incorporations took place at York, Coventry and elsewhere during the fifteenth century. In London the companies had magnificent halls, made gifts of money to the king and elected masters, wardens and a court of assistants, who were generally self-perpetuating. Thus they were oligarchic and soon the members had only a faint connection with their crafts, as is the case today.

Merchants were for the most part educated men who sent their sons and daughters to good schools. Though they usually married late in life, they had large families. Their average expectation of life was about fifty years. They were charitable both to the parish clergy and to monks, though they evaded, if they could, payment of tithes. The wealthier London merchants bought themselves estates in Middlesex and Surrey and often married their daughters into the landed gentry. In fact they considered themselves to be squires and gentlemen on equal terms with the knights of the shires.

If one thinks of these merchants, the big cloth manufacturers, the exporters, the lawyers (the Inns of Court came into being in the fifteenth century), the landed gentry eligible for knighthood and the yeomen owning sixty to a hundred acres of arable land as well as livestock, who 'could become gentlemen by getting into a lord's household and spending large and plenty',[11] as all belonging to the middle classes – the upper and lower bourgeoisie, if one likes to call them that – one can say that the 'rise' of these classes took place in the fourteenth and fifteenth centuries rather than the sixteenth and seventeenth centuries, as some historians have been arguing during the last forty years. Marxist historians have written of 'kulaks' instead of 'yeomen'. But the truth surely is that the 'middle classes' were as elusive and hard to define then as they are today. It is easier to write of the nobility, the knights and the gentry; the merchants and manufacturers; the husbandmen and labourers, without trying to invent a model society. One thing is certain: that is that greater social mobility existed in the late Middle Ages than ever before. The growth of the textile industry was one factor; the extension of sheep farming was another; the demand for the building of churches was a third. The towns were full of opportunities for the enterprising, and relatively free of class barriers. Sons of merchants could enter the professions or set themselves up as country gentlemen. 'Such restrictions on mobility as existed,' it has been said by an expert on the fourteenth century, 'were not absolute.'[12] The army and the Church also offered openings to younger sons. William of Wykeham, the famous Bishop of Winchester, who founded New College, Oxford in 1379, was the son of a serf.

To sum up, the fifteenth century saw the end of the 'manorial system', under which a peasant could not give his daughter in marriage or move house without the permission of his landlord. The overpopulation of the thirteenth century, which had provided the wealthier classes with the whiphand over their tenants and employees, disappeared with the pestilences of the fourteenth century that produced scarcity of labour and consequently a rise in real wages. By 1400 landlords everywhere had ceased to engage in arable farming for a profit. Land values fell, rents declined, higher money wages had to be paid: all these were factors gradually changing the national economy. But it would be wrong to assume that the ruling classes were materially worse off. The nobility benefited from the Hundred Years War, which ended in the middle of the fifteenth century, by obtaining booty and ransoms. Many of the greater landlords deliberately turned over to sheep and cattle farming. Arable land they preferred to let out for rent; but because the population was smaller, around about three million, they had to lengthen their leases and lower their rents. Wages rose and countrymen as a whole were better off. This may be attributed to a release of energy and enterprise by modest farmers and their families, who worked harder once they owned their own property.

Undoubtedly the fifteenth century was a good time for the lower classes, whether they were tenant farmers, peasant proprietors, tradesmen or shopkeepers. Indeed, it has been claimed that ordinary men and women attained a standard of life that was never reached again until England became fully industrialized.[13] Output increased; rent strikes paid off; serfdom virtually vanished. Luxuries were imported in exchange for cloth. Wage-earners, including agricultural labourers, were better off. It is true that they had to work long hours and were not paid for holidays. But the sumptuary laws – prescribing the food and apparel for each class in the community – indicate that workmen could afford better meals and clothing in the fifteenth than in the fourteenth century. John Gower, the poet and friend of Chaucer, writing in 1375 noted that although labourers did not eat wheaten bread 'they desired to be better fed than their masters, bedeck themselves in fine colours and fine attire instead of sackcloth'. Women, who were rather downtrodden in the early Middle Ages, also found work. Widows looked after their own holdings and took part in ploughing. Though women servants were paid less than men, women labourers were sometimes paid at the same rate as men. Women shone particularly as brewers.

Obviously the clothing of the rich and poor differed. Men reaping simply wore loose doublets and straw hats, sometimes with cloth stockings and ankle boots; ploughmen wore hoods under their hats, tunics, short trousers (*braies*) and mittens. Shepherds wore long smocks and hats on top of their hoods. By the fourteenth century the clothes worn by the upper classes were shorter and tighter, made of fabrics of varying colours. Ladies dressed in gowns, lacings and belts and were not ashamed to show the shape of their bodies, though their gowns were always long and had ample sleeves. The hood (*capuchon*) was worn by all classes, though men might put on hats and caps. Chaucer's yeoman wore a coat and hood of green, his miller a hood of blue, and his merchant a Flemish beaver hat.

Although the gentry classes were expanding, they were the people who were least happy in the fifteenth century. When Henry v was succeeded by a minor in 1422 and the resources of the English Government were wasted in vainly trying to hold and even extend Henry v's conquests in France, law and order broke down. 'Bastard feudalism', as it has been called, prevailed. The great dukes and earls, who are featured in Shakespeare's historical plays, usually had paid retainers numbering 200 or more whom they employed to overawe judges and juries in the law courts, intimidate sheriffs and uphold injustices. Complicated quarrels over property rights were thus seldom resolved fairly. Modest landowners were liable to be assaulted by gangs of ruffians who burnt down houses, ransacked churches and invaded private manors. The Paston family in East Anglia three times found themselves besieged in their own homes by armed bands sent against them by peers of the realm. Merchants were injured by widespread piracy. The Peasants' Revolt of 1381 was followed by the rising of Sir John Oldcastle in 1414 after he had been accused of heresy and escaped from the Tower of London, and by 'Jack Cade's' rebellion in 1450, which frightened the city of London. Between 1455 and 1485 England was divided by the so-called Wars of the Roses, a dynastic struggle, pictured in Shakespeare's plays about the reign of Henry vi, in which that king was finally defeated by Edward Earl of March, who assumed the title of King Edward iv. This aristocratic blood-bath preceded another civil war in which the future Tudor King Henry vii crushed Richard iii, the brother of Edward iv, at the battle of Bosworth.

Ordinary English people were comparatively little affected by these wars of dynasties and aristocrats, though the breakdown of law and order suggests a moral decline. To generalize about the frame of mind among the different classes in late medieval society is difficult. Yet in contemplating the fourteenth and fifteenth centuries in English history one cannot resist speculating on the question of whether the rich and ambitious or the poor and resigned were happier. It has to be remembered that life was short and incalculable and that most people believed that everything might be much better in an afterlife. The rich therefore spent large sums of money on building chapels and chantries and endowing monasteries in order to save their souls. The poor, when they thought about it carefully, considered that they were more likely to go to heaven than their masters.

It has well been said that 'the growth of a conscious, articulate, and moral fervour among the laity was a marked feature of the age'. Walter Langland in book v of *Piers Plowman*, entitled 'The Confession of Seven Deadly Sins and the Search for Truth', attributed the plagues and storms of the fourteenth century to the judgement of God on King and nobility as well as the mass of the people for their sins, and envisaged 'Reason' as telling wasters to go to work, ordering Lady Peacock to leave off clothing herself in furs, Walter's wife to stop wearing a head-dress worth 5 guineas and urging merchants to stop pampering their children. In their sermons the friars also condemned the sins of the rich, while John Wyclif, the Oxford theologian, and his followers, the Lollards, insisted that the Church consisted only of God's predestined elect, that the Bible, the whole of which was for the first time translated into English, was the source of eternal truth and that the official doctrine of transubstantiation was false. Wyclif stigmatized serfdom in any form as anti-Christian: hence the popularity of Lollardy with the lower classes. At the other end of the theological scale the mystics, such as Margery Kemp, stressed the need for every Christian to seek direct contact with God. We know that groups of simple people met in their own houses to read and discuss the Bible, and that even after the drastic measures ordered by Parliament against Sir John Oldcastle and his followers in the second decade of the fifteenth century Lollardy was not crushed, but lived on underground to merge into the puritan movement of the sixteenth century.

In the fifteenth century this puritan habit of mind turned against the monks and the friars. In Chaucer's *Canterbury Tales*, published towards the end of the previous century, they had been held up to ridicule. The monk in these tales was delineated as a huntsman with 'dainty horses' and greyhounds, and the friar as a wanton and merry fellow who kept pocket knives to give to pretty girls and 'knew the taverns well in every town and every innkeeper and barmaid too'. The Lollard authors even extended their disapprobation to ordinary parish clergy, saying that they were to be found

> At wrestling and at the wake,
>   And chief chanters at the ale;
> Market-beaters and meddling-make
>   hopping and hooting with heave and hale.
> At fair fresh and at wine stale
>   Dine and drink and make debate
> The seven sacraments set at sale,
>   How keep such keys of heaven gate?

The laity were also implicitly condemned for their behaviour in parliamentary statutes and royal proclamations. Tennis, football, golf, quoits and chess were all described as unlawful games. Only archery was encouraged. Wrestling, the owning of dogs, and of course poaching were forbidden to the lower classes. The hours when ale-houses might be kept open were prescribed; while gluttons had been pictured by Langland as eating and drinking 'a pint of the best' in the ale-house when they should have been in church, Chaucer's miller was envisaged as telling filthy stories in the taverns. Dances, 'scots-ales' and 'church ales', excuses for merriment, were all proscribed by the Church. In fact these prohibitions and denunciations reveal clearly enough how ordinary men and women tried to enjoy themselves in the later Middle Ages.

Thus one sees two sides of the coin. The poor accused the rich of deadly sins, which would take them straight to hell. William Caxton, the pioneer of printing at the end of the fifteenth century, begged 'the knights of England' to return to the good old days of 'chivalry' instead of going to the baths and playing at dice; and a one-time Chancellor of Oxford University wrote a book instructing the 'knightly class' about the virtues they should possess and the vices they needed to avoid. Dominican friars exposed the iniquities of the rich and idle, just as the Lollards did. On the other side, the ruling classes attempted to prevent their inferiors from entertaining themselves in the ways they relished and could afford, whether in the churchyard, the ale-house or on the village green or at fairs and markets, expecting them instead to toil from dawn to dusk and spend the rest of their time in church or practising archery. But in the words of the late Dr Coulton, 'in spite of squires and church synods, the working man did all he could to escape ... from the dullness of his working days'.[14] That is the only excuse for conjuring up a vision of Merry England in the Middle Ages.

Notes

1 W. Minchinton (ed.), *Essays in Agrarian History* I (1963), p. 41. Professor Titow describes the conditions in the thirteenth century as growing impoverishment unchecked until after the Black Death. Writing twenty-five years earlier John Saltmarsh in *History* VII (1941–3) said that by the thirteenth and fourteenth centuries 'a climax of material prosperity had been reached which was never to be surpassed', and thought the decline did not set in until the second half of the fourteenth century. But the consensus of opinion now is that a decline began before the Black Death.

2 M.M. Postan, *The Medieval Economy and Society* (1972), p. 152

3 A.H. Bridbury, *Economic Growth of England in the Later Middle Ages* (1962), p. 92

4 R.H. Hilton and H. Fagan, *The English Rising of 1381* (1950), p. 83

5 Postan, op. cit., p. 154

6 Cit. E. Powell, *The Rising in East Anglia in 1381* (1896), p. 52

7 E. Power and M. Postan (eds), *Studies in English Trade in the Fifteenth Century* (1933), pp. 11 seq.

8 Bridbury, op. cit., pp. 30 seq.

9 G.A. Holmes, *The Estates of the Higher Nobility in the Later Middle Ages* (1957), pp. 97 seq.

10 Bridbury, op. cit., pp. 75–6

11 Cit. A. Abram, *Social England in the Fifteenth Century* (1909), p. 76

12 May McKisack, *The Fourteenth Century 1307–1399* (1959), p. 346

13 R.H. Hilton, *The English Peasantry in the Later Middle Ages* (1975), p. 106

14 G.G. Coulton, *Chaucer and his England* (1921), p. 280

FIVE

The Coming of Commerce

The outstanding fact about the sixteenth century and the first half of the seventeenth century in England was the rise in prices, which was without a parallel until the incredible inflation in the twentieth century. The price of wheat and barley, essential for the making of bread and ale, increased five and a half times between the second decade of the sixteenth century and the fifth decade of the seventeenth. Several variations occurred between different foods, but the general trend applied to Europe as a whole. On the other hand, the price of industrial products rose much less, largely because the demand for them was more elastic than that for food. Everyone had to eat, but did not necessarily need to buy new clothes.

It used to be thought that the reason for this considerable rise in food prices was the influx of gold from Africa and silver from central and south America and the consequent lowering of the purchasing power of money. The American silver came chiefly to Spain, but the Spanish Government of Philip II, who ruled nearly half the known world, was almost bankrupted by the cost of large-scale warfare in Portugal and the Netherlands and against England at sea, the silver being dispersed throughout Europe in payment for munitions and for imports both of raw materials and food and clothing. But that situation did not arise until towards the end of the sixteenth century. In England earlier, however, the gold and silver coins (even the halfpenny was made of silver) were devalued, first in 1526 and then during the reigns of Henry VIII and his son, Edward VI, in the fifteen-forties by as much as 50 per cent. Each time the currency was debased after an interval prices rose. It was not until the reform of the coinage in 1560 during the reign of Queen Elizabeth I that confidence in the value of money was regained and in fact prices steadied during the fifteen-seventies; but as soon as the English were absorbed in war against the might of the Spanish Empire, following the threat from Philip II's 'invincible armada' in 1588, prices shot up again.

It is now generally agreed that the inflation of food prices was caused first not by the influx of bullion but by a sharp rise in the size of the population and an insufficient rise in the output of grain. As has been noticed, after the Black Death the population of England fell to about two million. By the end of the fifteenth century it started to rise again; and between the fifteen-twenties and the close of the sixteenth century it doubled, reaching nearly five million at the outset of the seventeenth century. Here are two contrasting illustrations. The first is the small village of Wigston Manor in Leicestershire, which is known to have contained 70 families in 1524 and is estimated to have housed 134 by 1603.[1] The second is London proper, which had a population of about 60,000 in the reign of Henry VII: that had doubled by the time James I came to the throne in 1603 and was bursting across its boundaries into Westminster and Southwark. This growth in the population can partly be explained by improved sanitation and fewer epidemics. Bastardy reached a record level in the reign of Elizabeth I. The illegitimacy ratio (derived from parish registers) grew high between 1550 and the first decade of the seventeenth century.[2]

Thus the demand for food mounted, while the supply of agricultural produce did not increase at the same rate. Elizabethan authors like John Fitzherbert pointed to a decline in the fertility of the soil and urged the need for more manuring to improve the yield of crops. A growth in the currency's volume and velocity of circulation further enhanced prices. Moreover since the enlargement in population occurred throughout the whole of Europe, food could not be imported cheaply. And when harvests were poor, as they were during the wet summers of 1594 to 1596, famine resulted.

It was the wage-earners – one-quarter to one-half of the population – who were worst hit by the price inflation, for prices rose more than wages: it has been estimated that the latter only doubled during the sixteenth century. Besides food the price of drink rose nearly sevenfold and that of fuel and light fourfold between 1500 and the outbreak of the Civil War in 1642.[3] In theory it is hard to understand how agricultural labourers survived. But mitigating factors were to be found. Where tenants held long leases rents remained stable; many of the rural population had side-lines; they owned cottage gardens where they grew fruit and vegetables; they might do part-time work weaving or mining and their wives and daughters could have been spinners or knitters. Thatchers, haywards and mole-catchers were in constant demand. In the Midlands and eastern England half the population kept pigs, and some had a cow or two. A large number of wage-earners moved into the towns where they would have been better paid. Apart from shopkeepers who sold food, drink and household goods, towns usually contained small domestic industries: during the reign of Henry VIII eighty-three cap-makers were at work in Coventry and fifty shoe-makers functioned in Northampton (today it is shoe shops that proliferate in towns). Undoubtedly the urban economy was variegated; but in most provincial towns a third of the inhabitants were too poor to be assessed for taxes.

In the countryside few villeins or 'bondmen', as they were now generally called, were left. The change from servile to free labour, begun some two centuries earlier, was virtually completed by the reign of Elizabeth I. A considerable number of customary tenants had by then become copyholders, that is to say, their landlords gave them copies of the manorial rolls which specified their rights in detail and which could be submitted as evidence in a law court. Others held leases which prevented their rents from being raised for twenty-one or even thirty-one years or during two lives. The average husbandman occupied twenty acres – or fewer when the soil was rich – from which he could supply his family with enough food and drink, except in a bad year. In some parts of England he might genuinely have been a mixed farmer: for example, dairy farming flourished in parts of Gloucestershire, Wiltshire and Somerset.

The rural class that fared best in Tudor England was that of the yeoman, the freeholder with some hundred acres at his command, who worked hard himself, employed a few men, ploughed his land with his own oxen or horses, sold his surplus produce in the local markets, served on juries, indulged in hospitality in his comfortable house, 'bountiful both to strangers and poor people', was a farmer on weekdays and a gentleman on Sundays. Hugh Latimer, Bishop of Worcester, and a yeoman's son, recalled the life of his father in a sermon: 'He had a farm of £3 to £4 a year. He tilled so much that he kept half a dozen men. He had a walk for a hundred sheep. My mother milked thirty kine [cows]. He kept me at school and married my sisters with £5 apiece.' Naturally some yeomen aspired to be gentry; it was not difficult to acquire a coat of arms, possibly by slipping a tip into the hands of the heralds who paid periodical visitations to different counties; other yeomen drifted into the higher status through marriage. But quite a few felt it was 'better to be the head of the yeomanry than the tail of the gentry'. After all, successful social climbers have always been liable to be sneered at. In *The Blind Beggar of Bednal Green* a contemporary playwright had a yeoman say to his son, who sought to be a gentleman:

Come, off with this trash,
You bought gentility, that sits on thee
Like Peacock's feathers cock't on a Raven.

The proficient yeomen farmers were not the only class to knock on the door of the gentry. Lawyers who had made their pile bought landed estates to improve their social standing. So did Crown officials and a number of merchants. But basically it was agreed that a gentleman was a man who could live 'without manual labour' and could afford to buy a coat of arms from the heralds. Queen Elizabeth was not keen on excessive social mobility. Only one duke existed in her reign and she had him beheaded. She also issued proclamations discouraging inferior gentry from assuming the title of esquire; she was chary of creating knights and even more so in adding to the peerage, though she made an exception in favour of her fancy man, Robert Dudley.

The emergence of the prosperous and public-spirited yeoman in Tudor England must not blind one to the general condition of the English countryside. It was the husbandmen, either copyholders or tenants at will, who constituted the bulk of rural society, some half or three-quarters of it during the sixteenth century. Although landlords found themselves unable to exact all the ancient feudal dues from their tenants, the husbandmen still had to make such customary payments as heriots, in addition to finding their rents, and had to work hard to provide subsistence for their families. The worst placed were the cottagers, who were employed as labourers and had little or no land of their own. For the comprehensive act known as the Statute of Artificers, which became law in 1563, laid down that the justices of the peace were responsible for assessing wages and that wage-earners must stay in the parish where they were born unless they received permission, recorded in a written testimony, registered by the local parson, of their right to leave. It was also enacted that during the spring and summer labourers must start their work at five in the morning and continue until seven or eight at night, with two and a half hours allowed for meal times. But it is questionable whether all these rules were obeyed and wage assessments fully enforced; yet real wages were certainly low and prices completely out of control.

While agriculture remained the principal occupation of Englishmen in the sixteenth and seventeenth centuries, industry and commerce were growing. One reason for this was that the general rise of prices stimulated industry, while the demand for manufactured goods fluctuated more than that for food and drink. A second reason was that England was at peace for longer periods than most countries on the European mainland. Thirdly, new technological inventions, such as blast furnaces and engines for draining mines, were introduced and cheapened the cost of production. Cannon foundries, sugar refineries and saltpetre works were being built. There were gig mills (which reduced the nap on the cloth by clipping), spinning wheels replacing distaffs and knitting frames for making stockings. Fourthly, the prejudice against the use of coal in preference to wood was being overcome and coal was becoming more widely applied to industrial purposes. Finally, in 1568 two joint-stock companies, were established – the Mines Royal, concerned chiefly with copper, and the Mineral and Battery Works, which made brass – both of which were pioneers of new processes, protected by patents, though they did not prove very successful.

Moreover the idea that internal communications were so bad as to handicap the movement of industrial goods has been exaggerated, even if it was bumpy to drive around in a coach. John Leland, the antiquary, who set out, as he told King Henry VIII in 1546, to see all parts of his 'opulent and ample realm', thought communications were quite good, with many stone bridges, though the road surfaces were generally poor. However, such products as coal and tin that were hard to cart over the roads could be carried along rivers or by coastal shipping around the island. No tolls were imposed on river traffic, as they were in other lands.

Cloth manufacture remained far and away the chief industry, at least until the middle of the seventeenth century. Exports, partly handled by foreign merchants, rose rapidly in the first half of the sixteenth century and steadily during the second half, while those of wool continued to decline, particularly after the staple town of Calais was lost to the French in 1557. 'If the office of Lord Chancellor had first assumed importance in Tudor times,' it has been said, he could have sat 'not on a sack of wool but on a bale of broadcloth.'[4] The early Tudor period has been called 'the golden age of traditional broadcloth manufacture'. Exports, mainly to the Netherlands and Germany, continued to flourish spasmodically until 1614. Most of these consisted of undyed and undressed or 'white' cloth. In that year King James I was persuaded to issue a proclamation forbidding export 'in the white'; since nearly half the cost of finished cloth went on dyeing it, a handsome profit was expected by the King and by an enterprising merchant, William Cockayne, a London alderman, who was granted a monopoly at the expense of the Merchant Adventurers.

The scheme, although it seemed promising enough, proved a fiasco and was soon abandoned, but cloth remained England's largest export until the end of the seventeenth century. This was partly because although the demand for broadcloth, made from short-staple wool, providing warm clothing, declined – broadcloth, as a Member of Parliament was to observe, 'is a heavy and hot wearing and serves but one cold corner of the world' – lighter cloth, known as 'the New Draperies', made from longer, coarser wool, began to gain customers. Its manufacture was increased when Flemings and Walloons, driven into exile by the ferocities of the Spaniards, settled in Colchester in Essex, Norwich and other parts of eastern England. The art of making fustian, a mixture of linen and cotton, was introduced into Lancashire, where rough cloth had been woven in the later Middle Ages. Previously fustian had been imported from Italy and south Germany; here again its manufacture owed much to refugees. The Privy Council licensed these immigrants to make 'bays' and 'says' and 'other outlandish commodities new to England'. Though such settlers were subjected to jealousy and xenophobia, they contributed handsomely to the strengthening of the cloth industry.

Other exports during the period included, as before, metals and minerals. The output of pig iron, made from ore since Roman times, was also improved by the expertise of immigrants, notably from Germany. Primitive blast furnaces were used chiefly in the Sussex Weald, but also elsewhere. Zinc ore, found in the Mendip hills, was alloyed with copper to produce brass, which had hitherto been imported. The tonnage of coal, dug from deeper mines, multiplied fifteen times between the mid sixteenth and mid seventeenth centuries. Only a small amount of it was exported because the need for it at home was paramount as timber became scarcer. Not only was it used for cooking and heating, but it was also employed in brewing, soap manufacture, iron production and other industrial processes. During the reign of Elizabeth I the reputation of English steel was enhanced and by the next reign it was claimed that the finest knives were made in England. Once again foreign workers, who settled in Sheffield, helped to revive a stagnant industry, which dated back to the Middle Ages. Lead and tin were exported in small quantities. The output and price of tin fell during the sixteenth century: it was then bought chiefly by London pewterers. But when the 'coinage duty' or tax on tin and the method of buying it by pre-emption were both abolished in the middle of the seventeenth century, the price doubled, the number of miners grew, and new works were opened.

Recognizable industrial establishments can also be discovered at this time, that is to say, as distinct from what are called 'country industries'.

The famous cloth factory of Jack of Newbury, employing 200 'pretty maidens' with milk-white 'kerchiefs' on their heads to do the spinning alone (backed by 200 men working the looms), appears to have been mythical; but undoubtedly a fairly large number of workers – engaged in mining, soap-boiling, glass manufacture and so on – serving one master on his own premises, were to be found in the Elizabethan age, although the 'putting-out' system, with men and women paid at piece rates and doing their jobs in their own homes, was the most characteristic form of employment.

A great many 'projects' were promoted, from pin manufacture to growing woad. *A Discourse of the Common Weal of this Realm of England*, written in 1549, advocated a whole programme of new trades. But, like Alderman Cockayne's bright idea for dye-works and dye-houses, they were slow to get off the ground and had to cope with Dutch competition. Two exceptions may be mentioned: gun-making and shipbuilding. London and Birmingham both had gun-making companies and plenty of artillery was available to the Parliamentarian side when the Civil War came, though Charles I sent his wife to buy cannon in Holland and France.

Of course, the reason why England was able to remain at peace for so long and develop industries was because it was an island. Therefore a fleet was essential. This consisted partly of armed merchant ships and partly of warships. In 1560 England had 50,000 tons of merchant shipping: by 1629, in the reign of Charles I (who deserves the title of father of the English navy more than Henry VIII), this was doubled. During the first half of the seventeenth century shipwrights concentrated on building heavily masted ships carrying cannon for the navy and privateering. They included first-rates and second-rates of 250 to 500 tons able to mount a hundred guns. This provided ample employment in the naval shipyards at London and Bristol. Merchant ships were mostly small (not more than 200 tons), but larger ships up to nearly 1,000 tons capable of reaching the Far East were built for the East India Company. A substantial number of merchant ships, especially 'flyboats' suitable for use in the Baltic, were bought from the Netherlands, where the Dutch shipbuilding industry was the most advanced in Europe, and also from Scotland.

The development of the shipbuilding industry and of a navy necessary to protect commerce, which was frequently menaced by pirates, was beneficial to the rapid expansion of foreign trade after 1660. Overwhelmingly the principal export continued to be cloth of various sorts. Its export was largely controlled by English merchants, though foreign merchants, particularly those belonging to the Hanseatic League, had previously managed about half of it and they continued to regulate two-fifths of the import trade.

Merchants who sold English cloth abroad had been known since the Middle Ages as Adventurers (though they were not very venturesome), as distinct from the Staplers who exported wool. They concentrated their business chiefly in the Netherlands, where Antwerp was the principal market. After the sack of Antwerp in 1576 the Merchant Adventurers searched for new markets and finally settled on Hamburg and Dordrecht. The Merchant Adventurers received a charter from Henry VII and had been recognized by an act of parliament as a regulated company in 1497. The company prescribed terms of apprenticeship, specified quantities that each member might export, made bye-laws and levied fines for breaches of its rules, but its membership was open to any trader willing to pay its fees. The members included not only export merchants in London, but affiliated members in other big ports such as Bristol and Newcastle. Undoubtedly 'interlopers', that is to say, exporters not belonging to the company, obtained a share of the business. Over this the company complained fiercely to the Privy Council, asserting that such competition lowered prices and raised the cost of imports, so 'bringing much evil and deceitful wares into the realm'.

The discovery of America and the West Indies at the end of the fifteenth century contributed only a little to the expansion of English commerce. The English were not conquistadors or at that time explorers. It is true that Henry VII granted pensions in turn to John Cabot and his son, Sebastian, who are believed to have been Genoese; they set out across the Atlantic in English ships to discover new lands that were open to trade. But John Cabot disappeared into the blue and his son, who appears to have discovered Hudson's Bay and Newfoundland, received a cold welcome when he returned to England: so he entered the service of Spain. Queen Elizabeth I was more amenable than her predecessors to persuasion about the merits of commercial expansion, but was attracted most by the idea of making a profit out of piratical adventures, especially when her country was embroiled in the long war against Spain.

The instrument of English commercial progress was the chartered company formed by enterprising merchants who were accorded exclusive privileges. Francis Bacon, the celebrated philosopher, who served Elizabeth I and James I, declared that 'trading in companies is most agreeable to English nature'. Such companies included the Muscovy Company (trading with Greenland and Russia), the Eastland Company (trading in the Baltic), the Levant Company (trading with the Turkish empire and Persia), and the East India Company, granted its charter just before the death of Queen Elizabeth. Trade with France, Italy and Spain in general was open to all, though French and Spanish companies had a fleeting existence. The only company that was concerned with crossing the Atlantic was the Virginia Company, in which the versatile Sir Walter Ralegh, statesman, admiral and historian, invested a fortune. The colony, which he set up, came to grief; but once tobacco was found to be a profitable crop, a Virginia joint-stock company managed for a time to pay its way. The first load of tobacco from Virginia arrived in England in 1614.

The East India Company also proved successful, especially after it obtained permission to establish a 'factory', that is to say, a trading station, north of Bombay. But from a financial point of view the Royal African Company, in which the courtiers of the early Stuart monarchs invested heavily, was outstanding. For not only did it bring back to England ivory, silver and gold as well as hides from west Africa, but it smuggled Negroes as slaves into the West Indies and later Virginia in return for tobacco and sugar. This triangular trade proved a godsend to English merchants for many years.

It has to be remembered that throughout the Tudor period the government, acting through Parliament (or by issuing proclamations in the monarch's name), interfered or, to use a neutral word, concerned itself intimately with the economic and social life of the country. It did so almost to as great an extent as have governments in the twentieth century. But whereas today governments make money available to assist industries enjoying a monopoly (such as coal and the railways), Tudor governments aimed by establishing monopolies to make money out of industry and commerce and thus reduce taxation. They even tried to prescribe in detail how craftsmen should do their work and how much they ought to be paid. This policy was embodied, as has already been observed, in the Statute of Artificers, which ordered justices of the peace to assess wage rates annually according to 'the plenty or scarcity of the time'. If the justices failed to undertake this duty they were to be fined £5, but if they attended sessions for the purpose they could pay themselves 5 shillings a day. In fact the government's reliance on the justices of the peace, who were overburdened maids of all work, stultified the effect of the act; some justices, for example, satisfied themselves simply by reissuing the previous year's assessment. Indeed, much of the economic policy followed by governments throughout early English history was vitiated by the fact that it was not enforced or not enforceable.

Broadly, governments tried to maintain employment in industry by prohibiting the import of goods that could be made at home, a system pursued or at least advocated in the course of most English history. They also attempted to ensure an even balance of trade. The author of the *Discourse of the Common Weal of this Realm of England* wrote in 1549: 'we must always take care that we buy no more of strangers than we sell to them'. That was why the export of raw wool had been periodically banned, why the manufacture of new kinds of cloth with the advice of experts from abroad was approved, why the exploitation of fishing was supported even to the extent of making Wednesday as well as Friday and Saturday into 'fish days', and why in the first year of Henry VII's reign an act was passed laying down that the wines of Guienne and Gascony could only be imported in English, Welsh and Irish ships; it was also enacted later that such ships must not have foreign masters or crews. These last acts were praised by Francis Bacon, because, he said, they changed 'the ancient policy of this realm from consideration of plenty to consideration of power'. For the same reason more than two centuries later the economist Adam Smith, otherwise a staunch believer in freedom of trade, approved the policy of the Navigation Acts, of which these two acts were the forbears, because they aimed at sustaining British shipping. But Smith was not to approve of 'bullionism', the view expressed by Queen Elizabeth I's chief Minister, Lord Burghley, who wrote: 'it is manifest that nothing robbeth the realm of England but when more merchandise is brought into the realm than is carried forth', since the adverse balance had to be paid for in gold or silver. Though it would be untrue to say that bullion was completely identified with wealth, the Government of Elizabeth I insisted that it needed a war chest with which to equal the flood of silver that sustained the Spanish Empire as it was waging war against England during the last fifteen years of the reign.

Under Elizabeth, who repudiated the Roman Catholic Church and assumed the title of Supreme Governor of the Church of England and who ruled the country with the assent of Parliament, a conscious, unified nation-state was evolving which, acting in the economic sphere, aimed to increase the power, wealth and prosperity of the land. Whether it acted in a misguided way or not, it directed its commercial and industrial policy to achieving these ends.

One problem that exercised Tudor governments was the 'enclosing' and 'engrossing' of land to make agriculture more efficient and profitable. Enclosing meant fencing in a piece of land that had hitherto lain open either in arable fields, meadows or commons, so that the cultivator could exploit the land as he chose and not have to clear it for common grazing at agreed seasons. Engrossing meant amalgamating two or more holdings into one in order to create larger units – economically advantageous but socially damaging. It also had similar ends in view to enclosure.

Enclosures were often made by the agreement of a whole village, and since it was natural enough to try to improve the productivity and profitability of the land this had been going on for some time. But the rising population and rocketing food prices in the sixteenth century accelerated the process. The precise motives for it varied. The expansion of the cloth industry during the fifteenth century, continuing up to the middle of the sixteenth century, meant that sheep farming had become more advantageous and required less labour than corn fields. The New Draperies did not need wool as fine as that used to make broadcloth. Sheep were also valuable for providing food. The Spencers of Althorp, a family famous in English history, for example, sold much mutton and lamb to the butchers in the reign of Elizabeth I. A foreign observer thought the English farmers were 'so lazy and slow that they do not bother to sow more wheat than is necessary for their own consumption; they prefer to let the ground be transformed into pasture for the use of sheep, which they breed in large numbers'. There was a saying: 'He that hath sheep, swine and bees, sleep he, wake he, he may thrive.'

It was the enclosure of arable land for use as permanent pasture that worried the government, for two reasons: first, it reduced the output of grain at a time when it was scarce and dear; secondly, by curtailing the demand for agricultural labour it created unemployment and provoked rioting where landholders ignored the traditional rights of villagers. On occasion riots degenerated into armed revolts. In the summer of 1549 Robert Ket, a Norfolk tradesman, led a large-scale revolt against the county's landlords, who, among other things, had been fencing in or encroaching on common land for grazing their sheep and cattle where the tenants also had grazing rights. Though the rebels were defeated and Ket was hanged at Norwich castle, the episode was a striking example of agrarian discontent. Nearly sixty years later a similar revolt wholly over enclosures took place in the Midlands, stemming from Northamptonshire. A lengthy series of acts was passed against enclosures for pasture (the first general statute was enacted in 1489) and royal commissions were appointed in 1517, 1548, 1565 and 1607 to investigate the matter. It was explained that 'when a man doth enclose and hedge his own proper ground where no man hath commons' it was 'very beneficial', but 'when any man hath taken away and enclosed any other man's commons or hath pulled down houses of husbandry and converted the lands from tillage to pasture' that was 'enclosure', which created unemployment, poverty and vagrancy. Sir Thomas More, who became Lord Chancellor in 1529, had condemned in his book *Utopia* noblemen and gentlemen who grew the finest and dearest wool and left no ground for tillage; a puritan, Philip Stubbs, explained in 1583: 'these enclosures be the causes why rich men eat up poor men as beasts do eat grass'; and John Aubrey, no puritan, writing in the seventeenth century, observed: 'Enclosures are for private, not public good. For a shepherd and his dog or a milkmaid can manage the land that upon arable employed the hands of several scores of labourers.'

It was in the Midlands, then one of the most densely populated parts of the country, where the majority of medieval villages had been surrounded by much common and waste, that the protests against enclosures were the loudest. For here enclosures were carried out pretty ruthlessly by large landlords and the peasantry had to appeal to ancient customs for redress in the law courts. In fact it was encroachment on the commons that most aggravated villagers. Where the soil was ill-drained, cold, heavy clay or chalk and limestone its use for sheep farming was understandable. It was the enclosure of fertile arable land when the price of grain was high that was harder to defend and led to social problems.

Actually the amount of land enclosed for sheep and cattle grazing in the Midlands was clearly exaggerated by contemporaries. Over two generations ago the findings of historical research concluded that less than 7 per cent of the total area of seven Midland counties was affected at that time, but such a blunt inference does not satisfy the requirements of quantitative historians or modern statisticians. At any rate, by the end of the sixteenth century the uproar over depopulation had largely subsided. An act of parliament in 1597 permitted the temporary conversion of arable land to pasture in order to restore it to good heart. King James I (1603-25) expressed the opinion that more land had been ploughed up in recent years from the waste than had been converted by enclosure from arable to pasture. Some experts on agriculture such as Thomas Tusser, an Eton and Cambridge man, who offered his advice to other farmers in verse and died bankrupt in 1580, thought that the common-field method of tillage was inefficient and uneconomic and advocated mixed farming. Depopulation was attributed, at least in part, to men moving from villages into towns. Although Charles I levied heavy fines for depopulation, by the time his son came to the throne in 1660 knowledgeable pamphleteers were arguing for more, not less, enclosure, and dubbed it in the long run 'an improvement'.

Elizabethan administrators – including such a well-informed character as the principal Secretary of State, Lord Burghley – were convinced that the enclosures, which, it was claimed, depopulated the countryside, were a main reason why so many beggars and vagabonds were to be found all over the country. The preamble to the Act for the Maintenance of Husbandry and Tillage, passed in 1598, insisted that they were 'a principal means that people are set on work, and thereby withdrawn from idleness, drunkenness, unlawful games, and all other lewd practices and conditions of life'. But in fact it is certain that enclosures played only a minor part in mobilizing an army of the unemployed and unemployable. During the fifteenth century wage-earners had not been too badly off and could afford to buy food, drink and clothing if they did not produce them at home. But Tudor England was relatively overpopulated, prices outstripped wages, and these wages were kept down (or supposed to be kept down) by justices of the peace. Unskilled labourers earned fourpence to fivepence a day and skilled labourers earned sixpence to eightpence when bread cost a penny a pound, cheese threepence a pound and butter fivepence to sixpence. Thus real wages were lower and the diet poorer than they had been in the recent past.

The rapid growth of population in sixteenth-century England and the rise in food prices were not exceptional, but a common experience throughout most of Europe. Hardly a country was not plagued by 'masterless men' unable to find work. One factor aggravating the situation in England was the suppression of the monasteries. For there almoners had usually provided a night's lodging and distributed food and money indiscriminately to all who came to them for help. This, however, had tended to create professional begging. The monks in the later Middle Ages had not attempted to come to grips with the root causes of poverty. After the dissolution greedy landlords, cowardly clergy and rich idlers were all denounced for giving birth to so much destitution. One clerical writer, William Harrison, the rector of a rural parish, claimed in his *Description of England* that 10,000 vagabonds or 'sturdy beggars' were 'on the road' between 1563 and 1572. In addition gypsies made their appearance in England at about this time and tramps, thieves and robbers were pretty numerous. But the bulk of the vagrants were young men and women aged between fifteen and twenty-five who were genuinely out of work.[5]

Apart from the able-bodied unemployed were the disabled, crippled and incurable invalids. London contained five hospitals: St Bartholomew's and St Thomas's for the sick, Christ's, which specialized in orphans, Bridewell, where vagabonds were punished and set to work, and Bedlam, for the mentally ill. In the capital, too, philanthropic merchants built almshouses or arranged for the distribution during their funerals of doles for the poor. A number of acts of parliament were passed ordering work to be found for vagrants, the erection of houses of correction, and the relief of the helpless poor by voluntary alms. In 1598, however, a statute fixed a compulsory maximum poor rate of twopence a head per parish, to be levied by permission of the justices of the peace, in order to build and maintain workhouses to employ rogues and sturdy beggars and provide relief for the 'impotent', while unpaid overseers of the poor were created to set those who were capable to work and apprentice unwanted children. A second statute ordered unlicensed beggars to be whipped and sent back to their birthplaces. The justices also tried to keep down the price of food and the export of corn was prohibited by statute when a bad harvest brought scarcity.

Life in the towns, to which the vagrants flocked, was, on the whole, better than in the countryside. London of course was unique, offering every kind of work from that of chimneysweeps to domestic service. It was far and away the largest port in England; it had 120 churches, its Inns of Court and lovely livery halls, vast houses and a Royal Exchange, opened by the Queen in 1570, and was surrounded by villages like Chelsea and Hampstead which it was destined to swallow up. In spite of endemic diseases its population grew rapidly and stimulated much building. James I is supposed to have said it had 'changed from sticks to bricks'. Bristol, Norwich and Exeter were other busy cities, though they had their ups and downs. Large villages, like Birmingham and Manchester, welcomed new industries, which were able to avoid the demand made by the craft gilds in the towns. (John Leland thought Birmingham particularly beautiful.) Such industries, or more strictly trades, included pillow-lace making, the manufacture of glass and the production of straw hats. In these lively communities ambitious members of the working class were not content to be mere wage-earners but became small masters and shopkeepers.

The sixteenth century was a splendid age for building, both in the towns and in the country; and we are lucky that so much of its architecture has survived, ranging from Elizabethan yeomen's farmhouses, the black and white timber-framed houses familiar in Cheshire and along the Welsh border, and scattered inns, to the palatial houses of the wealthy like Hatfield, Hardwick Hall, Audley End, Longleat and Montacute. We are reminded of mercantile prosperity by Exeter town hall or the buildings along Cheapside in London. But Tudor churches are few: it was a secular age. We have also learned how in Elizabethan times 'English provinces were incomparably more individual and distinctive than they are today'.[6] Only very important people had houses in London. When the landed gentry left their country homes they moved to town houses in county capitals like Exeter, Norwich or York; and they spoke not Oxford and Cambridge English but the language of their native parts.

In this age of building and rebuilding, the homes of gentlefolk no longer had walls of earth, low thatched roofs, a few wooden partitions and holes in the wall to let out the smoke. The new and enlarged houses had glazed windows, proper chimneys, plaster ceilings and painted walls. Stone usually replaced timber, which made the buildings more stable. Private houses could therefore be safely constructed on two floors, allowing for a parlour and several bedrooms besides the usual offices. Some rooms were warmed with coal. Modest houses and cottages did not cost much to build because labour was so cheap. Inside the houses furniture changed little. Beds and tables were elaborate and heavy. Cupboards were used to contain food and sideboards to display plate. Only a few chairs were to be found and they looked uncomfortable; stools and benches were the usual seats. But bedclothes were more inviting; straw pallets were replaced by down, and pillows superseded logs as head-rests.

Men and women dressed – or were supposed to dress – according to their station in life. Thus London apprentices wore blue cloaks, breeches of white broadcloth and flat caps. Merchants and other citizens and their wives dressed fairly simply, but the upper classes wore elaborate and heavy clothing, imitating French and Italian fashions. Gentlemen wore padded doublets (close-fitting body garments) covered by warm knee-length cloaks made of velvet or silk and often trimmed with fur, silk stockings and modern-looking shoes. Women also wore doublets, but their skirts and cloaks trailed on the ground. Ruffs were introduced at this time; so were scarfs, embroidered waistcoats, masks, fans and periwigs. Women painted their faces and dyed their hair, usually blonde, and bought perfumes and cosmetics. An Italian who visited London in the reign of Henry VII thought that Englishmen dressed 'in the French fashion except that their suits are more full and accordingly were out of shape'. The Reverend William Harrison did not approve of the clothes of the nobility and gentry. The idea that women wore doublets and men grew their hair long made it come to pass, he wrote, 'that women are become men and men transformed into monsters'.

Eating and drinking – despite the high prices – continued on a lavish scale among the well-to-do. Country gentlemen and city merchants, according to Harrison, were content with four, five or six dishes. They dined between eleven and twelve in the morning and supped between seven and eight in the evening. The Italian visitor wrote: 'They delight in banquets and variety of meat and food and they excel everyone in preparing them with excessive abandon. They eat very frequently at times more than is suitable, and are particularly fond of young swans, rabbits, deer and sea birds.' Table manners were not delicate. Only exquisite gentlemen used forks.

Beer, as distinct from ale, made from malt and flavoured with hops, was introduced from Holland during the Tudor period. A popular couplet declared:

> Hops, Reformation, bays and beer
> Came into England all in a year.

Quickly the growing of hops increased, though it was confined chiefly to south-east England. One of an ordinary wife's duties was malting, for beer was made in the homes of gentry and yeomen as well as in breweries. John Stow, a London chronicler, who wrote towards the end of the reign of Elizabeth I, said the price of ale was three pints for a halfpenny in the summer and a quart for a halfpenny in the winter. A physician in Henry VIII's reign deplored the huge consumption of beer, and in James I's reign a statute was passed penalizing drunkenness. Wine, though imported, was inexpensive. An act limiting its price was passed in 1536: this ordered that French wine should not be sold at more than a penny a pint. The Italian reporter observed that few people kept wine in their houses, but drank it in taverns. With the disappearance of the monasteries, which had often functioned as hotels, the number of inns multiplied, some of them being able to put up two or three hundred people at night. Fynes Moryson, who wrote at length about his travels, concluded that 'the world affords not such inns as England hath, either for good and cheap entertainments or the guests' own pleasure, or for humble attendance on passengers'.

Besides drinking in inns and taverns and overeating at home, amusements included masques and pageants, and plays were performed in London suburbs since they were not allowed in the city itself. Two of the earliest playhouses, the Theatre and the Curtain, were built in Finsbury and a third, the Rose, was built at Shoreditch. Here too was the Swan, while the Globe, where Shakespeare acted, was in Southwark. There was also a bear-baiting theatre at Southwark and a bull-baiting theatre on the south bank of the Thames. These theatres had to contend with much opposition. The Mayor of London wanted them banned altogether as corrupting the city youth. Actors were not allowed to perform on Sundays or public holidays or when an epidemic was raging. Because of difficulties with the lighting, plays were given in the daytime, thus interrupting the afternoon's work for their audience. Outside London many strolling players performed, as did minstrels, jugglers and acrobats, mainly in the courtyards of inns. Sports included football, surprisingly a much rougher game than it is today. Henry VIII set an example to the nobility by playing 'real tennis'.

The impressions recorded or deduced about the economy of England in the sixteenth and seventeenth centuries are contradictory. Admiral Sir John Hawkins thought that the wealth of England had trebled since the accession of Elizabeth I and Lord Burghley considered the country was 'abounding in riches'. Polydore Vergil, an Italian who spent much of the first half of the sixteenth century in England, conveys in his *Anglica Historia* the opinion that the Englishmen of his time were healthy and well fed and that the peasants were much better off than the peasants of his native land. Writing in 1587, William Harrison said:

> White meats, as milk, butter and cheese, which were never so dear in my time ... are now reputed as food appertinent only to the inferior sort, while such as are more wealthy feed upon the flesh of all kinds of cattle accustomed to be eaten, all sorts of fish ... and such diversity of wild and tame fowls as are either bred in our island or brought unto us from other countries of the main.

A Spaniard observed during the reign of Mary I (1553–8): 'These English have their houses of sticks and dirt, but they fare commonly as well as the King.' This reads like hyperbole; and the houses evidently improved after he left.

In contrast with these generalizations, we have the view, based on taxation returns, that 'In the larger towns of England ... fully a third of the population ... were so poor that they paid neither on the minimum level of wages nor the minimum level of goods.' As to the rural inhabitants, a great social historian expressed the view that 'the sixteenth century was poor with a poverty which no industrial community can understand'.[7]

The evidence about the large numbers of unemployed and unemployable, ranging from beggars to footpads, can hardly be denied, even if to blame it to any extent on enclosures of arable land to turn it into pasture is more than doubtful. At the end of the reign of Elizabeth I the ruling classes were noting 'the great decay of the people', the 'swarms of poor loose and wandering people', and 'the danger of famine'. Even the cloth industry, still the foundation of a valuable export trade, was far from being a gold-mine for ordinary workmen and women. Shakespeare blamed this on taxation in his play *Henry VIII*:

> ... for, upon these taxations,
> The clothiers all, not able to maintain
> The many to them 'longing, have put off
> The spinsters, carders, fullers, weavers, who,
> Unfit for other life, compelled to hunger
> And lack of other means, in desperate manner
> Daring the event to the teeth are all in uproar,
> And danger serves among them.

It has been contended that the age of the Tudors was a commercial age and became more commercial as the sixteenth century went on. Certainly it saw the birth of new regulated and joint-stock trading companies. Until the middle of the century only two such companies existed – the Merchant Adventurers, now seeking markets in Germany at the expense of the Hanseatic League, and the Eastland Company, which had long traded in the Baltic – but individual merchants pioneered by aiming to spread commerce as far as Russia, Persia and India. In 1569 the Pope was told that England largely depended on 'the merchandise that goes out of and is carried into the realm'.[8] It is likely, too, that a considerable amount of interloping and smuggling was carried on. One can name financiers and capitalists such as Sir Thomas Gresham, who boasted he could borrow any sum he liked in Antwerp; Sir John Hawkins, who made a fortune out of the slave trade, and Sir Lionel Cranfield, who became extremely wealthy as an exporter, importer and speculator before he became James I's Lord Treasurer. Even William Cockayne survived his vicissitudes to die a very rich man. Because of the profit inflation, that is to say, prices running away from the costs of production to the benefit of middle men, the sixteenth century was a period when financiers found a happy hunting ground. Lord Keynes wrote that 'never in the annals of the modern world has there existed so prolonged and so rich an opportunity for the business man, the speculator and the profiteer.'[9]

Similarly in agriculture, the landowner or sheepmaster, whether he was called a gentleman, an esquire or a yeoman, if he had an adequate acreage and could afford to hire a few men at the current rate of low wages, did very well for himself by selling wool to clothiers and food to the industrial areas of the country. He differed entirely from the medieval husbandman struggling to feed his family on what he could grow in his share of the village fields. Thus it can be said, and has been said, with equal conviction, on the one hand that sixteenth-century England was a country replete with riches; and on the other that because it was relatively overpopulated, with many unemployed and most wage-earners indifferently paid, 'Shakespeare's England' was 'a poor place'.[10]

Notes

1 W.G. Hoskins, *Provincial England* (1963), pp. 185 seq.
2 Peter Laslett, *Family Life and Illicit Love in Earlier Generations* (1977), chapter 3
3 These figures were kindly given me by Sir Henry Phelps Brown
4 P.J. Bowden, *The Wool Trade in Tudor and Stuart England* (1962), p. 40
5 A.L. Beier, 'Vagrants and the Social Order in Elizabethan England', *Past and Present*, 64 (1974)
6 Hoskins, op. cit., p. 86
7 R.H. Tawney, *The Agrarian Problem in the Sixteenth Century* (1912), p. 35
8 Cit. E. Lipson, *The Economic History of England* (1931), II, p. 185
9 J.M. Keynes, *Treatise on Money* (1930), II, p. 159
10 Sir John Clapham, *A Concise Economic History of Britain to 1750* (1949), p. 210

SIX

Setback and Recovery

By the sixteen-twenties the long-drawn-out period of price inflation, which had stimulated the economy but hurt the wage-earner, came to an end. It was followed by a trade depression that exercised the minds of the King's Ministers and Members of Parliament. Sir Lionel Cranfield, the merchant who 'started up suddenly ... from a base and mean original' to be surprisingly appointed Lord Treasurer in 1621, spoke of 'the want of money in the kingdom', 'the greatest dearth', and 'the decay of trade'. One feature of the depression was a decline in exports. The Dutch had forbidden the importation of dyed and finished broadcloths into their country from England; and by 1617 the value of cloth exports of all kinds, on which English commerce chiefly depended, dropped by nearly a third as compared with the value of those exported at the beginning of the century. Moreover the exports of 'New Draperies', introduced into East Anglia by exiles from the Netherlands in the later half of the sixteenth century, met with fierce competition from the Dutch, especially in the Mediterranean area. Exports of tin and lead were handicapped by export duties. As Germany had been the principal market for English broadcloth or 'Old Draperies', the disruption of commerce brought about after the outbreak of the Thirty Years War in 1618, which was to engulf much of Europe, further damaged English exports. Above all, currencies abroad were depreciated, which made exports difficult to sell profitably.

But foreign trade was not so essential to the English economy as it has since become. Other reasons for the deepening depression, less emphasized at the time, were a succession of bad harvests and plagues that devastated London and other towns. Unemployment and under-employment reached such a pitch that justices of the peace, though they had been given wide powers by the act of 1563, were unable to cope with the problems of the poor. Attempts to enforce minimum rates of wages for shearers, weavers, fullers and dyers failed, since the unemployed were eager to find work at any wage. The analysis of the situation by the ruling class and the cures suggested were mostly beside the point. The blame for an adverse balance of trade was laid on excessive imports, such as those of cattle from Ireland, wine from France and, above all, tobacco from Spain. The gains from cloth sold in Spain, which were said to have brought in £100,000 a year, thus went up in smoke. Finally the East India Company was castigated for exporting bullion, though the need to do so to pay for remunerative imports, such as spices, that could be re-exported, was strongly defended by the directors of the company.

The remedies proposed to overcome the adverse balance of trade were hardly new. The prohibition of the export of wool was urged on the ground that by cheapening its price the cost of producing English cloth would be lowered; and a ban on imports of grain, which was brought in from Poland and elsewhere, was advocated so as to help English farmers. It was argued that foreign merchants residing in England must be obliged to spend their money on English goods. More linen must be made at home and more fish caught from the sea. In some quarters it was demanded that the export trade in cloth should be thrown open to all comers instead of being left largely in the hands of the Merchant Adventurers, who had resumed their operations after the failure of the Cockayne project. Others simply wanted the Merchant Adventurers to be pressed into greater activity. Lastly, it was urged that the rate of interest on borrowed money, then usually about 10 per cent, ought to be reduced; but as no central banking system yet existed that would have been difficult to ensure. Clothiers attributed their industry's depression to high taxation and Customs duties.

The economic situation of the kingdom picked up in the sixteen-thirties. Wars against Spain and France, which ruined the royal finances, came to an end; and the assassination of Charles I's favourite, the first Duke of Buckingham, and his replacement by more cautious and economical Ministers, who cut down royal prodigality, was conducive to a revival of trade. The prices of wheat, barley and wool fell, so that real wages rose; the rate of population growth also slowed down. Although such taxes as Customs duties (known as 'tonnage and poundage') and ship money, levied to pay for the expanding royal navy, were felt to be grievances, they were paid. The rents of land rose. Exports of cloth recovered. Indeed, it has been said that 'from 1629 to 1635 the government of Charles I, like that of Pharaoh, was blessed with seven fat years'.[1]

It is doubtful if the average wage-earner gained much from this epoch of recovery, however. Unemployment and under-employment remained rife. Even those regularly at work were thought by contemporaries to be chronically below what they regarded as the poverty line. It was the general opinion that the country was overpopulated – 'pestered with people' was the phrase used – hence emigration was approved. It was also contended that the excessive growth of London had thrown the economy out of gear: 'it is no good state of body', declared a Member of Parliament in 1641, 'to have a fat head, thin guts and lean members'. Indeed, the King's Government attempted to develop Bristol and Exeter as rival centres of the export trade, especially during the Civil War in the forties, when they were two of the few ports left in Royalist hands.

It is likely that in London the standard of living was higher than in the countryside because its business was not dependent on the soil and the weather: it is true that Londoners had to buy their food from outside, but they could afford it. In the country at large the gentry and the enterprising yeomen, who could manage to save against a rainy day, did well enough, but the husbandmen and agricultural labourers were much less secure. They were unable to save; they had many children to support; their expectation of life at birth was less than thirty-five years, their wives were often ill-fed and died young: as Lady Stenton wrote, 'no farm labourer's wife can ever have felt well'.

If their way of life was uncomfortable, the independent poor nevertheless resented interference with it. Enclosures of lands in the Midlands and the draining of the fens in Yorkshire and Lincolnshire, initiated by Charles I in the hope of making a handsome profit for himself, led to local rioting. In the Isle of Axholme in Lincolnshire, where the fenmen made a living by fishing, keeping geese and hunting wild-fowl, they rose just before the beginning of the Civil War in revolt against the draining company, breaking down fences and destroying the crops. Later they pulled up the floodgates to allow the tides from the river Trent to drown much of the reclaimed land. In other parts of the country – in Wiltshire and Cornwall, for example – riots were provoked by arbitrary enclosures and the diminution of popular rights in the commons.

The 'fat years' were succeeded by lean years starting in the middle of the sixteen-thirties. In 1641 the citizens of London complained of 'a great decay of trade in the kingdom and great scarcity of money'. The prices of grain and wool fell and so did rents and exports of cloth, owing partly to increased foreign competition. The gentry and yeomen weathered the storms created by harvest fluctuations, but the position of the husbandmen and agricultural labourers, who constituted half of the population, worsened. Although an act passed in the reign of Elizabeth I required new cottages built for labourers to have four acres of land attached to them and a number of yeomen were indicted at quarter sessions for failing to provide them, by 1640 few agricultural labourers owned more than an acre or two; they were gradually losing their modest property rights and sinking to the level of a landless proletariat. It is true that where labourers lived in their masters' farmhouses they were pretty well-fed (and those, generally married men, who lived out mostly kept pigs and sometimes one or two cows), and that two-thirds of the cottages in the Midlands had two rooms; but the average wage of a shilling a day (without food or drink) did not go very far. 'Poverty and fear of poverty', it has been said, 'were a normal part of the social pattern of early seventeenth-century society.'[2]

By contrast with the precarious condition of the bulk of the rural population the position of the gentry and yeomanry had actually improved. The 'rise of the gentry', that is, of a middling landed class, can be traced back at least to the fourteenth century. The evidence of the building of country houses on a large scale, of the number of grants of arms and conferring of knighthoods during the first half of the seventeenth century and of the high average wealth of Members of Parliament at that time contributes to proof of the observation that the rise of the gentry was 'a simple fact'.[3]

The House of Commons, whose assembly in the autumn of 1640 was a first step along the road that led to civil war, consisted mainly of well-to-do landowners, lawyers and a number of merchants who for the most part were local men with local ties conscious of local grievances. To begin with, they had not the slightest intention of destroying the monarchical government, but they expressed indignation over the various ways employed to raise money for the King's purposes without the consent of the House of Commons, which had normally been called upon to vote any extraordinary taxation. Merchants resented the higher Customs duties they had to pay, while country gentlemen objected to finding ship money to enlarge the fleet when they lived in areas far from the sea. Farmers of the Customs, who had advanced considerable sums to the Crown, lost their leases and were made to disgorge heavy fines. Other minor grievances over the draining of the fens, the felling of timber in the royal forests, the fining of gentlemen who refused to accept knighthoods, the granting of patents, which were stigmatized as monopolies, and the attempts to regulate industry by the use of prerogative powers were all magnified to demonstrate the existence of a conspiracy against the people by evil counsellors of the King.

Up till the autumn of 1641 the reformist attitude of the members of the Commons was virtually unanimous. But after grievances over property rights had been met and the Commons turned to constitutional and religious questions, the mood changed, and the House became divided along no fixed lines. When civil war followed because the King refused to allow Parliament to approve his Ministers and officials and to take control of the country's armed forces, it proved to be a fratricidal conflict. Though immense research has gone into the matter, it was certainly not a class war. The most that can be said is that the majority of the aristocracy supported the King and most yeomen backed Parliament. But the bulk of the population was indifferent, except for the consciousness that the political conflict had interrupted and damaged trade.

As the war spread right across the country, from Cornwall to Yorkshire and Sussex to Lancashire, crops were destroyed, livestock seized, houses razed to the ground, men forcibly enlisted and farmhouses and cottages plundered. Vainly in areas not yet fought over men armed themselves with clubs in an effort to keep the war out of their counties. And to pay for the war the Parliamentarian leaders introduced new taxes, such as a direct tax on real and personal property known as the monthly assessment, and the excise, which was imposed both on goods manufactured at home, such as beer, and on a variety of imports. Both these taxes were highly efficient and exceedingly unpopular – 'extortionate', one historian (who is perhaps unconscious of the range of taxation in his own time) has called them. Yet by the end of the century they had become a fundamental part of the public finance of the kingdom.

Apart from these financial changes, what was the effect of the Civil War and the establishment of a republican government, following the defeat and execution of the King, on English economic and social life? So far as agriculture was concerned, the sales and transfers of land had many repercussions. All the estates belonging to the Crown and Church were sold to meet the expenses of a greatly enlarged army and navy. Some Royalist landlords were heavily fined, the fines usually amounting to one-sixth of the value of their property. The result was not catastrophic, because most Royalists succeeded in paying their fines and resuming the management of their estates, while the bigger landowners – the Duke of Newcastle, for instance – were able to regain their estates after the restoration of Charles II to the throne in 1660.

Nevertheless many Royalists with modest possessions were so encumbered with debts contracted during the Interregnum (1649–60), or caused by the expenses involved in getting back their estates, that they had to sell their land either to wealthier landowners or to successful merchants or rising yeomen. During the reign of Charles II, it has been pointed out, 'the hatred of the small squires and gentry for the great lords who were buying them out' was 'the theme of many contemporary plays'.[4] Often these great lords were not satisfied, as many of the manorial barons had been, to leave the running of their estates entirely to stewards and bailiffs, but turned themselves into 'improving landlords'. John Houghton, the author of *Letters for the Improvement of Husbandry and Trade*, wrote: 'The great improvement made of lands since our inhuman civil wars was when our gentry who before hardly knew what it was to think then fell to such industry and caused such an improvement as England never knew before.'

Other big landlords took the easier course of marrying rich merchants' daughters. Thus although the extraordinary expenditure forced upon the lesser gentry because they had been loyal to Charles I did not have any dramatic effects on their fortunes after his son's return, since they were able to borrow or mortgage their estates to meet their debts, in the long run many of them had to sell out and thus contributed to the enlargement of the great estates of hereditary landowners, who managed them in a more businesslike way and bequeathed them by entail.

During the Interregnum merchants too had their ups and downs. The Commonwealth Government was never able to make up its mind whether joint-stock or regulated companies trading overseas like the East India Company and the Merchant Adventurers were 'monopolies' and so, in Oliver Cromwell's words, 'prejudicial to the liberties of the people', or lawful bodies helpful to the national economy. These chartered companies therefore went through a difficult and uncertain time. They were obliged to lend money to the government; they had to put up with competition from interlopers; and their trade was dislocated by wars waged against the Dutch and Spanish. English shipping, however, was given the assistance of a Navigation Act in 1651, which confined the import trade to English ships or ships of the exporting country. This act was only partially enforced, but undoubtedly it benefited the mercantile marine, if not the shipbuilding industry; indeed, it was said that the number of home-built ships was insufficient to cope with the carrying trade.

Another more drastic Navigation Act was passed immediately after the Restoration and other such acts were passed by English parliaments in

1663, 1673, and 1696. One purpose of these acts was to monopolize the carrying trade to and from English overseas possessions in North America and the West Indies. The act of 1660 also enumerated certain commodities – they included sugar and tobacco – which had to be brought directly to England so as to promote the business of re-exporting, which had been of relatively little importance during the Interregnum, but was growing fast by the end of the seventeenth century.

A further objective of the act was to handicap the most powerful English rivals in the carrying trade, the Dutch. Unquestionably the number of English merchant vessels increased considerably between 1660 and 1750 (from an estimated 200,000 tons to 420,000 tons), but that might have come about anyway. Their employment was already growing before the act of 1651 was passed. And the Dutch were to be injured by the four wars in which they were involved during this period. Nevertheless, the policy embodied in the Navigation Acts represents an important aspect of a system of trade protection or economic nationalism that prevailed in England until the middle of the nineteenth century.

One other consequence of the events during the Interregnum was the disappearance of most of the Crown's economic rights. Henry VIII had instituted a Court of Wards to preserve feudal dues and services owed by tenants-in-chief; for wardship had allowed the Crown to benefit from the estates of rich orphans until they came of age. Besides wardship, tenure by knight's service, fee farm rents and purveyance were all abolished in return for the retention by the royal government of the proceeds from excise, first introduced by the Parliamentarians in 1643. Thus the medieval conception of the monarchy dating from the time of William the Conqueror, that all land was owned by the monarch and that all landholders held their properties directly from him, was abandoned, and 'the Statute Book' bore 'eloquent witness to the gathering strength of that landed class which was soon to dictate to the Crown'.[5] Instead of feudal dues the taxation of beer, wine and tobacco became permanent, a boon to all Treasurers and Chancellors of the Exchequer and a delight to puritans and conscientious doctors that has endured until present times.

Except in the years of bad harvests the price of grain fell steadily between 1660 and 1750. On New Year's Day 1668, for example, Samuel Pepys noted in his diary how his friends at dinner 'did talk much of the cheapness of corn, even to a miracle so as the farmers pay no rent, but do fling up their lands, and would pay in corn'. In the last two decades of the period average prices were the lowest ever known. Cheaper prices for wool also persisted, partly brought about by competition from Spain, partly owing to the continued prohibition on export, and partly because of a falling-off in the demand for English cloth abroad. Only the price of meat and dairy products kept up.

The Government was sufficiently perturbed about the low price of grain to introduce export subsidies in 1673. (This act lapsed in 1681, but was renewed in 1689 and continued until 1812.) Merchants were allowed to export wheat when the price fell below 48 shillings a quarter and exporters were paid a bounty of 5 shillings a quarter. Similar subsidies were paid on barley and rye sold abroad. Three consequences flowed from the low price of grain. First, because labourers were able to buy bread cheaply the value of real wages both in agriculture and industry rose. Secondly, the enclosure of fields where corn was grown so that they might be converted into pasture was no longer resisted by public opinion. The question was asked: 'since pasturage is more profitable than tillage why should enclosing landlords not lay down their arable land for grass?' From 1660 onwards enclosures could go forward by private acts of parliament or by the enrolment of enclosure agreements in the Court of Chancery. The prerogative courts, where enclosures had often been disallowed, were abolished.

The third and most significant result of the falling grain prices was that they encouraged farmers to experiment with new methods of husbandry and thus cheapen the cost of producing food and increase their own profits. Advice about how to do so was not lacking. As early as 1645 Sir Richard Weston published a book entitled *Discourses of Husbandrie used in Brabant and Flanders*; Walter Blith wrote *The English Improver and Improved* (1652); John Worlidge, himself a farmer, who invented a drill which made sowing easier, wrote in his *Systema Agriculturae* (1669) about how farming costs could be reduced; and John Houghton in his *Collection of Letters for the Improvement of Husbandry and Trade* produced a weekly paper which contained articles on agriculture, advice from experts like Worlidge, and lists of grain prices. Writing on *The Mystery of Husbandry: or Arable, Pasture and Woodland Improved* (1697), Leonard Meager remarked 'where the grounds are enclosed, how happily people live'.

The Royal Society, founded in 1662, of which Charles II was the first patron, set up a committee on agriculture (confusingly called its Georgical committee), which carried out experiments, instituted inquiries and published the results. Among the refinements advocated were first, the growing of fodder crops, such as turnips, to feed animals throughout the winter;

101

secondly, the use of artificial grasses – such as clover and sainfoin – to turn arable land temporarily into pasture for grazing (this is now sometimes called 'up and down husbandry'); thirdly, the growing of potatoes (recipes were published showing how to make them into puddings and custards to disguise their flavour); fourthly, the watering of meadows by digging trenches and controlling the flooding of grassland at different seasons; and lastly, stronger emphasis was put on the value of manuring, the fertilizers advocated including marl, ashes, pigeons' and hens' dung, sea sand and, above all, lime (though farmers needed to be careful with lime).

These agricultural innovations spread slowly from the gentry to the yeomen and thence to husbandmen, according to the benefits they offered to different classes of farming. Turnips had first been planted in gardens as vegetables, but Colonel Robert Walpole, father of the future Prime Minister, was growing them as fodder in Norfolk as early as 1673 and encouraged his tenants to grow them too. In the seventeen-twenties Daniel Defoe noted how the fattening of cattle with turnips had originated in East Anglia and expanded from there over most of eastern and southern England. Later in the sixteen-seventies Colonel Walpole started sowing clover, which was introduced into Suffolk at an early stage. Clover seed was imported in small quantities from Holland. Potatoes, like turnips, were first grown in kitchen gardens and only gradually planted in fields. The watering of meadows was an expensive business, especially as it was liable to be resisted by neighbouring farmers and led to litigation. As to manure, it was always scarce, as it still is today, while fertilizers needed to be applied scientifically.

Undoubtedly a phase of experiments and novelties in agriculture can be dated from the middle of the seventeenth century. Market gardening developed along the Thamesside, where orchards of apple and cherry trees were planted. Asparagus was grown there around 1685. Exotic fruits were not unknown. John Evelyn remarked on 'the great plenty of oranges' in Lord Sunderland's estate of Althorp in 1675 and of how Charles II had been presented with a pineapple tree, just as Oliver Cromwell had been earlier. Tobacco plants were cultivated in Gloucestershire, though this was strictly illegal as it competed with imports from the American colonies. With the lifting of the ban on enclosures cattle and sheep farming was concentrated in areas unsuitable for arable farming, for example in the Yorkshire Dales, where some farms had no ploughland at all. Ley grasses were sown to feed animals in fertile districts, while careful grazing, weeding and draining benefited pastures. Furthermore, attention was paid to the systematic breeding of horses, which had been of concern to the gentry since the early Tudor period. Sidney Godolphin, the future Lord Treasurer, imported Arabian horses. Finally, disafforestation and fen drainage continued in spite of frequent grumbling by the local inhabitants.

Nevertheless the evidence scarcely points to a 'revolution' or 'great leap forward' in agriculture in the seventeenth century. Farmers have always tended to be conservative. At the end of the century more than half the cultivated land still lay in open fields, where the customary communal husbandry was practised. It has been estimated that the amount of clover seed imported for ley farming was relatively small and opposition to growing turnips for fodder was even greater than that to growing clover. Turnip fields were mainly confined to Norfolk and Suffolk; they did not appear in Lincolnshire until the second quarter of the eighteenth century. It was the proximity of East Anglian ports to Holland that induced the trial there of new farming methods. Potatoes did not find favour as a staple item of diet for many years: they were largely grown to feed pigs. Indeed, it has been claimed that none of these crops became general until the four-course rotation of wheat – root crops – barley – clover became commonplace during the nineteenth century. On the whole, progress was slow. One pamphleteer, writing in 1675, gloomily remarked: 'it is our own negligence and idleness that brings poverty upon us'. The picture of 'early modern English farmers bursting with industry and enterprise' is difficult to sustain.

The number of very big landed estates grew between 1660 and 1750. At the top of the ladder were those belonging to the titled aristocracy: nobles often proved to be easy-going landlords, who might choose their tenants for social reasons rather than clamouring for the highest rents. The kind of tenants they liked were those with 200 acres or more, who paid their rent regularly and kept their holdings in repair. These magnates were able to supplement their incomes by holding political or Court offices, selecting their wives or their sons' wives judiciously and investing their money in mineral rights or commercial enterprises.

George I (1714–27) and George II (1727–60) ennobled very few commoners and the aristocracy scarcely increased at all during their reigns. It has been calculated that there were some 400 'great magnates' at this time, each owning not fewer than 10,000 acres of land.[6] Not all of them were really active. Some of them preferred to spend most of their time entertaining their relatives and friends, building themselves more and lovelier houses and furnishing them with paintings and other works of art collected from all over the world. Nevertheless a 'coherent oligarchy' or a 'charmed circle' did exist who jostled among themselves for social and political authority.

Beneath the titled aristocracy the gentry or squirearchy owned about three-fifths of the cultivated land in the country, with rentals amounting to between £1,000 and £5,000 a year. They represented counties and boroughs in the House of Commons, served as deputy lords-lieutenant, sheriffs or unpaid magistrates and overseers of the poor. Following the restoration of the Stuart monarchy in 1660 the number of small landowners declined, owing to the burden of taxation or harvest fluctuations or their own extravagance; and so, it seems, less social mobility prevailed than before, although merchants and professional men infiltrated the landed classes. It was an age of stability and conservatism. At the same time neither the small tenant farmers nor the agricultural labourers were materially worse off. The fear that had haunted the Elizabethan government, that the country would be depopulated because of the enclosure of arable fields for pasturage, was shown to have been groundless. Indeed the view was now held that the country was overpopulated.

In this period the bulk of the larger farmers were to be found in the corn-growing areas and a greater number of small farmers in the pastoral districts. There the farmers bought grain from the neighbouring arable regions (which was fairly cheap) to make bread, and they supplemented sheep and cattle grazing with dairy farming, pig farming, fishing, market gardening, carpentry, weaving, mining or other part-time occupations. Since most of them lived in hamlets or small villages they were free from the domination of squires, who, even if they were considerate to their tenants, could not alter their sense of servitude. The absence of a lord of the manor living on the spot gave the small pastoral farmers a sense of independence. They were perfectly content with being tenants, usually on leasehold, which was replacing copyhold tenures, and they did not require much in the way of fixed capital such as ploughs and mills.

It was rather different with the small arable farmers who owned their own land, for while it is an exaggeration to say they were being swept away by enclosures or being bought out of existence by big landowners, the fact remains that such farmers did suffer from the loss of commons and waste on which they had been accustomed to graze their few cows and pigs. But the disappearance of the smallholder, which dates from this time, also owed much to the fact that yeomen were willing to sell their freeholds and set up as large leasehold farmers instead.

What of the cottagers or agricultural labourers? The examination of 119 villages in Nottinghamshire has shown that the population of predominantly rural villages rose only less fast than that of villages in which manufacturing and mining took first place.[7] Even in villages where land had been enclosed for pasturage population grew slowly. The low level of food prices in the seventeen-thirties is assumed to have reduced the infant death rate and thus assisted the later increase in the size of the population. At the same time the bounty on corn encouraged the production of wheat and wheaten flour, as well as of barley and malt, for export. Hemp, flax and woad, as well as wool, were grown by substantial farmers, who needed to hire labourers. The dual economy of the pastoral areas – sheep and cattle combined with craftsmanship – gave adequate employment and a reasonable standard of living. By the beginning of the eighteenth century the English lower classes were better off than their European counterparts, and indeed they enjoyed their first golden age since the fourteenth century.

Although textiles continued to be the most important industry in the country, they were becoming more diversified. Besides the New Draperies a linen industry was developing, notably in Lancashire, where smallholders had woven flax, chiefly brought there from Ireland, since the sixteenth century, while the manufacture of stockings and knitted or woven underclothing was spreading. In his tour of Great Britain Daniel Defoe noted that the chief manufacture of Nottingham was the framework knitting of stockings, 'the same as at Leicester', and in Warrington he discovered a weekly market for linen 'called huk-a-back or huk-a-buk', so well known to housewives that he did not think it necessary to describe it. What the volume of textiles bought at home was cannot be calculated exactly; but to some extent the industry was protected from foreign competition, since the import of printed calicoes was forbidden in 1721 except for the purpose of re-exporting. In Norfolk Norwich 'stuffs' were made of silk and wool; elsewhere in East Anglia and in Devonshire bombazines, a twilled dress material such as was used for mourning, and kerseys, the coarse, narrow cloth made from long wool, were produced.

The aulnage system, introduced in the Middle Ages for the inspection and valuation of woollen goods, was unable to cope with all these varieties of textiles and was abolished in 1696. The coal industry extended from the north through the Midlands and mines were being deepened. The output in England, Wales and Scotland was three million tons from 1681 to 1690 and rose to six or seven million by 1760. New ironworks were being erected, more forges and slitting mills constructed, and coppices cultivated

105

as a source of charcoal. Iron was made into ploughshares as well as cannon, but not nearly enough was available for the needs of other industries and iron had to be imported from the Baltic countries and elsewhere. But in 1709 a Quaker ironmaster, Abraham Darby, began producing pig iron smelted with coke, a process that was to help the manufacture of iron castings. The tin industry was still in difficulties, but was rescued by the invention of tinplate during the reign of Queen Anne. Like tin, copper and lead were localized industries. More copper was being fabricated by the end of the seventeenth century. Salt continued to be in immense demand and so did beer; a large brewing industry was developing in London. Ale was consumed in enormous quantities; variety was given to it by warming it, spicing it, and sweetening it. Another lively industry was leather manufacture.

Foremost among new industries was paper-making. Thirty-seven mills existed in 1650 and by 1670 fifty or more were making brown paper. Huguenots – Protestants who fled from France in consequence of persecution – improved the technique of paper-making and by the end of the seventeenth century 150 to 200 paper mills were employing 2,500 to 3,000 workmen. Rags and water, necessary to produce the pulp from which paper was made, were in ample supply. Glazed pottery was another new industry, started at Stoke on Trent. The refugees from France contributed to the making of watches, beaver hats, tapestries and fine glass.

It may be an exaggeration to say that by now England had become a semi-industrialized country, but during the first half of the eighteenth century at least a quarter of its inhabitants were employed in mining or manufacture. Yet in 1750 agriculture still remained the largest occupation. Three-quarters of the working people lived in villages and hamlets.

In the second half of the seventeenth century foreign trade had begun to broaden. Up till that time exports had consisted overwhelmingly of woollen cloth, chiefly unfinished broadcloth, New Draperies, such as serges, and, cheapest of all, kersies, dyed and finished in England. But whereas at the outset of the century four-fifths of the total exports from London had been cloth, by the end of the century the proportion was three-quarters, which is still remarkable. By this time the value of all exports (it was not until 1697 that reasonably reliable figures, based on Customs returns, became available) was £6,419,000, including re-exports, and that of imports was £5,849,000. By 1750 the value of exports had risen to £10,000,000 and by 1760 to over £12,000,000. These figures do not take account of the profitable slave trade, or of wool smuggled out and tea smuggled in, though Customs officers were not above searching French ladies' petticoats for any contraband they could find. More English cloth was being sold in Spain, Portugal and Italy than ever before.

In fact the structure of foreign trade was distinctly changing. Trade with neighbouring countries like France, Spain and Portugal had always beeen open to all merchants. With the growth and diversification of English manufactured goods, the enlargement of the mercantile marine, the availability of more capital for investment and the success of individual exporters, who were becoming richer and more enterprising, the monopolistic trading companies set up by the government were no longer needed. The Merchant Adventurers lost their privileges in 1689, the Eastland Company was obliged to throw open its trade with the Baltic states in 1673 and the Muscovy Company, already decadent, faded away in 1698, though it continued to exist until fairly modern times. The Levant Company, which did business in Turkey, and the Royal African Company in effect lost their privileged positions by the end of the century.

The East India Company survived, although a rival company had been allowed to start operating in 1698. But the older company had far more experience and possessed valuable assets in its trading posts, warehouses and its own merchant ships. Both companies were organized on a joint-stock basis and by 1702 an agreement for their amalgamation was reached, which came into full effect in 1708. One other exclusive joint-stock company which survived was the Hudson's Bay Company, founded in 1670. It was chiefly concerned with the advantageous fur trade and, like the East India Company, built forts and trading posts in a distant part of the world. Here the government was eventually obliged to intervene to protect the company's interests against the French in Canada. By the Treaty of Utrecht (1713) Hudson's Bay territory and the whole of Newfoundland, where English fishermen sailed annually to catch masses of cod, were recognized as English possessions.

The progress of commerce, dating from the reign of Elizabeth I, meant that banking facilities were needed, if only to discount bills of exchange. Scriveners, business men who were authorized to draft documents and draw up contracts, acted as money-lenders during her reign as well as being investment brokers. During the reign of James I farmers of the Customs lent money to the Crown as advances. But the first recognized bankers were goldsmiths: this was natural, since they dealt in bullion and had a profitable side-line in melting down the heavier gold and silver coins which passed through their hands so that they could be sold as plate or exported as bullion. They also had 'running cashes', that is to say, they kept current accounts on which they paid interest and they issued transferable promissory notes which circulated like bank notes. These goldsmiths lent money to Oliver Cromwell and to Charles II on the security of taxes. But when in 1672 in order to pay for a naval war against the Dutch Charles II's Lord Treasurer suspended repayment orders, an action known as 'the Stop of the Exchequer', their confidence in themselves and the confidence of their customers in them were undermined. As a contemporary wrote:

> the people's fears that their money was not safe in the bankers' hands blighted them and since there being in their declension, the famous stop upon the Exchequer blasted them to their very roots, men being unwilling to trust money in their hands to lend to his Majesty

because, so it was pathetically alleged, the bankers in consequence of the Stop failed to pay out money deposited with them by widows and orphans.

The war waged by William III (1688–1702) against the French was much more expensive than Charles II's abortive war against the Dutch, which necessitated the Stop of the Exchequer. Although a land tax as well as enhanced Customs and Excise revenues provided substantial funds, they proved insufficient to cover the cost of overthrowing the strongest military power in the world.

Initially the Bank of England, founded in 1694, was simply the outcome of the Government's desperate need to borrow money. A group of business men then undertook to borrow £1,200,000 from the public and lend it to the Government at 8 per cent 'towards carrying on the war against France'. In return these gentlemen were permitted to form the Court of the Bank of England. The interest on the loan was guaranteed by the assignment of the yield of specific duties, and the Bank was allowed to deal in bills of exchange, handle bullion and act as a pawnbroker, but was given no exclusive privileges. Nothing was said in the act of parliament which created the Bank or in its charter about accepting deposits, issuing cheques or providing bank notes. Nevertheless it soon instituted a 'running cash', to which the goldsmith bankers contributed by opening accounts with it and thus making it the bankers' bank. It also began issuing notes of various amounts 'payable to bearer'. It was the reputation for business acumen and financial integrity of Sir John Houblon, the first Governor, and of members of the Court over which he presided, that explains the ease with which the money was raised for the Government and the Bank's ability to lend more money than it actually possessed in gold and silver coin to its customers.

The foundation of the Bank was followed by recoinage, managed by the celebrated scientist Sir Isaac Newton, which meant that clipped or unmilled silver coins were no longer to be accepted except for a time in payment of loans and taxes. This caused a scarcity of coin and a run on the Bank, which it succeeded in surviving. Exchequer bills were also issued at this time, carrying interest and charged against specific taxes, but they did not prove so readily acceptable as the Bank's own notes.

Before the Bank was founded another device to procure funds for the war had been tried. A million pounds was borrowed from the public to be paid for in the form of annuities. This was the origin of the National Debt. Thus both long-term and short-term government borrowing were instituted. By 1750 the National Debt stood at £78,000,000. Stockbrokers and stock-jobbers also came into being at about this time and were officially recognized by an act of parliament during the remarkable last decade of the seventeenth century. Quotations of stocks and shares prices were published, though the London Stock Exchange was not built until later.

The foundation of the Bank of England and of the National Debt had thus been necessitated by the needs of waging a long war against France (1689–97) in which England materially helped in the humiliation of the Sun King, Louis XIV. With its financial house in order the country was able five years later to face and win a second European war (the War of the Spanish Succession), this time not under the unattractive Dutch monarch, William III, but under Good Queen Anne, who boasted of her 'English heart'. Victory in this second war, which ended in 1713, created a rampant sense of national pride and established the first British Empire. Scotland had been united with England and Wales in 1707, and by the peace treaty England acquired not only the valuable fishing rights off Newfoundland and control of the fur trade, organized from Hudson's Bay, but also the Isthmus of Acadia (known later as Nova Scotia), where the fertile soil yielded crops and marshlands fed cattle. It also obtained a monopoly of the slave trade with Spanish America and permission to send one merchant ship annually to trade there, permission that was exploited to cover smuggling.

In the economic sphere imperialism was exemplified by the series of Navigation Acts intended to multiply shipping at the expense of the Dutch and other foreigners, by the quadrupling of import duties between 1690 and 1704, by the bounty on the export of corn, made permanent in 1689, by the ban on the imports of calicoes after 1701 and by the encouragement of 'infant industries' through prohibitions placed on other imports, such as linen and gold thread. On the other hand, the abolition of export duties began in 1699 and was completed after Sir Robert Walpole became the leading Minister in the House of Commons during 1722. Thus a tight system of protection – or a 'mercantile system' as it was to be called later – was introduced which endured for a century. After that free trade versus protection became the subject of virulent political controversy, only to be submerged when the European Economic Community was founded in the twentieth century.

England's financial and commercial progress was reflected in a steady reduction in the rate of interest, which was 10 per cent in 1625 and 5 per cent in 1714. The opportunity to invest in business rather than in land was welcomed. The Bank of England, the East India Company and dozens of smaller companies such, for example, as Sun Insurance, offered opportunities to do so.

Anticipating the opening of trade with the Spanish overseas empire, a South Sea Company was established and received a royal charter in 1711. It was not really a trading company but a finance company, which ambitiously aimed to outdo the Bank of England and the East India Company by loaning £10,000,000 to the Government and thus take over responsibility for most of the National Debt at a low rate of interest. The directors boldly promised to pay an annual dividend of 50 per cent on its shares. By June 1720 the value of its £100 shares on the Stock Exchange soared to £1,050. In its wake mushroom companies or 'bucket shops', as they were later called, were formed and had little difficulty in raising funds, so potent was the craze for financial speculation. But by the end of the year the bubble burst. The South Sea shares fell to £200 and many who had bought at a much higher price were ruined. The shock to the public credit was electric, since the company had been backed by the Government; even Walpole had invested in it. A so-called 'Bubble Act' had been passed by Parliament on 24 June 1720, declaring that the formation of joint-stock companies without a charter was illegal; and after an investigation during the winter some of the directors of the South Sea Company were sent to prison and all of them had their estates sequestrated. However, the company outlived its unfortunate beginning, carried on trade with South America for several years, and was not wound up until 1807.

English social life in the first half of the eighteenth century was ruled by an aristocracy that was rich and becoming richer. These noblemen monopolized positions at the Court of St James's and the most active of them obtained political offices, which, even if occupied for only a few years, generally proved lucrative. They built themselves palatial houses like Blenheim in Oxfordshire, Woburn in Bedfordshire, Cannons in Middlesex, Castle Howard in the East Riding of Yorkshire and Burley in Rutlandshire. They found handsome dowries for their daughters, generous allowances for their eldest sons, entertained lavishly and had domestic staffs ranging upwards from fifty to a hundred servants.

What is noticeable about the late seventeenth and early eighteenth centuries is that this 'small caste',[8] as it has been called, who never worried unduly about getting into debt, derived their incomes less from the rents of their vast acreages and more from offices and investments, from industry, mines, marriages and even speculation. It was not really a caste. John Churchill, first Duke of Marlborough, came from a modest Dorsetshire family; Sir Thomas Osborne, who became Duke of Leeds, and Sir Robert Walpole, who was created Earl of Orford, were country gentlemen, with no aristocratic ancestors, from Yorkshire and Norfolk respectively: but having earned their titles they merged into a group of peers who all knew each other and lived similar kinds of lives.

How did they relax when they were not at home or in London? The days of seaside resorts (Brighton was then a poor fishing village lapped by an unfriendly sea) or holidays abroad had not yet dawned, except that some of the nobility completed their education by going on Grand Tours of Europe, moving around France, Italy or Spain even when a war was in progress. But the well-to-do had a choice of spas where they could enjoy themselves during the summer months. Epsom was a very popular resort, conveniently near London, because there horse racing 'over those delicious downs' could be seen and mineral water drunk for health's sake from the wells. Tunbridge Wells was tricky because it was famed (as Daniel Defoe explained) for its 'gaming, sharping and intrigue'. Ladies could find 'all the felicities' there if they had money, but they needed to take care of their reputations. When he toured the country Defoe preferred Buxton to Bath. Buxton had only one decent hotel, owned by the Duke of Devonshire, at the bath itself; but the surrounding country was pleasant for coach drives, whereas Bath, he thought, was 'more like a prison than a place of diversion, scarcely giving the company there room to converse out of the smell of their own excrements and where the very city itself may be said to stink like a general common-shore [sewer]'.

The nobility patronized the theatre, prize-fighting and hunting. A foreign visitor was particularly impressed by the entertainment provided at Sadlers Wells in the village of Islington, north of London, where the proceedings started with a variety show, which included acrobats, rope dancers and men climbing ladders leaning against nothing, and concluded with a pantomime given in a pretty little theatre, where the audience ate and drank as they watched.

For ordinary folk the taverns, where huge quantities of beer were drunk, and spirit shops that sold cheap gin were the chief centres of relaxation *en famille*, gin being usually laced with fruit cordials. The ravages of excessive drinking offended the public conscience and acts of parliament were passed aimed at preventing illicit sales, which ultimately quartered the consumption of spirits in the middle of the eighteenth century. Increased imports of rum from the West Indies and tobacco from Virginia and Maryland, selling at a penny a pound, offered new indulgences. By 1750, too, more tea and sugar were being consumed. At coffee houses in London and elsewhere tea and chocolate, as well as wine, ale and punch could be bought and newspapers (which began to flourish in the reign of Queen Anne) were made freely available, as in modern French cafés. A Swiss visitor to the English capital in the seventeen-twenties was shocked at the amount of drinking: 'Could you believe it,' he wrote home, 'though water is to be had in abundance in London and of fairly good quality, absolutely none of it is drunk?' He also thought the English were large eaters, though their cooking was 'simple'.

Another thing that struck this visitor was the character and qualities of Englishwomen. 'You do not see many beautiful women in London', he informed his correspondents: countrywomen, however, he found charming and attractive, with complexions like lilies and roses; but Englishmen, he noted, did not spoil their women by flattery and attention; they preferred drinking and gambling to feminine society.

John Evelyn, who did not die until 1706 at the age of seventy-five, thought that English ladies had deteriorated since his younger days: whereas before 'they put their hands to the spindle and did not disdain the needle and were helpful to their parents', by the end of the seventeenth century they were reading too many romances and saw too many plays, including 'smutty farces'. But their dresses at least improved, in his view, for instead of 'the gorgeous brocaded robes, showing quilted and beaded under-skirts, the long hard bodice, stiffened with whalebone and encrusted with embroidery and gold lace', they turned to a more sober garb of velvet and satin, wore few but good jewels, and combed their hair naturally;

countrywomen dressed simply, a cap on their heads, a handkerchief in their bosoms and clogs on their feet.

By the time the Hanoverians came to the throne in 1714 women were able to buy their clothes more cheaply, at any rate Defoe thought so, because he wrote that 'almost everything that used to be wool or silk relating to the dress of women ... was supplied by the Indian trade': besides silk dresses, these included checked and striped cottons, printed calicoes, muslins, chintzes and other such fabrics brought in by the East India Company from India, Persia and China. Acts of parliament in 1701 and 1721 attempted to stem the flow of imports from India; their competition certainly stimulated the growth of the cotton industry in Lancashire, but that made little progress before 1750.

Looking at the economic position of England as a whole during the first half of the eighteenth century, it is clear that the condition of the labouring classes had improved considerably. As the size of the population was increasing only slowly, if at all, the supply of labour was limited, while the demand for workers in the expanding coal industry, the metal trades and the incipient cotton industry must have been considerable. Progress was reflected in higher production in the iron industry, for instance, now concentrated largely in the west Midlands and Wales, which doubled its output between 1700 and 1750, as well as in printing and paper-making, brewing, hosiery, building, leather manufacture and woollen textiles, where finishing processes had at last been mastered. With the building of workhouses and fairly heavy expenditure out of poor rates, the less capable must have been drawn off from the labour market.

After the two long wars against France had ended, prices (which reached their peak in 1710–11) began to fall – it has been claimed that average prices between 1730 and 1750 were the lowest ever known – and real wages rose. Whereas previously workers employed in their own houses were thought to have been better off than full-time labourers paid by weekly wages, the difference now was considered to be marginal.

Domestic servants, who were employed in large numbers by members of the nobility but also by quite modest households, were usually well treated and had ambitious ideas about the food they should be given. At Woburn the Duke of Bedford's servants were regularly visited by qualified surgeons who bled them several times a year and pulled out their teeth at their master's expense. Wages were not high, but servants were usually supplied with clothes as well as food and expected to be tipped by visitors, so that dining at a nobleman's house could prove quite costly: some servants doubled their wages with tips.[9] In yeomen's houses servants were looked upon as members of the family. In Samuel Pepys's time they might be beaten if they neglected their duties. Most servants were well fed and were paid an allowance for tea (or beer).

The Tory pamphleteer Charles Davenant considered that there was 'no country in the world where the inferior rank of men were better fed'. Daniel Defoe believed that the mass of the people ate well and drank well – 'three times as much as any sort of foreigners' – for they had, in his opinion, plenty of meat and beer. 'Even those whom we call poor people', he added, 'lie warm, live in plenty, work hard and need know no want.' Of course the enthusiasm of political pamphleteers needs to be taken with a pinch of salt, but Defoe himself was an employer and a widely travelled reporter, who ought to have known what he was talking about.

One fact is clear about England in the first half of the eighteenth century: this is that after the end of the European wars commerce boomed, partly because Robert Walpole as Prime Minister secured twenty years of peace and partly because the first British Empire furnished assured markets in North America, the West Indies and India, to which goods made in England could be profitably exported. By 1752 exports were valued at £5,400,000 and re-exports at £3,500,000, four or five times the figure a century earlier. More manufactured goods were exported and fewer imported. England was ceasing to be an underdeveloped country. Its industries, in which more capital was being invested, were prospering, and its agricultural output was large enough for grain to be regularly exported abroad.

The country had well-tried financial institutions, headed by the Bank of England; a Board of Trade had been set up in 1696, and commercial statistics were collected by an Inspector General of Customs from 1699 onwards, showing a lively export trade and a favourable balance of payments. Agricultural methods were improving, industry was becoming more varied, and the standard of living of the wage-earning classes was higher than anywhere in Europe. Because of all this and the long period of peace during the early eighteenth century England was an affluent country.

Notes

1 H.R. Trevor-Roper, *Archbishop Laud* (1962), p. 298
2 Charles Wilson, *England's Apprenticeship 1603-1763* (1965), p. 120
3 J.H. Hexter, 'Storm over the Gentry', *Encounter*, 56 (1958), p. 32
4 H.J. Habbakuk, 'English Landownership 1680-1740', *Economic History Review*, x (1940), p. 11
5 G.E. Fussell, *Economic History Review*, ix (1938-9), pp. 68-71; Phyllis Deane, *The First Industrial Revolution* (1979), pp. 40-1
6 G.E. Mingay, *English Landed Society in the Eighteenth Century* (1963), p. 19
7 J.D. Chambers, 'Enclosure and Labour Supply in the Industrial Revolution', in E.L. Jones (ed.), *Agriculture and Economic Growth in England* (1967), p. 115
8 J.H. Plumb, *Sir Robert Walpole: the Making of a Statesman* (1956), p. 6
9 Dorothy Marshall, *The English Domestic Servant in History* (1969), pp. 17-19

SEVEN

The Industrialization of England

During the eighteenth century, in spite of the disturbances brought about by five wars, culminating in the dramatic contest with the empire of Napoleon Bonaparte, the economic progress of England was outstanding in Europe.

Measured in terms of commerce, sustained growth can be dated from the seventeen-forties; and had it not been for the war against Spain (widening into war with France), which caused the downfall of the pacific Sir Robert Walpole in 1742, it might have continued even more rapidly. As it was, an extraordinary increase in England's export trade had to await the conclusion of peace in 1748. Before the next war began exports (including re-exports) had doubled in value as compared with the position at the beginning of the century. Payments to the forces and subsidies to allies assisted the export trade during the Seven Years War (1756-63). Victories in this far-flung struggle, which embraced North America, the West Indies and India, directed by the eccentric genius of the first William Pitt, later Earl of Chatham, opened up new markets for English goods outside Europe. 'The principal dynamic element in the English export trade during the middle decades of the eighteenth century', it has been observed, 'was the colonial trade, which created the largest free trade area in the world.'[1]

At the same time internal demand for goods was growing. The population of England and Wales, which had been increasing slowly in the first half of the century, rose by three million between 1760 and 1801, when the first official census was taken, reaching a total of more than nine million. The population of London was over half a million, while that of Birmingham doubled during the second half of the century and that of the sprawling towns of Manchester and Liverpool trebled. In general the fertility of married couples was higher in the industrial areas than in rural parishes. Families with three or four children were numerous among the poor; the gentry were even more prolific. The illegitimacy ratio was high, rising sharply during the second half of the century, particularly in the north-east and west. But the illegitimate were generally unwelcome: every year babies were allowed to die of exposure or starvation. The size of the population was determined partly by a higher birth rate in some areas, partly by a lower death rate, the result of improved hygiene and medical knowledge, and partly by more skilful midwifery. Though malaria and influenza were commonplace, the epidemics that pulverized society had come to an end with the Great Plague of 1665.[2]

Another factor contributing to the economic advance was that though harvests were occasionally poor, the price of grain had been cheap until the middle of the century, as was evidenced by substantial exports. This cheapness raised the value of the incomes of consumers of bread, who could afford to buy manufactured goods out of their earnings. Indeed, the opinion has been hazarded that labourers were actually prepared to work harder in order to be able to buy articles hitherto beyond their reach, like household gadgets and gardening tools for men and cotton dresses and crockery for their wives, and thus raised their standard of living. Writing in 1776, Adam Smith cautiously remarked that 'the real recompense of labour . . . has during the present century increased perhaps in a still greater proportion than its money price', and another famous economist of the time, the Reverend T.R. Malthus, noted that from 1720 to 1750 the price of wheat had fallen, while wages had risen, so that labourers were definitely better off.

In the mid eighteenth century agriculture was still the largest pursuit, occupying three-quarters of the population. In fact the new methods of cultivation which were then taking hold, the sowing of clover and the planting of turnips and potatoes, actually required more labour. They also enabled more livestock to be fed and to survive the winter, their manure enriching the soil on which crops were grown. England was becoming a country of meat and potato eaters, though the really poor still had to manage on bread and cheese.

While bountiful harvests kept prices low there was little impulse for radical changes. But from 1760 onwards prices rose and the number of acts of parliament permitting enclosure grew fast. Between 1760 and 1844 over 2,500 private acts were passed and over four million acres enclosed. Enclosure made the rich richer, but did not necessarily make the poor poorer. These enclosure acts heralded the end of the communal arable farming so long characteristic of much of the Midlands and south-east England and allowed owners to put their land to more profitable use by systems of mixed farming.

Proposals for enclosure were referred as a rule to committees consisting chiefly of local Members of Parliament. Once the committee approved, enclosure commissioners, who were interested parties or represented interested parties, carried out the detailed arrangements. Invariably the smaller farmers, who had to bear their share of the considerable cost of enclosing land, and villagers with no legally defined rights were worst hit. Yeomen farmers, as has already been noted, were starting to disappear before the end of the seventeenth century. On the other hand, the ordinary agricultural labourer was better off; employment was plentiful and the heavy demand for food during the wars against France kept up the level of his wages. The sowing of waste land and the cultivation of the commons for arable crops after enclosing gave him more work.

It was not until towards the end of the Napoleonic wars that England became a net importer of grain. However, an act of parliament, passed in 1815, prohibited the import of wheat from abroad unless the price of home-grown wheat was above 80 shillings a quarter. This meant that in order to benefit English farmers the price was being kept artificially high. But Parliament had to recognize one of the lessons of war, namely that an island needs to be capable of producing sufficient food as a second line of defence to prevent its people from being starved when the flow of imports is being impeded by enemy action. Without an efficient agriculture the two German wars of the twentieth century might well have been lost. Paradoxically the invention of the submarine in 1911 was to prove a boon to English agriculture.

In the eighteenth century rising food prices were in part owing to the needs of war time. They were steady during the first half of the century, rose by 30 per cent in the seventeen-fifties and doubled during the war against revolutionary France. Whereas before 1760 the incomes of landlords only grew slowly, afterwards their rents rose and their debts were paid off. As has been the case throughout much of modern history, it was the big farmers who profited most from the growing public demand for food. It has been estimated that by 1790, 400 great landowners had incomes of £10,000 a year, 700 to 800 wealthy gentry enjoyed incomes of between £3,000 and £4,000 a year, and 3,000 to 4,000 squires had incomes of between £1,000 and £3,000 a year,[3] while 10,000 to 20,000 owner-occupiers lived on £300 to £1,000 a year.

An aerial view of the defences of Maiden Castle, one of the many prehistoric hill forts in Dorset, the country of the Celtic tribe of Durotriges. To the right can be seen the rectangular fields which typified Celtic agriculture.

A Celtic torque or necklace of twisted gold.

A decorated cup from Waternewton (near Castor on Nene), one of the most industrialized areas of Roman Britain. (Third century AD; height nine inches.)

Above This aerial photograph taken at Market Deeping, Lincolnshire, reveals the strips into which open fields were divided from Anglo-Saxon times onwards.

Left A gold clasp from the seventh-century Sutton Hoo ship-burial. Believed to have belonged to an Anglo-Saxon king of East Anglia.

Below An Anglo-Saxon silver penny struck at Canterbury in the later part of the ninth century (actual diameter $\frac{3}{4}''$). The silver coinage dating back to the seventh century was evidence of the growth of trade in England.

Scene from an Anglo-Saxon manuscript showing a harpist, smith and ploughman.

This silver sword pommel, four inches long and decorated with writhing snakes, was found in Fetter Lane. It dates from the temporary Danish occupation of London in the second half of the ninth century.

One of five or six thousand castles built by the Normans in England: Rochester Castle, owned by William the Conqueror's half-brother, Odo, Bishop of Bayeux and Earl of Kent.

The Peasants' Revolt: Wat Tyler, leader of the Kentish rebels, meeting his death at Smithfield on 15 June 1381. King Richard II (centre), who had asked what the demands of the rebels were, watches him being struck down.

A knight on horseback with his wife and daughter-in-law, who wear the long, close-fitting dresses which became fashionable in the fourteenth century.

A lady weaving wool into cloth, England's biggest export in late medieval and early modern times.

Sixteenth-century bakers at work, from the manual of the Bakers' Company of the City of York.

Above left An example of Elizabethan architecture: the hospital (almshouse) founded by the Earl of Leicester at Warwick in 1571.

Left English shipbuilding expanded rapidly during the reigns of the first two Stuarts. Heavily masted ships carrying cannon were built for privateering. In this engraving armed merchant ships capture a Spanish-manned vessel carrying gold from Peru.

Top Visscher's Long View of London and Southwark, seen across the Thames in the early seventeenth century.

Above Longleat, one of the great country houses built in the classical style during the reign of Elizabeth I: a seventeenth-century painting by Jan Siberechts.

Above Eighteenth-century low life: an inn scene by Hogarth (1747).

The old East India wharf at London Bridge, painted *c.* 1756 by Samuel Scott. The East India Company enjoyed a monopoly of the trade with India until it was ended by Parliament in 1813.

Agriculture remained the largest occupation in England until after the repeal of the Corn Laws: an idealized country scene as illustrated by Stubbs's *Haymakers* (1785).

The distributive trades expanded enormously in the late eighteenth and nineteenth centuries. While shopping centres increased, open–air markets, which had flourished since the Middle Ages, remained popular: Norwich market, as depicted in a painting by Cotman (1806).

Boulton's and Watt's engineering factory at Soho outside Birmingham, where they manufactured steam engines capable of turning machinery.

Ironworks for casting cannon and a boring mill at Coalbrookdale, *c.* 1788. It was in Coalbrookdale that Abraham Darby's use of charcoal as a fuel paved the way for the rise of Britain as the world's largest iron producer.

The opening of the Liverpool to Manchester railway on 15 September 1830: George Stephenson's 'Rocket' won the prize for the best locomotive, which proved capable of carrying passengers at a high speed. The Chancellor of the Exchequer, William Huskisson, was knocked down and killed at the opening ceremony.

The viaduct over the Sankey Canal, 1831. On the top of the viaduct ran the Liverpool to Manchester line.

Strikes induced by hunger and poverty followed the end of the Napoleonic wars: a cartoon showing the bread riots of 1830 contemplated by a puzzled John Bull and his dog, from a contemporary magazine.

The middle classes enjoying themselves at Ascot races in the eighteen-forties.

The squalid living conditions of the London poor: Doré's *Over London by Rail* (1871).

The Dinner Hour, Wigan, a painting by Eyre Crowe showing women workers at the cotton mills (1874).

An example of social conscience in late Victorian England: the chocolate firm of Rowntree (like that of Cadbury, both run by Quakers) provided lawn tennis for its employees in their spare time.

Edwardians relaxing on the river: a sketch by Bernard Partridge in *Punch*.

The suffragettes symbolized the movement for sexual equality, finally achieved in the nineteen-seventies. Their leader, Emmeline Pankhurst, is here shown being arrested outside Buckingham Palace in May 1914.

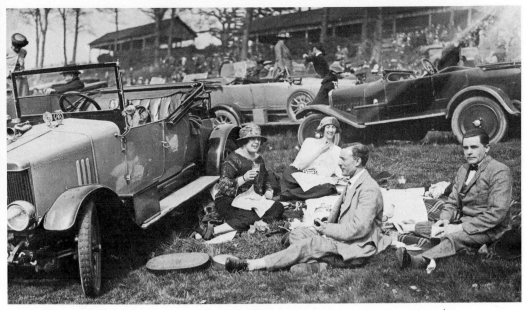

Middle-class families began to savour the benefits of cheap motor cars in the nineteen-twenties: a group photographed picnicking on a Bank holiday at Easter, 1923.

At the same time large-scale unemployment became rife in the early twenties: unemployed ex-servicemen singing to and collecting money from a London theatre queue in 1925.

Families sheltering at Holborn Underground station during the German bombing of London in the Second World War.

Despite the Race Relations Act, a multiracial society in England sometimes created problems and sometimes sparked off riots. Policemen are seen preparing to move in on rioters at Brixton in south London during April 1981.

The farmers in the Home Counties possessed the advantage of a large and secure market in London and its suburbs. East Anglia and Leicestershire were centres of up-to-date management. It was in East Anglia that the second Lord Townsend earned the nickname of 'Turnip Townsend' and Thomas Coke, another enlightened aristocrat, presided over meetings of farmers at his great house of Holkham, while in Leicestershire the grazier Rober Bakewell improved the breeding of sheep and horses.

Thus, on the whole, in the second half of the eighteenth century agricultural enterprise was encouraged by the better prices obtainable for food. Wool and leather were also in demand. That was why enclosures went ahead so rapidly, why landowners provided finance for technical improvements, why ordinary farmers became more ambitious, why new tools and ploughs were introduced and why a semi-official Board of Agriculture was established in 1793. Finally, the country showed itself capable of producing sufficient food for its people at home as well as for the armies and fleets engaged in warfare.

As has already been seen, it was because of a prospering agriculture and a growing population that the demand for manufactured goods had increased. Industry was further helped by an expanding foreign and colonial trade, particularly in the last two decades of the century. It has been pointed out that 'after 1782 almost every statistical series of production shows a sharp upwards turn. More than half the growth in the shipments of coal, more than three-quarters of the increase of broadcloth, four-fifths of that of printed cloth, and nine-tenths of the exports of cotton goods were concentrated in the last eighteen years of the century.'[4] And in spite of the renewal of the war against France in 1803, during which Napoleon attempted to stop the sale of English exports throughout his empire (by the Berlin Decree of 1806 and the Milan Decrees of November 1807), by 1815 exports from Great Britain had more than tripled in value as compared with those in the decade 1761-70. Out of a total of £37,000,000, £17,100,000 worth of goods were sold in the New World where, thanks to the supremacy of the British navy, Napoleon's decrees could not reach.

Among these exports cotton goods were becoming more and more important. Cotton or 'cotton wool', as it was usually called, had first been mixed with linen yarn to produce fustian, a coarse cloth, previously imported from Germany and elsewhere. It was spun and woven in cottages by men and women with the help of children, the materials being supplied by middlemen employing 'putters-out' and arranging for the finishing of the cloth, which was paid for by piece rates. Spinners carded and spun the

119

cotton and weavers wove the cotton weft and the linen warp, the breadth and length of the threads across the loom.

It was the demand for the pure cotton cloth and dresses imported from India and sold at little more than the price of fustian that exerted pressure on English manufacturers to imitate the Indian calicoes and checks: their production was stimulated by an act passed in 1721, prohibiting the import of all printed and painted calicoes and other cotton goods except muslins and neckcloths. Raw cotton was plentiful, being bought chiefly from the West Indies and the Levant, and later from North America and Brazil. The experience gained in manufacturing fustian and linen in Lancashire and the relative cheapness of labour there meant that the county was to become the heart of the cotton industry for a period of nearly 200 years.

The industry developed rapidly. Measured by the amount of raw material imported, the output multiplied tenfold between 1760 and 1785. The invention of the flying shuttle or wheel shuttle by John Kay, a clockmaker, which doubled the weaver's output, came into general use in the 1760s, and James Hargreaves's 'spinning jenny' accelerated the work of the spinners. Both these machines could be employed in the operators' own homes. But it was the application first of water power and then of steam power to the working of cotton machinery around the end of the century that decidedly quickened the production of cotton goods and cheapened their cost. Spinning was first mechanized; the power loom followed later. These inventions came in response to the growth of the cotton industry from the middle of the century onwards: they did not start the steady growth of the industry, but they made it leap forward.

The size and the expense of the new machines meant that they needed to be purchased by capitalists and to be housed in factories. The first factory containing water-driven machinery in Lancashire was built in 1777 by Richard Arkwright, a barber and wig-maker, who had invented both a carding machine and a spinning frame. By 1811 two-thirds of the cotton spun in Lancashire came not from cottages in villages but from factories in industrial towns.

The weaving looms were more complicated than the spinning machines. Power looms were in fact not introduced on any considerable scale until the reign of Queen Victoria. Capitalists were hesitant about embarking on the investment required, and the hand-loom weavers, who had built sheds attached to their cottages, where they did their work, were vociferous in defending their means of livelihood against novelties. Yet even without the immediate introduction of mechanized looms the progress of the cotton industry was astonishing. The soft, lime-free water available in Lancashire and the proximity of the port of Liverpool, convenient for the import of raw materials and the export of finished goods, all contributed to the growth of the new industry. By the end of the Napoleonic war it had outstripped the woollen industry in its economic significance for the nation.

No other industry in eighteenth-century England expanded as speedily as cotton. Iron, one of England's oldest industries, showed marked progress. At the beginning of the century the demand for iron was high, notably for making agricultural implements. But it was then cheaper and easier to import it from Sweden than to buy it at home. The reason was that iron ore had to be smelted with charcoal, obtained from partly burnt wood; but timber had already become scarce during the previous century and most of the trees in the Sussex and Kent Weald, where iron had long been produced, had been felled because wood was also needed for building ships. As has been noted, Abraham Darby had succeeded in smelting cast iron in furnaces with coke obtained from coal. But his discovery was a well guarded secret; by 1775 the number of blast furnaces using coke was fewer than thirty. Moreover, coke was not then employed in the forging of pig iron (crude iron) for conversion into wrought iron, which was needed for industrial machinery. Cast iron was required chiefly for cauldrons, pots, kettles, fire grates and other smallish articles.

In 1784, however, a naval agent or supplier named Henry Cort invented a process known as puddling for converting pig iron into wrought iron in a reverbatory furnace. The pig iron was reheated with coke, then stirred with rods until the impurities were burnt away, and was finally passed between rollers. Thus Cort's invention 'had the effect of freeing the forge-masters from their dependence on the woodlands, just as Darby's discovery had freed the furnace owners'.[5] Cheap wrought iron was of immense value to industries such as shipbuilding and engineering, just as cast iron was to agriculture and home life. The output of pig iron shot up between the mid seventeen–eighties and the start of the nineteenth century almost as sharply as did that of cotton goods. By the end of the eighteenth century iron was being exported for the first time; from 1800 to 1850 a fifth of the pig iron produced in England was exported.

Although ten tons of coal were needed to produce one ton of pig iron, supplies of coal were ample; so the iron industry shifted away from Sussex to areas like South Wales, Yorkshire, Derbyshire and parts of the Midlands, where ore was to be found and collieries were established, thus reducing the expense of transporting coal to the ironworks. Coal had long ceased to be mined from outcrops. Shafts had to be sunk and the problems presented by carbonic acid or marsh gas and water in the mines overcome. Early in the century the invention by Thomas Newcomen, an ironmonger in Devonshire, of a steam engine for pumping water out of mines enabled seams in or below water layers to be mined, and thus increased production. James Watt's steam engine, invented in 1775, made pumping cheaper and more effective. The invention by Sir Humphry Davy of a safety lamp in 1815 reduced the danger of explosions from firing the gas and permitted dangerous seams to be worked. By 1829 the output of coal had risen to 16,000,000 tons a year, as compared with only 4,750,000 tons in 1750.

Miners were usually rough and independent characters (as they still are), who did not relish working long hours, especially as they often had a bit of land to cultivate. Not only boys but women were employed in carrying the coal that had been hewed along the underground passages and up ladders to the surface, but by the seventeen-eighties Newcomen's steam engine had been adapted to lift baskets of coal to the top of the shafts. Coal miners were paid either at piece rates or by the hour. In some cases they might have to hew and draw the coal and deliver it to customers as well before they received their pay. It was in fact the delivery of the coal that was the bottleneck in the industry. The coming of canals and railways solved this problem.

Of other industries, woollen textiles and pottery were the most notable. Woollen cloth manufacture was now chiefly concentrated in the south-west, East Anglia and Yorkshire. Up till the end of the eighteenth century it was still the most profitable export. But it was not as cheap to make as cotton because it was mainly produced by the 'putting-out' system, which meant that the work was divided between carders, spinners, weavers, fullers, dressers and dyers, all paid for at piece rates; it had then to be sold in a variety of markets besides the most famous, Blackwell Hall in London; secondly, the power loom, operated by water or steam, made slower progress in the wool industry than in the cotton industry and so fewer factories were then set up, which meant a reduction in overhead costs. Furthermore the demand for woollen textiles was less elastic than that for cotton goods. By the beginning of Queen Victoria's reign the value of woollen exports was only a quarter of the value of cotton exports.

English pottery, which was rather crude during the first half of the eighteenth century, was, like ironwork, handicapped by the scarcity of charcoal needed for baking the clay. This drove the industry nearer to the coal mines: a large number of small factories were built in north Stafford-shire. There Josiah Wedgwood established in 1769 his famous pottery works, which he named Etruria after the district in Italy where classical vases had been discovered. He was a man of vision and foresight who employed artists to design his neo-classical 'creamware'. The duller clays of Staffordshire were mixed with clay bought in Cornwall and Devon-shire. Wedgwood took a close interest in the development of transport, installed a steam engine in his factory and built a village for his workpeople. But the conditions in the industry as a whole were far from idyllic, particularly for the boys employed.

By the end of the eighteenth century industry 'had ceased to be the handmaid of commerce, but had become its mistress'.[6] Between 1770 and 1830 the national income had nearly doubled. What were the causes of the spurt forward, which had contributed to the victory over Napoleon and paved the way to Victorian affluence? In the first place can be put the rise in population, which increased the size of the home market for all sorts of goods. But a large population does not necessarily lead to economic progress, as the histories of India and China demonstrate. Secondly, the innovations and inventions, particularly in the textile, iron and coal indus-tries, stimulated the division of labour in the processes of production, reduced costs and therefore also prices. Hundreds of patents were taken out and some inventions were cumulative: that for using coke for smelting was one, the pumping of water from coal mines another.

It has been asserted that 'the new methods, new ideas and new departures in organization were discovered not mainly because they were needed but because we wanted them and were well enough off to try them out and accept the changes they brought'.[7] But one should not underestimate the inventive genius of the British people. The spirit of discovery was first fostered by Francis Bacon; it was exemplified by the experiments of the Royal Society; the genius of men like Isaac Newton and Robert Boyle made them pioneers of modern physics and chemistry; and the twentieth century has given us men like Lord Rutherford and Sir Alexander Flem-ing. A fascinating point about the inventions of the eighteenth century is that most of them were the discoveries of more or less uneducated men like John Kay and Henry Cort.

Another factor was the amplitude of cheap capital to invest in industry. The establishment of the Bank of England and the reform of the currency at the end of the seventeenth century created a money market based, after the South Sea bubble had burst, on public confidence. Following the success of the Bank of England private concerns had multiplied; but these banks were vulnerable because they were not allowed a joint-stock basis until 1826 and were limited to partnerships of six. By 1821 some 60 banks were functioning in London and another 370 throughout the country, all issuing their own notes. The Bank of England did not have the power and authority that it has now; and many country banks went bankrupt in the early nineteenth century.

Though the rate of interest had been low throughout most of the eighteenth century (it was 3 to 4 per cent in 1750) it does not seem that the enterprise of private bankers was particularly helpful to industrial and commercial progress: they provided short-term credits for working capital, but were reluctant to engage in long-term investment. Most of the fixed capital for manufacture was found by industrialists ploughing back their profits. The fact that the rate of interest is low does not necessarily increase investment in industry, as has been proved during the twentieth century: high interest rates normally prevail during booms, low during slumps. What is essential is confidence. It is not evident that the percentage of the national income invested was exceptionally high, or that savings rose substantially before the second quarter of the nineteenth century dawned.

One other factor in promoting economic advance was the liberation of trade from some of its medieval shackles. Sir Robert Walpole had freed English manufacturers from export duties, though he retained them on raw materials, notably wool, for he was no advocate of free trade. The publication of Adam Smith's *Inquiry into the Nature and Causes of the Wealth of Nations* and Jeremy Bentham's *Fragment on Government* in the seventeen-seventies, however, influenced informed public opinion in favour of more freedom for commerce and industry in order to secure the greatest happiness of the greatest number. Adam Smith argued the case for promoting international division of labour: 'if a foreign country can supply us with a commodity cheaper than we can make it', he wrote, 'better buy it off them with some part of the produce of our own industry, employed in a way in which we have some advantage'. As an instance he suggested that good claret and burgundy might be produced from grapes grown in Scotland, but their cost would be thirty times that of wines imported from France. Forty years later another economist with business experience, David Ricardo, published an *Essay on the Influence of the Low Prices of Grain on the Profits of Stock* in which he condemned import duties on corn.

After the end of the American War of Independence William Pitt the Younger, who was Chancellor of the Exchequer as well as First Lord of the Treasury for eighteen years, lowered the tea duty and other import duties and negotiated a trade treaty with France, which reduced the duties on French wine and brandy, and obtained in return reductions of French duties on textiles, pottery and hardware. But Pitt did not believe that free trade was a theory that could be quickly put into effect. In 1825 Thomas Huskisson as President of the Board of Trade reduced other import duties, but his reasons for doing so were financial rather than economic.

Free trade as the battle cry of progress awaited the reign of Queen Victoria. Such changes as were made in the tariff played only a minor part in helping industry before and after the war against revolutionary France. On the other hand, the apprenticeship laws were modified; compulsory apprenticeship in the woollen textile industry was abolished in 1809 and in all other industries during 1814. The impulse for their abolition was humanitarian.

Of all the inventions and innovations in British industrial history during the eighteenth century, James Watt's steam engine was the most significant. Hitherto power to drive machinery had been provided by animals, wind or water, all of which were slow and unreliable. Watt's first steam engine, patented in 1775, was a great improvement on that of Newcomen. After Watt entered into a partnership with a Birmingham industrialist, Matthew Boulton, he patented in 1782 an engine with a rotating movement capable of turning machinery instead of the vertical movement required for pumping. The policy of Boulton and Watt was restrictive: they controlled the manufacture of their engines under licence, insisting on high standards of workmanship. In 1795, instead of being consultants, they opened their own engineering works at Soho outside Birmingham. It was not until their patent expired that these steam engines proliferated. In 1800 1,200 of them were in operation. They were invaluable to the two growth industries – cotton for spinning and iron for blowing the blast at furnaces using coke – as well as furnishing mechanical power for forging. Moreover, since coal was necessary to produce steam it gave a boost to that industry. Once the use of coal as power was added to its value for heating and cooking, the supreme importance of British coal mines was fully recognized.

It was largely to facilitate the carriage of coal that canals were built. The first canal in England, known as 'the Sankey cut', was sponsored by the Liverpool Council; the second, constructed by the second Duke of

Bridgewater four years later in 1761, joined up his coal mines in Worsley with the cotton town of Manchester; later it was linked with the river Mersey. These canals halved the cost of coal in Liverpool and Manchester. In 1770 a canal between Liverpool and Leeds was begun; it was to join up with the river Humber and Hull, enabling goods to be carried right across the country. The lock, first invented in the fourteenth century, was employed to carry water up- and downhill. But the engineering problems involved in building these canals were formidable. The aqueduct across the river Irwell, built by Bridgewater's self-educated foreman engineer, James Brindley, created a sensation. The canals took a long time to complete; it was forty-six years before the Liverpool–Leeds canal was finished. The Grand Trunk canal, begun by Brindley in 1767, was not finished until seven years after his death. This canal connected Lancashire and Cheshire with the Midlands, while the Grand Junction canal linked the Midlands with London. The Oxford canal was used to carry coal there from the Midlands; the Kennet and Avon canal joined the river Severn with the Thames so that goods could be brought along it from Bristol to London.

The money for building these canals was raised privately and their construction was permitted by acts of parliament. For a time they were extremely profitable, but they had marked disadvantages. As each canal was paid for by its users, the company owning it was not much concerned with through traffic from one canal to another; consequently the canals often had different levels and depths and sometimes goods had to be trans-shipped from one waterway to another. Secondly, since they took such a long time to build, some of them wasted national resources. By the middle of the nineteenth century they had been largely superseded by the railways. The reason for this was that carrying goods by horse-drawn barges along canals was a leisurely business. Manchester merchants complained that it took longer to bring their raw material from Liverpool than it did to carry it by ship across the Atlantic.

The canal era (1760–1830) coincided with a considerable improvement in the roads, which had been unsatisfactory ever since Roman times. Theoretically the parish authorities were responsible for their upkeep, amateur surveyors being allowed to use a local tax on real property, levied by the justices of the peace, to pay for the work or to employ labourers for the purpose. The first Turnpike Act, passed in 1663, permitted a local company to form a trust to build and maintain lengths of road, recouping itself by levying fees on travellers at turnpike gates. During the first half of the eighteenth century the central government had been more concerned over laying down regulations about the weights of loads than over building new roads to meet the needs of traffic. It was an instance of the way in which money was easily made available for investment, and of the fact that industry urgently required better transport, that by 1830 turnpike roads covered a distance of 23,000 miles (out of a total of 128,000 miles).

The turnpike roads were far from popular. The toll gates could be avoided by horsemen, but wagons and coaches were subject to irritating delays and sometimes to arbitrary increases in charges. They were disliked by drovers because the hard roads hurt the feet of their cattle. Turnpike roads were built only over short stretches, ten to twenty miles long, where they were thought likely to be most profitable; in London, for example, toll gates were sited at Hyde Park Corner and near where Marble Arch now stands; and most of the country still had nothing but grass tracks, impassable in winter.

The names of three engineers who built new roads are well known: John Metcalf, who was blind yet organized the construction of roads with adequate drainage in Lancashire and Yorkshire; Thomas Telford, surveyor of the road from London to Holyhead through north Wales and designer of the Menai Bridge; and John Macadam, whose name is associated with a method of road-making which involved using layers of broken stone, each subjected to pressure before the next was laid. Such roads inaugurated the era of flying coaches and quickened the delivery of the royal mail. But they were not so valuable for carrying bulky cargoes as were the canals and later the railways.

One of the most extraordinary facets of the prosperity of England in the second half of the eighteenth century and the beginning of the nineteenth is that it was not materially injured by wars. The East India Company, it is true, went through a difficult period. When late in 1773 it was allowed by the Government to sell tea cheaply in America, paying the duty and eliminating colonial merchants and smugglers, the American reaction was swift and fierce; coercive measures by the British Government followed, angering the Americans even more.

It was because of this well-meaning but ill-timed attempt to let Americans buy inexpensive tea that they became a nation of coffee drinkers. Whereas the consumption of tea rose enormously in the eighteenth century, the English, for their part, did not take their coffee seriously. A Frenchman noted that the English 'attach no importance to the perfume and flavour of good coffee ... their coffee is always weak and bitter and has completely lost its aromatic flavour'. Writing in 1782, a German traveller said: 'I would always advise those who wish to drink coffee in England to mention beforehand how many cups are to be made with half an ounce or else people will probably bring them a prodigious quantity of brown water which . . . I have not yet been able wholly to avoid'.[8] During the American War of Independence that followed the fiasco over tea the official figures of British exports plummeted, for in turn the French, Spanish and Dutch came in on the American side, so that European as well as American markets were lost.

Yet within a year of the signature of the Peace Treaty of Versailles, recognizing American independence in 1783, exports exceeded those of the last years of the colonial period; and the ten years when Pitt the Younger was peace-time Prime Minister were among the most prosperous in English history. During the early years of the long war against revolutionary France British iron and steel provided weapons, and cotton and woollen textiles uniforms and blankets. Although ultimately nearly half a million men served in the army and navy, the number of workmen required to sustain the needs of the forces overseas was much smaller than those required in the twentieth century. Agriculture sufficed to produce most of the food wanted, except in years of bad harvests; and while grain prices rose, so did the wages of farm workers. Furthermore the contribution of the potato to the final victory must not be underestimated.

The loss of foreign markets again brought temporary distress, but the burgeoning cotton trade discovered new markets in South America and elsewhere. Imports of raw cotton, the best index to the success of the industry, had actually doubled by the time the Peace of Amiens was signed in 1802. The output of iron and steel more than doubled. Well over half the British exports at this time went to the United States of America. Indeed, the total value of all exports doubled and that of imports rose substantially. Timber had to be bought – first from the Baltic and later from Canada – for the building of ships, but the extension of the docks in London and other ports, essential to the expansion of the mercantile marine, went ahead, cheap iron replacing timber in their construction.

After the renewal of the war Napoleon, having been forced to abandon his attempt to invade England by the defeat of his fleet at the battle of Trafalgar in 1805, aimed to damage his enemy ('the nation of shopkeepers') by boycotting all British exports to Europe; he was in a position to do so because in the following year he was able to compel the Tsar of Russia to close his ports to British ships. The 'Continental system', as Napoleon called it, succeeded in reducing British exports to Europe for a time, but in 1809 total exports reached the record value of £50,000,000. Moreover poor harvests in 1808 and 1809 required the import of food, much of which, ironically enough, came from France and was paid for in gold. This was permitted by Napoleon because, unlike Adam Smith, the French Emperor equated wealth with precious metals and hoped to bleed his enemy of them. In 1811 British exports fell to the value of £32,400,000, but after the French army's retreat from Moscow in 1812 the Continental system collapsed. Its most harmful consequence was to involve England in a war with the United States, fought at sea and on the land frontier of Canada. But the war did not last long enough to damage trade seriously.

What were injurious to the economy in the years 1793 to 1815 were the financial costs of the war against France. While Pitt the Younger remained Prime Minister he tried to pay for a large part of them out of taxation rather than by borrowing. The income tax was introduced in 1799 at the rate of 2 shillings in the pound. Two years earlier, because of heavy borrowing by the Government and loans to allies, the Bank of England, which had now in effect assumed the functions of a central bank, ran short of gold and a panic set in; prices of stocks fell and many bankruptcies followed. The Government was obliged to relieve the Bank of its obligation to pay cash against its notes. The price of gold then rose and the value of the pound fluctuated, causing retail prices to rise and real wages to fall. Though this created discontent, the Government's policy of raising taxes to meet much of the cost of the war was effective in keeping the rate of inflation within reasonable limits, while the increase in prices stimulated industry.

By the time the war ended in 1815 Great Britain might claim to have become the emporium of the world. The income tax was abolished in 1815; the gold standard was restored in 1821. By then, although the population of England and Wales had risen to over twelve million (with two million in Scotland), prices were beginning to fall following the war-time inflation. The outlook was excellent for the wealthy landowning classes and the industrious middle classes, whose placid existence is pictured in the novels of Jane Austen and in Charles Dickens's *Dombey and Son*, 'for whom the earth was made to trade in'.

But what of the wage-earners? English wages in the second half of the eighteenth century were higher than those in France and lower than those in the newly founded United States of America. Their real value varied in accordance with the price of bread and whether the country was at war or peace. Agricultural workers were better off in war time, but other workers were not necessarily so because 'the proportion of the energies of Englishmen that went into the production of exports was extraordinarily high' and the export trade both to Europe and America was interrupted by wars.[9] In between the wars, shortages of workers in particular industries occurred, for an integrated national market for labour was lacking. Coal miners were needed after the Seven Years War, which led to higher wages being offered them; and Josiah Wedgwood had difficulty in finding workmen for his potteries in 1769, when he wrote that 'almost everybody wants hands'.

Wage-earners were by no means unvociferous. Whenever bad harvests and a consequent rise in food prices threatened them with hunger they rioted. In 1740-1 demonstrators burnt down mills and attacked corn dealers and bakers. By the seventeen-sixties, when the population was growing fast, this pressed upon the supply of food. London was usually plentifully provisioned; indeed, the sight of grain being shipped through the countryside to the capital provoked the anger of famished spectators: but in 1767 the metropolitan poor became equally restless as, owing to a bad harvest, the price of the quartern loaf rose steeply. In other parts of the country coal heavers, who unloaded ships arriving at docks, merchant seamen and silk workers were all clamouring for higher wages, either rioting or going on strike. The Government was reluctant to call out troops to suppress the disorders, and the interference with normal trade was such that to some extent at least they made their point and enlisted public sympathy. Rural magistrates, usually country gentlemen, often pitied hungry strikers and encouraged them to turn their wrath against rich farmers and profiteering middle men who kept up high prices for grain, thus showing indulgence to rioters who were agitating for higher pay.

Nevertheless those who struck for better wages in the eighteenth and early nineteenth centuries were rarely sufficiently united to win a victory. Local trade clubs, the successors to the medieval journeymen's and craftsmen's gilds, were the characteristic wage-earners' organizations of the time rather than national trade unions. Skilled workmen, shipwrights, for example, were the most successful at forming strong unions. Some of the clubs were benefit societies more than unions and less militant than they might have been. Because of the lack of unified force among workmen employers were able to apply to Parliament for a ban on combinations and for the imposition of maximum rates of wages in their own particular industries.

Strikes induced by hunger and poverty were not the only symptoms of unrest. The substitution of expensive machinery, which had to be housed in factories, for the spindles and looms that were worked by hand in the cottagers' own homes aroused the hostility of textile workers. It was not simply because of the fear that their earnings would be cut by the competition of factories that this fundamental social change was disliked, but because domestic workers, not being strictly disciplined by their employers, could organize their lives to suit their own convenience, calling upon their families to assist them when necessary and allowing them to take a day off from work when they felt like it. They often did not work on Mondays. Men who worked in factories were required to do twelve- to sixteen-hour shifts, starting early in the morning and, when artificial lighting improved, through the night.

After a clergyman named Edmund Cartwright invented a power loom that could be operated by steam in 1789 it was taken up by cotton manufacturers during the war against Napoleon and later by the woollen textile industry. The hand-loom weavers, who had enjoyed their last period of prosperity before the war, were shocked by the economic and social consequences of mechanization; for among other things the new looms could be handled by boys and girls. The hand-loom weavers soon took demonstrative action. When Cartwright's first steam looms were installed in a cotton mill they were destroyed by incendiaries before the equipment was completed. Wool-combers were equally opposed to the introduction of machinery and shearers tried to obtain the prohibition of gig mills, on which the work could be done more quickly.

In protest about the unemployment created by mechanization workers calling themselves Luddites resorted to a campaign of smashing the new apparatus. Their name may have come from a boy named Ludlam who, to spite his father, broke a knitting frame. The Luddite movement began in the hosiery and lace industries and then spread to the cotton and woollen mills during the later part of the war and after. But all such protests by agitation and violence proved vain. The number of power looms rose from 2,400 in 1813 to 100,000 in 1835. Although the number of hand looms in use remained considerable, the attempts of their operators to compete with the power looms in factories formed the most depressing chapter in the economic history of the early nineteenth century. Some Luddites were hanged and others were transported for life.

It was in response to social unrest during the Napoleonic wars that Combination Acts applicable to all industries were passed by Parliament.

The first act of July 1799 was aimed against combinations of masters as well as of workers. Some employers would have preferred statutory minimum wages as a safeguard against strikes. In 1824, owing to the initiative of radical Members of Parliament, the Combination Acts were repealed. The acts had not been very effective either in preventing employees from striking or restraining employers from price-fixing. Strikes by both spinners and weavers demanding higher wages were frequent in Lancashire between 1815 and 1830. They usually collapsed, owing to want of adequate strike pay or sufficient support from other unions.

The repeal was followed by attempts to form national unions, the most ambitious of which were a National Association for the Protection of Labour, sponsored by John Doherty, an Irishman who had settled in Manchester as a cotton spinner, and a Grand National Consolidated Trades Union, founded in 1834 under the influence of Robert Owen, himself a mill owner with advanced ideas. The first, which claimed to have recruited 100,000 members, disintegrated in 1832 through internal squabbles; the second, which boasted 500,000 members, including women, foundered for much the same reasons and was converted into a less belligerent society. Both these organizations were a kind of response to the passing of the first Reform Act of 1832, with its modest transformation of the constituencies and the electorate. Many radicals had pinned their hopes of industrial reforms on the election of a more representative Parliament with a membership sympathetic to the aspirations of the wage-earning classes. But the Reform Act was of direct benefit only to the middle classes.

The epilogue to the political and social drama of the early eighteen-thirties was the decision in March 1834 of the magistrates of the village of Tolpuddle in Dorset to condemn six labourers to transportation for seven years because they had administered oaths to fellow members of a union: for the abolition of the Combination Acts had left intact the right to convict labourers of conspiracy under the common law of the land.

One reason for the discontent that prevailed after 1815 was the treatment of poverty. The functioning of the Elizabethan Poor Law, which laid responsibility for dealing both with the able-bodied poor, usually unemployed, and the impotent poor or unemployable on justices of the peace, had never proved satisfactory. Poor rates had been levied and workhouses built, but the problems of the unemployed and under-employed had not been solved. After the outbreak of the war against France the magistrates of Speenhamland in Berkshire had begun in 1795 to give outdoor relief on a scale based on the price of bread and the size of the family concerned.

Relief was also given to the underpaid whose earnings fell short of that scale, thus subsidizing the wages of the lowest-paid workers. The Speenhamland system spread throughout the country, particularly in southern England, but it applied only to rural areas. As a result the annual expenditure out of the poor rates grew from £2,000,000 in the seventeen-eighties to £6,000,000 in 1812.

After the war ended in 1815 poverty increased, especially among agricultural labourers. Landlords and farmers had invested capital in equipment such as threshing machines and tedders to spread and dry hay and extended their operations to less fertile soil in the expectation that the higher prices obtained for food in war time would continue, but they were disappointed, even though they were protected by the Corn Law of 1815. A Member of Parliament claimed in 1816 that many small farmers were becoming pensioners on the poor rate. At the same time the miserable plight of the hand-loom weavers was only one instance of the way in which mechanized processes in industry were creating pockets of poverty. Wages fell when demobilized soldiers and sailors were flooding the labour market. Some industries that had profited from war conditions lost ground and had to dismiss workers.

By the eighteen-twenties the position began to improve somewhat, since the standard of living of wage-earners was helped by a fall in the price of food. Yet the problem of poverty remained. In 1832 a Royal Commission was appointed to suggest remedies. It urged that relief should not be left entirely to the parishes, as it had been since the sixteenth century, and that a Board of Commissioners should supervise the regulation and building of workhouses. By the Poor Law Amendment Act of 1834 parishes were grouped into 'unions' and a Board of Guardians, elected by rate-payers, was appointed to carry out the regulations of the Commissioners. Though relief in aid of wages had been condemned, it was in fact continued. On the other hand, the total amount of relief was cut down because many who were offered relief only if they entered a workhouse refused it. In fact during the eighteen-thirties unemployment was not excessive and real wages were reasonably good in most manufacturing industries.

But what were the conditions of those at work like? Factory workers were, on the whole, better paid than either agricultural labourers or domestic servants, but money was not everything. Agricultural labourers usually had a garden or patch of land on which they could grow fruit and vegetables and sometimes had a pigsty. Their cottages could be of stone or brick, with glazed windows. Meals could be elaborated with game, for in spite of ferocious penalties laid down in an act of 1817 poaching was widespread, usually commanding public sympathy and even on occasions the connivance of the village constable. The position of domestic servants was by no means bad: 'the servants' table', wrote the author of *The Complete Servant* in 1825, 'is usually provided with solid dishes and with ale and table beer'. Upper-class servants, like the clerk of the kitchen, the chef, the butler and the valet, had well-furnished, comfortable rooms and pickings from the family table.

By contrast, factory workers had to toil for long hours in stifling conditions in rooms that were dirty and badly lit. Women and children were also employed for long hours in factories, particularly in the cotton industry. Mill owners contracted with Poor Law authorities for batches of pauper children to serve as apprentices, who were lodged in sheds adjoining the factories, where they were liable to catch fever in insanitary surroundings. An act of parliament of 1819, out of keeping with the attitude of *laissez-faire* that then prevailed, prohibited the employment of children under nine in cotton mills and restricted the hours of work for older children to twelve a day. But as no factory inspectors were appointed the act was easily evaded. However, fourteen years later another act laid down that children between the ages of nine and thirteen employed in all textile factories (except silk) should not work more than forty-eight hours a week and inspectors were appointed to enforce its clauses. Night work was forbidden to all persons under eighteen and they were not to be required to work for more than twelve hours a day or sixty-nine hours a week. It also legislated for two hours a day of schooling for children working in the textile industries. Loopholes in the act were plugged in 1844, when night work was forbidden to women. Gradually, enlightened public opinion was persuaded that because of the need to protect women and children who worked in mills and mines it was necessary to reduce by law the appalling hours of factory labour.

Though coal miners were relatively well paid, the iniquitous truck system was commoner in it than in other industries. Mine owners set up shops on the premises of the mines, where for one reason or another the men and their wives were expected to spend at least a part of their wages. In remote areas where few shops were to be found, manufacturers might actually pay their workers in truck, that is to say, in goods instead of money.

In the industrial towns housing conditions were generally bad. In Manchester, for instance, many workmen and their families lodged in damp and unhealthy cellars. As the cost of building rose in the early nineteenth century, houses put up by jerry-builders at rents workmen could afford were small and crowded together, like the back-to-back houses still to be seen in some northern towns. Overcrowding reflected the growth in the population. Nevertheless the death rate also rose after 1831: this was the result of inadequate sanitation and polluted water supplies. It was scarcely surprising therefore that cottage labourers, accustomed to being masters in their own homes, however humble, and working such hours as they thought necessary for the good of their families, were reluctant to submit themselves to the discipline, long hours and unhygienic conditions that unquestionably prevailed in the majority of factories.

The contrast between elegance and squalor, between the ideals of the so-called Romantic Movement of early nineteenth-century England and its industrial realities, is striking. Anyone who reads the novels of Jane Austen, describing the life of the country gentry of her time, where the main excitement was who was going to marry whom and the best way of avoiding boredom, learns little of what was happening on the battlefields of Europe or in the crowded cities. The French Revolution sparked off lyrical poets like Wordsworth, Shelley and Keats, who rejected the ordered classical universe of Dr Johnson and his circle, stood for liberty and personal freedom and found city life distasteful. In London one could see the beautiful houses built by the Adam brothers and John Nash on the one side and the slums of Westminster and the East End on the other. The aristocratic portraiture of Reynolds and Romney was far removed from the paintings of Turner, whose later work may be seen to symbolize the advent of the age of steam.

In his novel *Hard Times* Charles Dickens painted a memorable portrait of an imaginary Coketown:

> It was a town of red brick, or brick that would have been red if the smoke and ashes had allowed it .... It was a town of machinery and tall chimneys out of which interminable serpents of smoke trailed themselves for ever and ever, and never got uncoiled. It had a black canal in it, and a river that ran purple with ill-smelling dye, and vast buildings full of windows, where there was a rattling and trembling all day long, and where the piston of the steam-engine worked monotonously up and down, like the head of an elephant in a state of melancholy madness.

There were produced 'the elegancies of life' that 'found their way all over the world'.

Another contrast could be drawn between the dark, smoke-laden towns of the industrial north and Midlands and the pleasurable, leisured existence in such seaside resorts as Southend, Broadstairs, Brighton and Weymouth. Bath was still a popular resort with the well-to-do, but the beauties of the Lake District had only just been discovered. Lydia Bennet in Jane Austen's *Pride and Prejudice* thought Brighton heavenly and her more mature sister, Elizabeth, was disappointed at not being able to visit the Lake District.

However fairly the landscape of the early nineteenth century is depicted, it is hard to forget its grimmer aspects. It is true that a German visitor, writing in 1828, said that 'outside some of the northern factory districts and the low quarters of London one seldom sees rags and tatters, as seldom as broken window panes and neglected cottages';[10] but wherever coal mines and ironworks were to be found, a blackened country came into being. Factory workers had little to cheer them at their toil or at home except mugs of beer or cups of tea. Apart from a few notable exceptions, employers were mostly self-made men who were far from being philanthropic. When in 1797 the copper miners in Cornwall were faced with starvation and threatened their masters with violence, John Wilkinson, who made a fortune out of armaments, advocated the use of a press-gang and the lowering of the miners' wages to teach them a lesson. Many of the ironmasters were nonconformists, who lived austere and frugal lives, but had little of the milk of human kindness. They were opposed, for instance, to the building of a theatre in Birmingham: yet workmen and their families badly needed distraction from the stark daily round.

England was in the process of being divided into two nations, on one side the industrial north and Midlands, on the other the rural south and east. Scattered around were benevolent landlords occupying gracious houses which few today can manage or afford. The census of 1831 recorded huge numbers of domestic servants, nearly 700,000 of them, who catered for the comforts of the upper and middle classes.

The invention of mechanical means of manufacturing textiles drew many families away from the countryside, graced by the landed gentry and their minions, into the ugly towns of industrial England. William Cobbett, once a farmer and always a journalist, deplored the way in which the 'Lords of the Loom' had attracted countryfolk into their factories to make 'many work for the gain of a few'. He thought of such capitalist employers as 'greedy, grinding ruffians' who were changing men, women and children into their slaves. But another journalist, Edward Baines, a Yorkshireman, proclaimed that in his opinion 'manufacturers' had 'transformed heaths, deserts, quagmires, bogs and scenes of desolation into lands of fertility and abundance'. No doubt both would have admitted that a new rich and a new poor had been created, peopling the divided society of which the novelist and statesman Benjamin Disraeli was to write, between whom there was no intercourse and no sympathy.

It was ironical that the opening year of the reign of Queen Victoria, which we now look back upon as the most prosperous in English history, should have been a year of recession, hunger, much poverty and unemployment, heralding the first of those periodic social and economic crises in peace time that have since punctuated the story of industrialized England.

Notes

1 Ralph Davis, 'English Foreign Trade 1700–1774', in W.E. Minchinton, *The Growth of English Overseas Trade in the 17th and 18th Centuries* (1969), chapter 2

2 J.D. Chambers, *Population, Economy and Society* (1972), pp. 37 seq.; Peter Laslett, *Family Life and Illicit Love in Earlier Generations* (1977), chapter 3

3 G.E. Mingay, *English Landed Society in the Eighteenth Century* (1963), p. 54

4 T.S. Ashton, *An Economic History of England: The Eighteenth Century* (1955), p. 125

5 T.S. Ashton, *The Industrial Revolution 1760–1830* (1968), p. 54

6 J.H. Plumb, *England in the Eighteenth Century* (1950), p. 81

7 H.L. Beales, *The Industrial Revolution 1750–1850* (1958), p. 49

8 André Parreaux, *Daily Life in England in the Reign of George III* (1969), p. 37; *Carl Philipp Moritz in England in 1782* (introduction by P.E. Matheson, translated 1924), p. 33

9 Cf. John B. Owen, *The Eighteenth Century 1714–1815* (1974), p. 305

10 H. Meidinger, *Reisen durch Grossbritannien und Irland* (1828), p. 27

EIGHT

The Victorian Age

By achieving its victory over Napoleon the British Government acquired a far-flung empire in several fits of absence of mind. Imperialism, sought in pursuit of glory, as with the French conqueror, had little appeal: colonies were appreciated for their trade or their use as naval bases. The West Indies, for example, were valued for their sugar and India for its tea. But otherwise colonies were regarded as expensive luxuries. Canada, which had not much except furs to offer, needed to be protected from American expansion; Australia was chiefly a dumping ground for convicts; New Zealand was as yet only a field for missionaries. The Cape of Good Hope, like Heligoland, Mauritius, Malta and the Ionian Islands, all obtained by treaty in 1815, were ports of call for the British navy. However, the second British Empire bought a large part of England's exports, although the United States, the heart of the first British Empire, still took a fair proportion of them. The fruit of peace was not immediately prosperity. The war had cost £1,000,000,000, so taxation remained high. Bad harvests caused depressions in 1826 and 1829. But by 1832 employment was becoming plentiful and the cost of living was lower than during the war. More money was available for investment, the rate of interest being as little as 4 or 5 per cent. Yet it was a serious recession with which the reign of Queen Victoria (1837-1901) opened.

In fact this recession continued intermittently until 1841. In the summer of 1837 50,000 workers were unemployed or on short time in Manchester alone: an influx of impecunious Irish labour was partly responsible. The price of bread shot up and instances of death from starvation were recorded in the newspapers. The cost of administering the Poor Law rose, though not to the same extent as it did after the end of the war. In 1840 the infant mortality rate among the wage-earning classes was one in four. Commissioners appointed under an act of 1834 – the charter of the rate-payer, it has been called – had to abandon the idea of not giving any outdoor relief and in fact thousands of families were allowed a shilling or two a week. Those who were lucky enough to be employed, for example in the textile industries, were often required to work a seventy-two-hour week.

It has been observed justly that 'the imagination can hardly apprehend the horror in which thousands of families were then born, dragged out their ghastly lives and died'.[1] No wonder that an Anti-Corn-Law League, aimed at reducing the price of bread, was founded in 1838, or that in the same year the London Working Men's Association drew up a 'People's Charter' demanding annual parliaments, universal male suffrage, equal electoral districts, the removal of property qualifications for Members of Parliament, payment of Members and a secret ballot, all in the optimistic belief that a House of Commons so reformed would assuage the grievances of the poor. The Chartist movement failed; but the Anti-Corn-Law League led by Richard Cobden, a self-made man, and John Bright, a textile manufacturer, triumphed by persuading the Tory Prime Minister, Sir Robert Peel, to abolish the laws in 1846. This meant that the export of grain was no longer subsidized and the import of corn could not be prohibited, procedures that had been habitual since the thirteenth century. The supporters of repeal were largely business men in Manchester and elsewhere who were able to contribute or collect ample funds to back the movement. Some of the working men's leaders, however, far from regarding it as a moral crusade, feared that should repeal result in reducing the price of bread it would be employed as an excuse for lowering wages. Fergus O'Connor, the Chartist leader, said: 'it will make the rich richer and the poor poorer'.[2]

The repeal of the Corn Laws did not have the evil consequences forecast by landowners and big farmers (Lord John Russell, the Whig leader, had feared that the struggle over repeal would be injurious to the aristocracy to which he belonged). The price of wheat remained fairly steady, around 50 shillings a quarter, until the eighteen-seventies (except during the Crimean War of 1854-6). The profits earned by growers of grain were dependent on a yield of about twenty-six bushels per acre. Owing to the high cost of carrying goods by sea corn imported from America was never cheap for a generation after the repeal. It was only with the opening of the prairies in the Middle West and the introduction of steamships that foreign competition in the sale of food became acute. The cost of transporting grain from Chicago to Liverpool fell by nearly a third between 1873 and 1884. It was then that rents, incomes, prices and wages in the English countryside slid catastrophically downwards.

Yet before the dismal seventies farmers were trying hard to put their house in order. An enormous improvement in drainage, which made heavy soils more workable, was taking place; enclosures were more or less completed and an increase in output was obtained, not so much by bringing commons and wastes into cultivation as by enriching the land under the plough, eliminating fallow years, and using more manures and fertilizers such as superphosphate and guano (fish manure), which was imported. Capital was invested in land and labour-saving machines were introduced, lowering the costs of ploughing and sowing seed. The Royal Agricultural Society, founded in 1838, and the Rothamsted Experimental Station, set up in 1842, offered advice to farmers on scientific matters. Mechanization proceeded apace, but the number of people employed on the land had diminished little by 1851. Although the population as a whole was growing rapidly the country still managed to produce 90 per cent of the food it needed. In fact, the big and medium-sized farms earned good profits for their owners, making them more affluent than they had ever been until today: 'that English farming was the best in the world all the world acknowledged,' wrote a historian of the Victorian age. Mixed farming made great headway between the early 1850s and the early 1870s, when the prices of fat stock fed on cheap grain were often high.

However, after 1877, because of foreign competition, arable farming (which employed four men an acre) declined and the membership of the National Agricultural Labourers Union, started by Joseph Arch in 1872, fell significantly from 100,000 to 23,000 in 1879. By then agricultural labourers had grown accustomed to three-bedroom cottages, were paid 12 to 14 shillings a week and ate wheaten bread that cost fivepence or sixpence for a four-pound loaf. They fed on pork or bacon and drank beer or elderberry wine. Who could then have dreamt that self-contained rural village life would virtually disappear in the twentieth century, or that the country would be in danger of starvation once wars encompassed the entire globe?

Before the repeal of the Corn Laws Peel had reduced or abolished a large number of duties for fiscal, not free-trade, reasons. A Committee on Import Duties had reported that 94.5 per cent of the total Customs revenue was derived from duties on only seventeen items. But Peel retained a 5 per cent tax on imported raw materials and 12 per cent on partly manufactured goods. He maintained the duties on wines and spirits and reimposed income tax at sevenpence in the pound to meet the expense of simplifying the tariff. After the victory of what has been called the Manchester School over the Corn Laws, free trade gradually took hold. Imperial preferences were swept away, though preferences on sugar were retained until 1854 and on timber until 1860. The Navigation Acts, protecting the mercantile marine, were repealed in 1849. With further assistance from Mr Gladstone England became the free-trade country *par excellence* during the second half of the nineteenth century.

Protection was no longer deemed necessary, because no longer were there infant industries crying out to be fostered. Imports could be paid for by a booming export trade. The growth in exports, in which cotton goods predominated, was, in relation to the population, far higher between 1840 and 1860 than ever before or since. After cotton, other industries such as coal, iron and steel, woollen textiles and 'invisible exports' (for example earnings from marine insurance, shipping and overseas investment) also contributed to national prosperity. Lloyd's Society of Underwriters had been founded as early as 1771. Capital was invested not only in the British Empire but in Central and South America and in the United States. The Baring brothers and the Rothschilds were pioneers in such foreign investments and were the outstanding merchant bankers of the time. Indeed, more money was invested overseas than at home. British industry largely financed itself by ploughing back profits. Few private firms sought investment from the public until towards the end of the century, and the banks were still reluctant to tie up their resources by loaning money to buy fixed capital. Although limited liability was introduced in the eighteen-fifties, family businesses were slow to convert themselves into private or public companies.[3]

The railways, like the canals, were the outcome of private enterprise, which by quickening the transport of goods cheapened them. Iron rails had been used to move coal from pit-heads and steamboats had carried traffic on rivers during the second half of the eighteenth century. On the earliest railways the locomotives that moved wagons, particularly uphill, were stationary. Furthermore, on these railways customers were allowed to run their own trains, drawn by horses as well as by hired locomotives, just as they used their own barges along the canals. No fewer than nineteen Railway Acts were passed by Parliament during the first two decades of the nineteenth century permitting the construction of lines to carry coal in south Wales alone.

George Stephenson, a self-made man who worked in the collieries, built his first locomotive in 1814. When in 1825 a company opened a railway to carry mineral traffic between Stockton and Darlington, a distance of eight and a half miles, Stephenson was appointed company engineer and persuaded his employers to replace horses with steam engines to draw the trains. The company then engaged on a larger project, a railway between Liverpool and Manchester, offering a prize for the best locomotive, and this was won by Stephenson's 'Rocket', with a fantastically lengthy funnel, built in 1829. In 1838 another company constructed a railway from London to Birmingham and the Great Western Railway developed a line between London and Bristol at the same time. In the forties new railways were rapidly built and companies amalgamated. The Midland Railway and the London and North-Western Railway came into being. Every effort was exerted to attract passengers. For the purposes of refreshment the railways advertised 'magnificent salons, luxuriously furnished, warmed and illuminated, and buffets where attendants neither desire nor expect tips'.[4]

One of the results of the building of railways by private enterprise was that in a mania for quick profits lines were duplicated. For example, one could still choose alternative routes between London and Birmingham and between London and Manchester in the first half of the twentieth century. Secondly, since the railway companies had to buy up land in towns and villages they were often compelled to put their stations away from the town centres, as at Oxford and Cambridge. By 1870 the basic network was virtually complete, covering a total distance of 6,000 miles. The railways soon became effective rivals to the canals in carrying goods and to the turnpike roads for passenger traffic.

The building of the railways had significant social and economic consequences. They were invaluable alike to manufacturing industry, to the export trade and to agriculture. The railways enabled farmers to send perishable goods to distant town markets and to collect their raw materials from factories and ports: this fortified agriculture, in spite of the repeal of the Corn Laws. By 1870 a larger acreage was under the plough than ever before or since. The building and manning of the railways stimulated employment directly and indirectly in Victorian England. Walter Bagehot, the political theorist, and Charles Dickens, the novelist, both thought the railways were democratic institutions. When a general Railway Act was passed in 1844 it required companies to provide trains running each way along their lines every day except Good Friday and Christmas Day, at a rate of twenty miles an hour, stopping at all stations and with a maximum fare of a penny a mile. This 'parliamentary train' might be deemed democratic. But it is doubtful whether the introduction of first-class carriages (intended for gentlemen), second-class carriages (intended for gentlemen's servants) and third-class carriages (for the rest) did anything to eliminate class distinctions. Trains did, however, reduce the isolation of rural life. 'The railroad', it has been claimed, was 'the Magna Carta of people's motive freedom'. And possibly the novelty of this form of transport made fellow passengers more affable and sociable than they generally are today. The poor, argued *The Economist* in 1851, benefited from 'this vast invention. How few among the last generation ever stirred beyond their own villages. How few among the present will die without visiting London.'[5]

Parliament continued to be exercised about the employment of women and young persons (up to the age of eighteen) in textile factories. An act passed in 1847 limited their working day to ten hours or fifty-eight hours a week. This act has been considered by some historians as more meaningful than the repeal of the Corn Laws, but it did not result in a ten-hour day for adult men, whose working hours were not the subject of legislation until the twentieth century. In any case the act allowed women and young persons to be worked in shift or 'relay' systems, as they were called, entailing longer hours for men, and it permitted the employment of children to help them during an afternoon shift when the women and young persons had gone home. A compromise was reached with a Factory Act of 1850 which provided for a sixty-hour week for women and young persons, prohibited their doing night work and required the closure of textile mills at 2 p.m. on Saturdays. Further Factory Acts extended regulations to other industries than textiles. Gradually the restriction of adult working hours became a reality.

The 'sweating' of women in retail millinery, dressmaking and tailoring, particularly in London, was notorious. George Augustus Sala in his book *Turn Round the Clock* (1859) related how he saw seamstresses and milliners' workwomen bound for the dress factories in London's West End with 'pinched faces, eager faces, sullen faces' and 'with large mild eyes', wondering at the necessity of working a twelve-hour day or longer to make ballroom dresses for countesses and marchionesses.[6] An act of 1891 belatedly attempted to deal with this form of exploitation, but only limited working hours to twelve a day. The sweating of sewing-women has persisted in one form or another until the present day.

Further acts affecting industrial employment followed during the last twenty years of the nineteenth century. An Employers' Liability Act of 1880 required employers to insure their workpeople against the risks of their calling. An act of 1895 limited the working hours of children to thirty a week. Finally, the Factory and Workshop Consolidation Act of 1901 marked the progress achieved during the Victorian era: it even empowered the Home Secretary to regulate processes in industry and matters of health by departmental orders. The struggle for social reform had been long and arduous. Indeed, the conditions in which men, women and children were called upon to work in factories, workshops and mines had been so degrading as to shock contemporaries as well as posterity.

From the economic point of view the long reign of Queen Victoria may be divided into three periods. The first and shortest, covering the initial thirteen years of the reign, was one of trouble and unrest, with many strikes in Lancashire and the Midlands. When in July 1838 the House of Commons refused to consider a petition for the People's Charter, bearing 1,200,000 signatures, a convention, meeting in Birmingham, actually threatened a general strike, though the Chartist leader, O'Connor, recoiled from any kind of 'physical force'. The Chartist agitation reached its apogee during the years 1838 to 1842, when both wholesale and retail prices were rising.

Although after that real wages improved, a bad harvest in England in 1845 and the failure of the potato crop in Ireland in 1846 brought an end to the brief period of prosperity and ensured victory for the excellently organized campaign for the repeal of the Corn Laws, a victory which split asunder the Tory Party. The state of the Lancashire cotton mills was so bad from the point of view of the men, women and children employed in them that the series of Factory Acts already outlined was forced through Parliament. The antagonism between capital and labour was ventilated in pamphlets and in O'Connor's newspaper, *The Northern Star*. Robert Owen, himself a successful manufacturer and mill owner, argued that capitalism could be eliminated by socialism: by socialism he meant workers' control of industry, not control by the State. Such co-operation, he believed, could be established without a revolution. It would scarcely have been surprising if the revolutions that took place in France, Austria and Italy had infected England. But partly because O'Connor was no revolutionary the Chartist movement collapsed. To those who believe that individuals count in history, it would appear that the statesmanship of Sir Robert Peel and the Duke of Wellington averted the danger of complete upheaval in the hungry eighteen-forties.

The second period of the reign was heralded by the opening of the Great Exhibition in the Crystal Palace, erected in Hyde Park during 1851, the year after Peel died. It was largely the inspiration of Prince Albert, Queen

Victoria's husband, and while foreign countries contributed to the 10,000 items on display, most of the exhibits were advertisements for the industrial progress of the United Kingdom, which was then gathering momentum. Thackeray could boast that 'these, England's arms of conquest, are the trophies of her bloodless war!'

England was then beginning to benefit from the events of the tempestuous early decades of the century, such as the building of the railways and the introduction of labour-saving devices into the textile industries. The insanitary conditions of work of the labouring classes had been exposed and condemned and were to some extent remedied. Effective acts of parliament mitigated the harsh working life in the cotton mills; a Mines Act of 1842 had forbidden the employment of women and young children underground; in 1848 a General Board of Health was set up, though improvements in hygiene came slowly. Responsible trade unions were established, such as the Miners' Association in 1841 and the Amalgamated Society of Engineers in 1851. The first meeting of the Trades Union Congress took place in 1868. For the managerial class and the skilled workers at any rate salaries, real wages and working conditions became better, so that output rose. Some employers realized that they could increase production by means of incentives rather than by insisting on long hours. A habit of taking Mondays off, notably in Birmingham, always a wealthy city, was winked at by employers, as it often is now.

Although a temporary setback took place during the American Civil War (1861–5), when a big reduction in imports of raw cotton damaged the industry in Lancashire, commodity prices rose, the economy flourished – it was one of the fastest growing in the world – and unemployment virtually disappeared. From the material point of view the mid Victorian period was the high-water mark in English history. The upper and middle classes were pampered: in 1871 nearly 16 per cent of the population were domestic servants, a higher proportion than those employed in agriculture or textiles. Although wage-earners did not necessarily possess comfortable housing, satisfactory conditions or easy lives, let alone social equality, it can be claimed that the population as a whole enjoyed a richer and more varied standard of living as a result of industrialization. One feature of the age was the growth of retail outlets. The number of shops increased enormously, replacing pedlars and, to a lesser extent, street markets. A network of wholesale dealers, commercial travellers and local shops covered everything people needed to buy. London saw the beginnings of the 'super store'. Covered markets, such as that at Oxford, which still survives, were introduced in many industrial towns.

The boom that took place during the mid Victorian period came to an end in 1873, when the third period of this reign, the late Victorian era, may be said to have begun. Wholesale prices began to fall and continued to do so intermittently until 1896. This was the first but not by any means the worst of the depressions suffered in modern times. It was partly international in character and so reduced the demand for the export of goods, services and capital, the rate of progress of all of which slowed down. Great Britain was particularly badly hit because by this time its head start in industrialization had ceased to be an advantage, as the United States of America and Germany were speedily expanding their manufactures and protecting their industries with high tariffs. While the population of England and Wales continued to grow fast (from 22,712,266 in 1871 to 29,002,525 in 1891), the value of exports per head declined during the same period. Great Britain's share of the total world output of coal, pig iron, steel and cotton fell and went on falling until 1914. In the United States scarcity of labour stimulated the invention of mass-production methods, such as conveyor belts, while in Germany academic scientific research invigorated the chemical and optical industries.

It may well be that English business men who prospered in mid Victorian times were too complacent; some of them, it has even been suggested, were living on their capital. Mr Dombey did not worry unduly about his company's affairs, as he passed his time in Leamington Spa courting a beautiful widow. Money was easily borrowed and profits flowed in, though sometimes they were smaller than expected. Why should managements bother about changing techniques when everything looked rosy? As a rule, unskilled labour was ample and could be employed for long hours without interference from powerful trade unions, real wages being reasonably satisfactory. On the other hand, highly skilled and intelligent operatives were not numerous: some inventions, in the steel industry, for instance, had to be abandoned because of this scarcity. Consequently industrial discoveries or improvements were then fewer than in the United States or Germany. Moreover, such inventions were no longer the brainwaves of self-taught men like Newcomen and Cort: they required an educational background. Men were expected to enter industry as boys, at the very latest by the age of thirteen or fourteen, to learn their trades as they went along, even if they were the sons of successful business men. Well-educated men were siphoned off into the professions. The British manufacturer, it has been said, 'was distinguished more for his commercial experience than by his technical skill'.[7] It has also been contended that industry was less vigorous and adaptable than it might have been at this stage in English history.

Undoubtedly, the remarkable growth in exports characteristic of Victorian England had begun to slow down after the eighteen-seventies, but it is questionable whether industrial productivity declined substantially. It has been estimated that the market value of the goods and services produced by the national economy (the gross national product) doubled between 1870 and 1900 and the explanation may well be that domestic consumption increased at the expense of exports. Even if industrial output might have grown faster with the aid of technological improvements, the fact remains that the reign of Queen Victoria ended in another boom and a rise in the standard of living of the working classes.[8]

At the end of the century agriculture was even more subject to foreign competition than manufacture. It is true that during the eighties remissions of rents, a fall in tithes and relief for some farmers from the burden of rates arrested impoverishment. But both landlords and tenants found themselves in difficulties. Because the area devoted to growing wheat and barley was very substantially reduced, so was the number of agricultural workers, many of whom drifted into towns or emigrated. Fertile arable land was converted into grass to feed sheep and cattle. The price of wheat plummeted – it fell to about 22 shillings a quarter in 1894, as compared with 56 shillings in 1877 – and so did the earnings of yeomen and tenant farmers. The creation of a Board of Agriculture in 1889 and the setting up of a Royal Commission in 1893 did nothing to halt the decline. With its agriculture in disarray and its export industries suffering from foreign competition, the economy of England was less buoyant than it had been earlier. But this was not so much owing to innate deficiencies as to changing circumstances throughout the world, especially in North America.

The nineteenth century saw some of the most remarkable transformations in English social history. Gas lighting enabled factories to stay open through the night. In 1798 Boulton and Watt's Soho factory was first lit by gas in open burners instead of by oil lamps and candles. Part of Pall Mall was illuminated by gas in 1807, being supplied by mains from a central works. In 1812 what was to become the London Gas Light and Coke Company was formed; other companies introduced gas lighting in provincial towns. Besides factories, concert halls and assembly rooms installed gas light; but it was not until the eighteen-eighties that gas was extensively used for cooking and heating. England lagged behind other countries in gas-work chemistry – such as the production of dyes and drugs from the by-products of the gas-making process – and the employment of gas furnaces or engines in industry.

Progress with electricity was also slow: it did not begin replacing steam power or gas until towards the end of the century. To start with, it was used only for telegraphy: railway companies erected telegraph poles along their lines. An Electric Telegraphy Company held a monopoly from 1846, but it sold out to the Post Office in 1870. Electric tramways were first successful in Liverpool; they were substituted for horse-drawn trams in Leeds in 1891. Four years later Bristol had electric trams and other towns followed suit. In 1889 the first underground electric railway was built from Edgware Road in London to King's Cross.

Better lighting in factories and workshops and improvements in public transport (London obtained its first omnibuses as early as 1829) meant that shift systems could be organized in industry through day and night, reducing overhead costs and enlarging output.

The most striking aspect of social change during the reign of Queen Victoria was the widening and strengthening of the middle classes in the community. No satisfactory definition of these classes has ever been evolved, but they were undoubtedly the product of industrialization, which increased the numbers of business men and their clerks. Their existence and characteristics were recognized and described by Victorian authors, who were mostly middle-class themselves. As Lord David Cecil has observed, 'the formidable cloud of a sternly moral tone' which hung over the novels of George Eliot derived from 'that great middle class which between 1750 and 1850 gradually became the predominating force in England'. In earlier English history one thinks in terms of an upper and lower gentry and a business community, comprising retail as well as wholesale merchants. Apart from lawyers, merchants (usually representing ports) were the only members of the House of Commons who were not landed gentry, while voters were nearly always subject to the advice and influence of the aristocracy and local landowners. In the eighteenth century it was not difficult to buy a seat in the House of Commons, which was regarded as a very agreeable coffee house and a highway to the House of Lords.

The first Parliamentary Reform Act in 1832 gave the vote in the boroughs to all who occupied houses or offices the annual value of which exceeded £10. In the counties, in addition to the 40-shilling freeholders, the vote was given to tenants who paid an annual rent of £50 or more.

Thus it could be claimed that modestly off members of the middle classes had become electors everywhere. The Municipal Reform Act of 1835, by abolishing existing close corporations and replacing them with councils elected by rate-payers, reduced the powers of the justices of the peace, who had in effect controlled local government since the Middle Ages. But it was not until 1888 that the County Councils deprived the gentry of their administrative authority, which had been traditional in country life. These political changes reflected social changes.

Though thus restricted by law, the influence of the nobility and landed gentry lingered on. In some constituencies long-established families continued to enjoy almost a prescriptive right, hallowed by time, to seats in Parliament. The Church and the Army were still mainly the provinces of the landed gentry, but members of other professions – lawyers, physicians, surgeons, civil engineers and the like could be deemed members of an upper middle class, in which successful merchants, sailors and financiers could also be included. The lower middle class consisted chiefly of minor officials, shopkeepers and clerks, some spruce and some shabby.

A large number of the middle classes were nonconformists. William Cobbett had noticed how Methodists and Quakers were prominent in business life. After the repeal of the Test and Corporation Acts in 1828, which since the seventeenth century had excluded dissenters from all public offices, the magistrates' benches began to be filled by nonconformists. It has been pointed out that during the mid Victorian period the mayors of several large towns were Unitarians. Congregational chapels were largely attended by middle-class tradesmen. The number of Baptist chapels multiplied fourfold between 1801 and 1851. The nonconformists made big strides forward in the industrial areas of Lancashire, Yorkshire and Wales, as the wide variety of chapel buildings still to be seen there bears witness.

Chapel-building continued fast throughout the mid Victorian era; but only half the population was avowedly religious. Church-going was an upper- and middle-class practice. In 1850 few urban working-class people attended any form of service. This was hardly surprising when one considers the long hours which most of the wage-earning class were required to work. Sundays and Christian holidays were their sole recognized days for relaxation. Only the Salvation Army, formed in 1879, with its brass bands, cheerful singing and popular paper, *The War Cry*, made much impact on the religion of the poor.[9]

The urban masses sought consolation from the drabness of their existence not, as in the past, by contemplating a celestial life to come, but by drinking alcohol, watching sports and betting. Excellent excuses for drink were that it acted as a painkiller, moderated gloom and enhanced festivity. Though many ordinary men and women drank when they could afford it, the heaviest drinkers were Irish immigrants, who earned enough money to buy it by undertaking the dirtiest jobs, such as building the underground railways. By an act of 1834 public houses were permitted to stay open from five in the morning until midnight: an earlier Beer Act allowed excise officers to issue retail licences to anybody who paid a fee of 2 guineas (£2 10p). Nonconformists, the Salvation Army and modern historians have all been exercised over the evils of alcohol, and the temperance cause was prominent among the lobbyists of the Victorian era.[10] In fact the number of on-licences and the consumption of alcohol per head of population have fallen considerably since then.

The public house was the working man's club, as it still is. (Rich men's clubs also proliferated during the first half of the nineteenth century.) Judging by the behaviour of Miss Abbey Potterson, proprietor and manager of the 'Six Jolly Fellowship-Porters' in Dickens's *Our Mutual Friend*, one may suppose that good order was kept in them. Outdoor amusements included horse racing, dog racing and even pigeon racing, particularly popular in the Potteries. Cock-fighting and bull-baiting had been banned by acts of parliament in the eighteen-thirties. Though ferocious prize-fighting was popular with spectators, less bestial sports existed. The laws of cricket were not formulated until the second half of the century. It is hard to decide whether cricket was a democratic game. In so far as it was played extensively on village greens, it may be said to have been so. But cricket on the highest level, as played on Lord's Cricket Ground, established on its present site in 1814, was patronized by the aristocracy, who betted heavily on match results; and the distinction between 'Gentlemen' and 'Players' was retained until 1962. The Football Association was founded in 1863 and once the game was professionalized it attracted large 'gates'. Sir Robert Peel was said to have been one of the best football players at Harrow school, where he was educated. At Rugby school the other, amateur, form of the game was introduced, from which it spread to most public (that is, private) schools: the Rugby Union was formed in 1871. Other games – lawn tennis, croquet and golf – were played chiefly by the middle classes.

By way of indoor entertainments the theatre held its own, but wage-earners had neither the time nor the money to patronize it. Between 1850 and 1870, however, taverns and public houses were building halls where singers, comedians, acrobats and jugglers performed before audiences who sat at tables and drank. From these evolved the music hall, which after a rollicking period of success in the early days of the twentieth century, survived the First World War unscathed, but began dying after the war of 1939–45. Because it became mainly a family entertainment (particularly in the theatres owned by Sir Oswald Stoll), its vulgarity was restricted. In the second half of the twentieth century this form of amusement has resumed its late-Victorian aspect, delighting wage-earning families in northern England, nights for men only being interspersed with shows for all.

The late Victorians were concerned with more serious matters than music-hall turns and public houses. The education of the children of the poor, which had been frowned upon during earlier centuries because it reduced family incomes, was advocated by enlightened politicians. Elementary education progressed fairly rapidly, the number of children at school multiplying fivefold between 1801 and 1858. Then in 1870 an Education Act laid down that all children in England should be given the opportunity of learning the three R's (reading, writing and arithmetic) and elected school boards were set up; but it was not until 1891 that elementary education became compulsory and free. For the benefit of the middle classes 'public' schools were founded, mostly boarding schools like Marlborough and Wellington. Girls' schools started in 1856.

As to higher education, London University, uniting University College and King's College, had been founded in 1836; it was cheaper to be educated there than at Oxford or Cambridge. Moreover it was radical and secular in its outlook and not dominated by the classics. On the whole, however, higher education was alien to the middle classes. As has been noted, boys going into business were expected to leave school early, start at the bottom of the ladder, and work their way upwards. This practice persisted until the mid twentieth century. In any case it was not until then that university education was made freely available to promising boys and girls whose parents could not afford to pay all their fees and expenses.

For the higher education of women Girton and Newnham Colleges were founded at Cambridge in the eighteen-seventies, but though women were allowed to take university examinations, degrees were not conferred on them.[11] At Oxford Lady Margaret Hall and Somerville were opened in the eighteen-eighties, these colleges being kept well away from the men's colleges. It had not been until 1871 that all posts as well as degrees became open to nonconformists at Oxford and Cambridge. They were among the last citadels surrendered by the Church of England.

Progress in popular education was reflected by the successful establishment of W.H. Smith's bookshops and bookstalls at railway stations (though the circulation of newspapers was not yet large) and by the expansion of public libraries, both of which took place in the eighteen-sixties. Other amenities that may be credited to the later part of Queen Victoria's reign included the building of museums and art galleries and the spread of public parks. Such open spaces had been singularly lacking in the industrialized towns of the late eighteenth and early nineteenth centuries.

Looking back on the Victorian age from the viewpoint of the nineteen-twenties or thirties, those who were then young – and the author was one of them – formed strong impressions or prejudices about it. The first impression was that respectability and narrow-mindedness were its key characteristics. The second was that England's place in the world then stood supreme, because so much of it could be painted red on the map as being British possessions (indeed, it was thought a misfortune that we no longer ruled the upstart United States of America) and because our swift progress in industrialization had given us incredible affluence. Thirdly, the Victorians were regarded as philistines, whose execrable taste had left its marks on our towns and cities, particularly in the north of England. Lastly, we thought that women and children had been exploited and maltreated, the descriptions of men's greed and cruelty riveting our attention on the pages of Dickens's and Mrs Gaskell's novels. Of course, all these notions were partial and inexact.

The search for respectability was essentially confined to the expanding middle classes in society and was stimulated by religion. The family was sacrosanct. The father was expected to be ambitious for himself and his children and to increase his income by industry and abstinence. The mother had the duty not merely of supervising the household and correcting the behaviour of her children, but also of raising the tone of her husband's mind 'from low anxieties and vulgar cares'.[12] 'Home', it has been said, was 'a place of rest for the husband where a woman finds her highest pride in the sweetest humility and the tenderest self-suppression.'[13] Family prayers, family attendance at church or chapel and family holidays were unifying habits. A suitor was expected to ask a father's permission to court his daughter. Fidelity was the supreme virtue in marriage. Love was deified and women were idolized. A good example was set by a virtuous, domesticated and happily married Queen.

All this we tended to look upon as a mixture of prudery and hypocrisy. But we were shocked to discover that Charles Dickens, the proponent of middle-class respectability, had a mistress who was an actress, and surprised that Gladstone, the pattern Victorian Prime Minister, had as his hobby (which kept him out at nights) the reformation of prostitutes. We forgot that the Victorians themselves produced some of the most outspoken critics of the middle-class belief in infinite progress and infinite goodness. Matthew Arnold, Thomas Carlyle, John Ruskin, J.A. Froude, William Morris and Lord Morley were all in their different ways contemptuous of the competitive industrial society of their time, condemned the tendency to cant and hypocrisy and deplored the current emphasis on the 'moral' side of life at the expense of the intellectual and artistic.

Lord Palmerston, a typical Whig aristocrat, who was Foreign Secretary and then Prime Minister, was considered to epitomize the best aspects of imperialism. We thought of the British Empire, as ruled by him and his like, as an institution managed chiefly for the benefit of the governed. The colonies we regarded as a trust and our duty, we felt, was to educate them in parliamentary democracy. It was only when the Empire disintegrated that it was realized how valuable the colonies had been to us economically and how much our trade had depended on their ready-made markets. Moreover, the men who had actually governed them in the Indian or colonial Civil Service recognized with a shock what a comfortable life they had led overseas when they returned to a servantless England.

It was customary to sneer at the Albert Memorial, at Sandringham, the favourite home of Queen Victoria, and even at the Crystal Palace. Victorian Gothic was a joke; the Pre-Raphaelites were condemned for trying to imitate medieval art; painters like Frith and Landseer were castigated for being sentimental. But we scarcely grasped that photography, another triumphant discovery of the Victorian period, had been the underlying reason for the development of the post-Impressionist and abstract painting we admired so much, since the kind of paintings done by G.F. Watts, Edwin Landseer and other Victorian artists could be successfully rivalled by photographers. Today we no longer look upon the Victorians as philistines. In fact it is generally accepted that Pugin, Barry, Gilbert Scott, Philip Webb and Norman Shaw constituted a distinguished list of architects. And many people have come to prefer mock-Tudor cottages and Victorian Gothic churches to purely functional buildings.

As to the exploitation of the wage-earning classes, it has to be recognized that the social conscience of the Victorians was also aroused by it. Hence the long series of Factory Acts, the establishment of factory and health inspectors, and the creation of mechanics' institutes and philosophical and

153

literary societies aimed at providing spare-time occupations for all who needed them. A century that opened with the Combination Laws ended with effective trade unions. A burden to working men of all classes were the long hours they were required to toil for a modest reward. The author's grandfather was a journeyman hatter. In the mid Victorian period he went to work at six in the morning and continued until nine or sometimes ten o'clock at night. Later, to supplement his income, he taught at a Ragged School for four evenings a week. As he worked all Saturday, he rarely saw his children in their waking moments except on Sundays.[14] But that a career could be opened to talents was shown by the fact that his eldest son rose to be Vice-Chancellor of Birmingham University and his youngest a leading Civil Servant, both being knighted for their services to the community.

The changes in the social outlook and the economic structure of England during the nineteenth century were certainly the most remarkable in its history until the twentieth century, when the speed of change quickened. How one looks back upon it depends chiefly on when one was born. The reign of Victoria has been described as an age of Steam and Cant. But equally it can be said that it was guided by a genuine belief in Progress and Goodness.

Politically, much was made of the virtues of the ballot box, but it could be used by men only. It is true that women, who in earlier centuries were admitted to few occupations, now had wider opportunities of employment; but they suffered from exploitation and were denied equal rights. Hardly any women were appointed factory inspectors. The newspapers, which became cheap in the mid nineteenth century, were chiefly devoted to politics and sport and were uninterested in women readers. A tract written by the famous radical economist and philosopher John Stuart Mill, hesitantly published by him in 1869, entitled *The Subjection of Women* and advocating their independence, made a profound impression. A year after this a Married Women's Property Act allowed women to retain control of any money they earned by trade or investment. Only in the last quarter of the century was a choice of worthwhile higher education opened to them. Further acts of 1882 and 1893 gave wives the same rights with regard to property as unmarried women. Marriages could take place in registry offices and divorce was made a little easier (before 1857 it was almost impossible for those who were not rich). These reforms were quite inadequate. Of all the social transformations that have taken place in the twentieth century, the emancipation of women from the position they held in Victorian times is the most significant.

154

It is hard to decide which event in the nineteenth century made the greatest impact on society: the invention of the steam engine, say, or the gas lamp or the establishment of police forces in London and elsewhere. From the economic point of view it was surely the growth of big cities and the alteration in the balance between manufacturing industries and agriculture. The decline in industrial supremacy had admittedly also begun: whereas in 1870 Great Britain produced one-third of the world's output of manufactured goods, by 1900 the proportion had fallen to one-fifth. Yet though 'there were several years of bad trade ... the economy as a whole flourished'.[15] It needs to be remembered that England was finding new markets for the products of its staple industries in primary producing countries, where, unlike in Europe, protective tariffs did not have to be overcome.[16] Moreover, the value of invisible exports, particularly investments in American railways, compensated for setbacks in visible exports. In fact at the end of the Victorian period real wages and incomes were still growing; but compared with the galloping progress in the middle of the reign, the economy had started to slow down.

Notes

1 G.M Young, *Victorian England* (1936), p. 25
2 Cit. G. Kitson Clark, *The Making of Victorian England* (1952), p. 135
3 William Ashworth, *An Economic History of England 1870–1939* (1972), pp. 94, 147, 179
4 J.H. Clapham, *The Railway Age 1820–1850* (1926), p. 400
5 Cit. E. Royston Pike, *Human Documents of the Victorian Golden Age* (1967), p. 41
6 ibid., p. 49
7 Phyllis Deane, *The First Industrial Revolution* (1979), p. 285
8 Donald N. McCloskey, 'Did Victorian Britain Fail?', *Economic History Review*, 23 (1970–1); D.H. Aldcraft, 'McCloskey on Victorian growth: a comment', and D.N. McCloskey, 'Victorian Growth: a rejoinder', *Economic History Review*, 27 (1974)
9 K.S. Inglis, *Churches and the Working Classes in Victorian England* (1963), pp. 118 seq.
10 Brian Harrison, *Drink and the Victorians* (1971), chapters 10 and 11
11 My mother went to Newnham and always resented the fact that she was not allowed to take a degree

12 Walter E. Houghton, *The Victorian Frame of Mind 1830–1870* (1957), p. 351
13 Quoted from an article on 'Womanliness' by Elizabeth Lynn Linton in the *Saturday Review* in 1871 by Jennie Calder, *The Victorian Home* (1977), p. 126
14 James Ashley, 'My Autobiography' (1907), edited by Sir William Ashley, MS in my possession. Ragged Schools were voluntary institutions, established by philanthropists for the benefit of the poorest children. They started to disappear after the Education Act of 1870
15 Ashworth, op. cit., p. 241
16 See the arguments of C.K. Harley and D.N. McCloskey on 'Foreign trade, competition and the expanding national economy', in *The Economic History of Britain since 1700*, II, R.C. Floud and D.N. McCloskey (eds) (1981)

NINE

The Golden Age
of the Middle Classes

The period between the ending of the 32-month war in South Africa, known as the Boer War, in 1902, and the First World War, which began on 4 August 1914, was one of relative economic stability, but not advance. The population continued to grow, but not so fast, owing partly to the practice of birth control, at any rate by the middle classes, and partly to a continuous reduction of the death rate, particularly among young children. The rate of income tax during the Boer War was 1s 3d in the pound and in 1914 it was 1s 2d in the pound. Incomes grew more slowly than they had done in the Victorian age. Though money wages rose a little, so did the cost of living: consequently the value of real wages hardly improved at all. In London skilled workmen's real wages were actually lower in 1914 than they had been in 1901, which admittedly was a peak year.

To some extent the higher cost of living, which diminished the value of money wages, was compensated by better social services, a higher standard of sanitation and medical treatment, and enlarged educational opportunities: all these were paid for out of direct taxation, which fell chiefly on those with good incomes. Few people were unemployed: by 1913–14 their number had fallen to a mere 2 per cent of the insured population. Hours of work tended to become shorter. It was exceptional for them to be determined by act of parliament for male adults. Usually they were the subject of negotiations by trade unions, whose membership amounted to about four million in 1914, as compared with two million at the outset of the century. When the Coal Mines (Eight Hours) Bill, which reduced the number of hours worked daily in this hazardous industry, was passed, Winston Churchill, the President of the Board of Trade, declared grandiloquently that 'the general march of industrial democracy is not towards inadequate hours of work, but towards sufficient hours of leisure'.[1] The middle classes continued to grow in size and to flourish. About a fifth of the occupied population can be assigned to the upper and lower middle classes in 1911. Fifty years later the fraction was about one-third.

At the opposite end of the human scale poverty continued to afflict what has been called 'the submerged tenth'. Investigations that were carried out by philanthropists indeed suggested that towards the end of the nineteenth century the fraction was nearer one-third in London and York. Though these towns were not typical, it has been observed by an impartial economic historian that 'there can have been few times when the lot of the very poor was more miserable than in the early years of the twentieth century ... they lived in squalor, misery and insecurity, worse fed than ever'.[2] Would-be recruits for the army during the Boer War often had to be rejected because of their low physical condition. It is also significant that over 13,000 pawnbrokers were in business in different parts of the country, as compared with 5,000 fifty years later. Men and women would pawn their best clothes on Mondays and redeem them at the end of the week so as to have a little money in their purses.

At the beginning of the twentieth century nearly a million and a quarter men and women were still employed in agriculture. Rural labourers were paid a maximum of 18 shillings a week. The output of cereals continued to decline and the area devoted to arable cultivation to contract. Farmers naturally concentrated on providing the fresh food that was most wanted by the home market, such as milk, butter, cheese, fruit, beef, mutton and pork; but they met with competition from imported frozen and chilled meat from as far afield as New Zealand, which was cheaper. Total production did not fall, but its value did so until the war of 1914. So agriculture contributed only a modest amount to the national income. Rents fell, workers left to labour in the towns, and tens of thousands emigrated to the United States and Canada, the annual departures reaching nearly half a million a year in 1911–13.

By contrast, British manufacturers and mining continued to expand. Up to 1914 the staple industries, coal, iron and steel, textiles, shipbuilding and mechanical engineering, played the most important part. According to the census of production taken in 1907 the first three of these industries contributed 46 per cent of the total national output. Output did not increase as rapidly as it had done during the early years of the nineteenth century, but it outstripped the growth in population. These staple industries did not, of course, stand still. Mechanization by the use of steam power and to a lesser extent of electric power was increasing, larger factories were built and more capital was invested in them. Some attempts were made, particularly in the coal and cotton industries, the steel industry and shipbuilding, to meet the needs of changing times. For example, the demand was for steamships rather than sailing ships, and more steel was wanted for bicycles than for railways.

Nevertheless the fact remained that the pattern of industry did not change dramatically between 1870 and 1914. To a large extent capitalists were contented with established methods of production and trusted to the continuing demand for their goods from old customers: it has even been asserted that Edwardian industrialists were fonder of yachting and shooting grouse than of attending to business.[3] Neither in mining nor textile manufacture were any revolutionary changes introduced. During this period the main advances in industrial techniques and business organization were taking place in Germany and the United States, not in England. A boom, which was enjoyed throughout much of the world between 1909 and 1913, confirmed the complacency of English business men. Since no scarcity of labour prevailed and money could be borrowed easily, they had little incentive to be unduly adventurous.

The staple industries contributed a large part of all British exports, which paid for imported raw materials and food. In 1911–13 textiles, coal and machinery provided over half such exports. The value of all exports (including re-exports) had risen by 90 per cent since 1901, or, recalculated at constant prices, by 46 per cent. This was a slower rate of increase than during the Victorian epoch; but as imports became cheaper, a smaller amount of exports (visible and invisible) was needed to pay for them. While exports of coal more than doubled in value and iron and steel fully held their own, the increase in the sale of textiles was smaller, but they still formed the main part of total exports. Three-fifths of British exports and re-exports were sold outside Europe, particularly in countries belonging to the British Empire such as India, West Africa and Australia, where markets were widening. A quarter of the total output of British goods was exported in 1913. Great Britain was still the largest exporter in the world. In addition, invisible exports were expanding. Merchant shipping was extremely prosperous, while investments abroad doubled between 1900 and 1914: the value of dividends from these investments is estimated to have amounted to £200,000,000 in 1913. Thus a large part of the profits earned by British industry was invested abroad rather than at home.

By contrast, wage-earners were relatively less well off than their employers. Free trade affected them in two opposite ways. The sale of goods made by cheap labour in India and elsewhere undercut the price of work done at home, for example in the cotton industry. On the other hand, the British working classes had the benefit of inexpensive imported food. But the tendency of many wages to fall and unemployment to rise in 1908–9 created unrest. It was not until 1914 that real wages began to rise. The gap between the poor and the rich was still pronounced. Half the national income went to 12 per cent of the population.

While before 1914 the staple industries were the principal source of industrial growth, new industries were being developed, if slowly. These included rayon, dyes, telephones, photographic apparatus, wireless apparatus, aluminium, motor cars, aircraft and plastics, chiefly bakelite. But because the staple industries remained so profitable the economy was overcommitted to them, and therefore the adjustment to new lines of manufacture was extremely cautious.

What did enjoy an era of rapid growth was the distributive trades, that is to say, retailing, advertising and the like. Distribution constituted the biggest single economic group in the community, while other consumer services, such as catering and entertainment, also expanded. It has been calculated that these 'non-productive' groups employed about half the working population. But 'non-productive' is a pejorative word. For the provision of services is simply part of the process by which a consumer gets an end-product: it is no use a concern manufacturing food or clothes unless it can find a way of reaching customers with them. Hence the need for advertising, which has never become more comprehensive than in the twentieth century.

What is equally striking in the economic life of the early twentieth century is the large number of women in employment. According to the census of 1901, 1,690,000 women were employed in domestic work, including charwomen and laundresses; a further 712,000 worked in dressmaking and 663,000 in the textile industries. By 1911 women constituted about 30 per cent of the working population, two million being engaged in domestic service: many more women did part-time work which went unrecorded. After the war came in 1914 women were employed in the army and navy, on the land, in munition works and other factories and in public transport. It was no wonder that the suffragettes secured their first triumph in 1918, when women over thirty were given the vote.

Another feature of the early twentieth century was the beginning of what was to be popularly known in the forties as the Welfare State. As has been noticed, apart from the Factory Acts, which applied to women and children, the Victorians had been reasonably happy with *laissez-faire*, following Adam Smith's advice that industry could be guided by an invisible hand to a prosperous state without interference from the government. Why did the mood change? It was partly because real wages ceased to rise, partly owing to the strengthening of the trade union movement, and partly to political pressure exerted by the Labour Party, which had been formed in 1900 and won fifty-three seats in the general election of 1906. It was also owing to the exertion of two outstanding Liberal Ministers, David Lloyd George, who was Chancellor of the Exchequer, and Winston Churchill at the Board of Trade.

The case for helping the wage-earning classes by government action was underlined by a temporary depression during the first half of 1907, when 800,000 were unemployed. In 1908 strikes or lock-outs took place because employers were trying to reduce wages in the shipbuilding, engineering and cotton industries. The Conservative Party's solution to economic difficulties of 'tariff reform', that is to say, the imposition of duties on imports that competed with goods made at home, was to be rejected by the electorate in 1910. Churchill thought that the 'lines of cleavage in the community ... were becoming social and economic', and that 'the social field lies open: there is no country', he claimed, 'where the organization of industrial conditions more urgently required attention'.[4]

So the Liberal Government pushed through, besides the Coal Mines Act, an Old Age Pensions Act (1908), a Trade Boards Act (1909), a Labour Exchanges Act (1909), a National Insurance Act (1911) and a Shops Act (1912). These acts were extremely modest in their scope. The Trade Boards Act, which provided for the fixing of a minimum wage rate, for example, applied only to four 'sweated industries' and 200,000 workers. The Old Age Pensions Act arranged for a pension of 5 shillings a week, paid for by the government, to persons over seventy whose income was not more than a miserly £21 a year. The National Insurance Act, which was financed by contributions from employees (4d), employers (3d), and the Exchequer (2d), in its first part insured workers with modest wages or salaries only against sickness and in its second part insured workers in only seven industries against unemployment, the maximum benefit being 7s 6d a week for the first five weeks. The labour exchanges, which opened in 1910, were entirely voluntary. The Shops Act stipulated that shop assistants should have intervals for meals and that there should be one early closing day a week, but otherwise left the question of working hours alone.

These limited and hesitant steps towards the Welfare State and the strengthening of the trade union movement meant that wage-earners were made more conscious of their needs and of their importance to the community at large. The Trade Disputes Act of 1906 exempted unions from actions for tort, while the decision taken in 1911 to pay Members of Parliament out of public funds enabled trade union leaders, should they be elected, to play their full part in the House of Commons if they did not receive salaries from outside sources. Four hundred and forty-seven Labour candidates stood in the general election of 1918 and fifty-nine were elected, all of whom had been put forward by trade unions. Articulate representatives of the working classes both inside and outside Parliament pointed out that nothing had been done by the Government to improve wages. Indeed, the National Insurance Act had provided for compulsory deductions from wages. Between 1907 and 1909 railwaymen, dockers and even music-hall artists went on strike for higher wages, and at the same time a temporary recession created unemployment. Again in 1911–13 a wave of strikes and lock-outs affecting coal, cotton and the transport industries swept the country. However, on the whole England was undoubtedly enjoying a high degree of prosperity when the First World War broke out.

The First World War took politically-minded English people by surprise. In 1914 they were more agitated over the Irish demand for Home Rule, the antics of the suffragettes and the threat of industrial action by the Triple Alliance of railwaymen, transport workers and coal miners to fight 'capitalism' than over events in the Balkans. The Government was unprepared for a large-scale war on the European mainland and in any case assumed that Hohenzollern Germany would soon be defeated in alliance with the French. It was only when a military stalemate produced by trench warfare and the terrible expenditure of lives made in trying to overcome it were realized that measures essential to victory were undertaken at home. An industrial truce was proclaimed, but it was not until March 1915 that the trade unions agreed to the 'dilution of labour' by allowing men from other trades and women to work in key industries. They also consented (except for the coal miners) to submit disputes to arbitration for the duration of the war. The Defence of the Realm Act (nicknamed 'Dora') and the Munitions Act, both passed in 1915, gave the Government far-reaching powers. Yet another year passed before conscription was introduced, and it was not until December 1916 that Ministries of Labour, Food and Shipping were established. By 1917 the railways, coal mines and the cotton industry had all come under the control of the Government.

The danger of German submarines ('U-boats') sinking so much merchant shipping as to menace the country with starvation caused a convoy system (opposed by the Admiralty) to be set up. At the same time the Ministry of Agriculture redoubled its efforts to promote the production of more food at home. As a result nearly 60 per cent more wheat and potatoes were grown than before the war. Ironically, food rationing was not imposed until February 1918, but was continued until 1921.

The economic and social consequences of the war were profound. Since 750,000 men were killed in the fighting, there was 'a missing generation' which otherwise might have furnished the future leaders of industry. The consolation – which was to prove delusive – was the belief that the League of Nations, founded in 1919 and inspired by American ardour, though the United States Government refused to join it, would settle future international disputes by conciliation or joint action.

Secondly, the war had led, as has been noted, to the partial emancipation of women. But the vote was not given until the age of thirty, because it was feared that otherwise women would swamp the men and rule the country. Women could become Members of Parliament. They were freely admitted to most professions and to the universities, though Cambridge continued to refuse them degrees. They – or some of them at least – assumed a gossamer badge of equality by 'bobbing' their hair. They smoked cigarettes in public and clothed themselves in a way that flattened their breasts. But they had to wait ten years before they were given the vote on the same terms as men, and another fifty years before they all wore trousers, were paid at the same rates as men and were allowed to enter mixed colleges at Oxford and Cambridge. Moreover, owing not so much to the war as to a freakish distribution of births, there were, according to the census of 1921, about a million more women than men between the ages of twenty and forty, the marriageable time. The existence of 'surplus women' enabled men to retain their sense of superiority. Women, on the other hand, continued to resent the double standard of sexual morality enshrined in the divorce laws, which implied that adultery was a less serious offence for men than for women.[5]

After the war the staple industries began to decline. In general this was owing to the loss of foreign markets, particularly in devastated Europe: Germany had been one of England's best customers. Outside Europe countries had been induced to raise their production of food and raw materials; consequently when the war ended they found themselves with an excess, prices fell, and they could not afford to buy as many imported manufactured goods as before. Lastly, other countries, less hit by the war, such as the United States and Japan, were competing directly with British exporters and erected tariff barriers to protect their own industries. The coal industry was injured by the greater use of oil. Moreover before the end of 1920 Germany began paying reparations to France, one of our best customers, in coal dug in the Ruhr. Because of the enormous production of coal during the war the best English seams were exhausted, so that output per man declined. Cotton was not only damaged by foreign competition, based on cheap labour, but its machinery was for a large part obsolete, and it had a new rival in rayon. Owing to the destruction brought about by the U-boat campaign shipbuilding had been vastly expanded; but once it had met the immediate needs of peace-time trade at home and abroad, it was left with surplus capacity.

From the financial point of view the cost of the war can be exaggerated. It is true that the national debt multiplied fourteenfold, but this merely created a huge transfer payment within the country. Debts owed abroad, particularly to the United States, were another matter. For whereas the Government had reason to hope that these would be offset by the repayment of debts owed to it by its late allies and by reparations from Germany, in fact such hopes proved delusive: for example, Russia's debts were never repaid because of the Bolshevik revolution. As to private investments in the United States, most of which had been sold on the instructions of the Government to protect the value of the pound in terms of dollars and to prevent the purchase of war materials from becoming too expensive, these had been replaced by 1929 and the interest they earned helped to pay for imports.

Another consequence of the war was the buttressing of the trade unions. The Government had gradually realized that in order to accelerate the output of munitions and warships and to stop strikes from interrupting war work it was essential to negotiate with them. The unions were promised that in return for their accepting the relaxation of their rules, the Government would use its influence 'to secure the restoration of previous conditions in every case after the war'. The Government also promised higher wages and bonuses, which it was able to guarantee absolutely once industries came under its direct control. Incidentally the war also enhanced the authority of shop stewards, that is to say, workmen elected by their mates to represent them in dealings with their employers. By 1920 the membership of the unions had more than doubled, rising from 4 million in 1914 to 8.3 million.

So powerful had the unions become that they were able to make a purely political impact. Their sympathies lay with the Soviet Government when the Poles were fighting the Russians in 1920. That May London dockers refused to load or coal ships carrying munitions to the Poles, and the British Government acquiesced in the ban. In the following August representatives of the Trades Union Congress joined those of the Labour Party in forming a Council of Action, which urged unions to instruct their members to go on strike if the Government intervened in the war by backing the Poles against the Soviet Union. 'Hands off Russia!' was the cry. Again the Government gave way.

But the chief demands of the unions were of course for higher wages and shorter hours. An economic boom was enjoyed between the date of the armistice and the spring of 1920. This was brought about by the need to replace deficiencies in consumer goods and raw materials caused by the war, by the recovery of much of the export trade, by a wave of speculation and by a natural feeling of optimism about the future. Consequently the demands of labour were mostly met: wage rates increased, and so did prices. But in some industries – steel, for example – real wages undoubtedly improved. During the short post-war boom many workers caught a glimpse of prosperity they had never known before. In several industries hours were reduced, usually to an eight-hour day, but the forty-hour week, acclaimed as an ideal by all parties in industry, was never translated into legislation.

One post-war law was a limited success: a new Trade Boards Act (1918) led to the creation of joint industrial councils, consisting of employers and trade union representatives, to discuss problems in specific industries as well as wages and hours of work. Over fifty such councils had been set up by 1920. An Industrial Courts Act (1919) established a permanent Court of Arbitration and permitted the Ministry of Labour to appoint courts of inquiry in cases where arbitration was not acceptable. Finally a National Industrial Conference, attended by 500 representatives of trade unions and 300 of employers, presided over by the Minister of Labour, met in February 1919 and produced an agreed report. This has been regarded by some historians as a noble scheme and by others as a magnificent confidence trick practised by the Government to choke off labour unrest: in any case it proved a damp squib and has long been forgotten except in history books.

The sunny prospects held out to all classes in the community during 1919 and 1920 were soon dimmed. Strikes by the police, the railwaymen and cotton operatives were soon settled, but in 1921 a tragic chapter in the history of the coal industry opened, which did not close until after another world war.

During the First World War the industry had come under the control of the Government and wage demands by miners had been granted. After the war the Miners' Federation asked for a 30 per cent increase in wages, a six-hour day and the complete nationalization of the industry. Most of the coal owners were reactionary and most of the miners' leaders aggressive. To avert a crisis a commission under a judge, Sir John Sankey, was appointed and agreed to by the miners on the understanding that their wages would not be reduced. The first report of the commission recommended increases in wages and a seven-hour day, and condemned the chaotic system of management. Its final report contained no agreed recommendations, though Sankey himself favoured nationalization. The miners, supported by fellow trade unionists, insisted upon 'Mines for the Nation'. This was the last thing the Government wanted; it was anxious to wash its hands of the problem as quickly as possible. After all, because of large requirements for coal both at home and overseas the industry seemed to be facing a promising future. A rise in wages was granted, but by February 1921 the Government, realizing the industry was surprisingly becoming depressed as the post-war boom burst, suddenly announced that the mines would be decontrolled on 1 April.

To meet the new situation the coal owners promptly asked for a reduction of wages and refused to accept the idea of a National Wages Board, which the miners wanted. When the miners rejected the new terms they were locked out. Railway workers and transport workers promised their full support to the miners by stopping any movement of coal. The scene was set for a confrontation. The miners' allies called for a strike on 15 April and received the moral support of the TUC and the Labour Party. The Government reacted vehemently to the menace of what amounted to a national strike, and declared a state of emergency. The railwaymen and transport workers backed down. To all who sympathized with the miners 15 April 1921 became known as Black Friday. The miners returned to work after an agreement had been reached with the owners by which wages would vary in accordance with ascertained profits; a minimum rate was also fixed, the reduction in pay being eased somewhat by a government subsidy.

From the Government's point of view it had got out of direct responsibility for the management of the industry in good time. Exports of coal fell once the French army withdrew from the Ruhr, which it temporarily occupied in 1923 to enforce the repayment of reparations, for it was then that the Germans began paying reparations by exporting coal to France. British exports reached their post-war peak in 1924 and then declined (exports to France in 1923 were 18,800,000 tons and in 1925 10,200,000 tons). By then 100,000 mineworkers had lost their jobs. The sale of cotton goods abroad also declined because of the growth of the industry elsewhere, especially in India and Japan. Exports of cotton yarn fell by nearly half between 1912 and 1938, and cotton piece goods in 1938 were only one-fifth of the exports achieved in 1912. The markets for iron and steel also contracted, partly because of the French acquisition of Lorraine, with its vast iron ore fields and coal mines. The production of pig iron was also hit by the use of scrap. Finally, British shipyard capacity, which had been substantially enlarged by 1920, was never fully utilized.

All of these staple industries, together with the docks, the railways and agriculture, provided less employment in the nineteen-twenties than they had done before. Gradually new industries were developing; in textiles rayon and artificial silk, and in transport motor cars and motor bicycles. House-building needed a variety of workmen, from bricklayers to carpenters; it was subsidized first by the Addison Act of 1919, secondly by the Chamberlain Act of 1922 and thirdly by the Wheatley Act of 1924, each Housing Act becoming known by the name of the Minister responsible. The first encouraged local authorities to build subsidized houses; the second subsidized private enterprise; the third subsidized houses built by municipalities at controlled rents. Other developing industries offering a large amount of employment were electrical engineering, chemicals, printing and publishing. Compulsory school attendance up to the age of fourteen and the expansion of secondary schools and universities after 1918 created a big reading public, which induced a number of well-educated gentlemen to try their hands at publishing. The most enterprising survived.

Several of the important new industries were based on discoveries made before 1914. Signor Guglielmo Marconi, one of the founding fathers of wireless, for example, arrived in England in 1896, but his company did not become really prosperous until 1920. During the war the Department of Scientific and Industrial Research was set up to stimulate inventions. The Board of Trade licensed twenty-four research associations during the five years after the war, of which the most celebrated was the Medical Research Council.

Giants began to dominate industry during the inter-war years. The

Central Electricity Board, created by act of parliament in 1926, was given responsibility for the wholesale distribution of electricity. It initiated the building of 'the grid', that is to say, high-voltage transmission lines carried on pylons, which some thought disfigured the countryside. By the time the Second World War began it covered the whole country, the amount of electricity generated had multiplied sixfold, and it proved invaluable to industry. It also increased the amount of electricity available in the houses of people who could afford radios, electric cookers, refrigerators, washing machines and vacuum cleaners. Thus it was a blessing to the middle-class housewife. Another giant was Imperial Chemical Industries, which was also founded in 1926 by amalgamating four big firms whose works were scattered up and down England. Its guiding genius was Sir Alfred Mond, who had been Minister of Health and who was an outstanding financier and a keen Zionist. Another Jew, Lord Leverhulme, built a huge combine concerned chiefly with making soap and margarine. Courtauld's and British Celanese, ultimately to amalgamate, pioneered rayon and artificial silk. Samuel Courtauld, whose company had international interests, usefully devoted his millions to patronizing modern art.

A distinction can be drawn between the combines established by private enterprise and such organizations as the British Broadcasting Corporation, the Electricity Board, the Port of London Authority and the London Passenger Transport Board, the last being set up in 1933. They have been called semi-public concerns, and met with the approval both of Socialists and Conservatives. Their conception reflected the spirit of compromise for which the English have often been said to be famous. It would be difficult to decide whether they worked better or worse in the service of society than the semi-monopolistic giants built by private enterprise. But the largest single economic group was to be found in the distributive trades. These included wholesalers, departmental stores like Selfridges and Harrods, food shops and restaurants like J.S. Lyons and the Express Dairy, chain stores like Woolworths and Boots, fish-and-chip shops, advertisers and door-to-door canvassers. It has been estimated that the number of persons employed in these trades rose from 1,773,000 in 1920 to 2,039,000 in 1929, and it continued to rise even during the depression that followed.

Adjacent to these trades stood the entertainment industries. The coming of 'talking pictures' in 1928 enlarged the number and size of cinemas, while the establishment of the British Broadcasting Corporation (born out of the British Broadcasting Company, started in 1922), incorporated by charter, had some three million people listening to the programmes and presumably owning wireless sets. Although newspaper owners grumbled about the news broadcasts put out by the BBC, serious competition did not really arise until the coming of television after the Second World War. In fact broadcasting stimulated the circulation of newspapers, which reached its peak in the nineteen-twenties.

The development of new industries had its impact on the geographical distribution of the population. London grew fast. Greater London had a population of 8,202,818 in 1931 out of a total population of under forty million in England and Wales, while the populations of north-east England, Lancashire and Wales all fell and that of the Midlands increased. No one who visited Cumberland, east Lancashire or the Rhondda Valley in the nineteen-twenties had any doubt about the poverty and misery caused by the economic depression. Birmingham and Coventry presented an entirely different picture. Middle-class suburbs, such as Victoria Park in Manchester and Edgbaston in Birmingham, were carefully planned. Garden cities dated back to the beginning of the century. Some favoured industrial workers, like the employees of Cadbury's, the chocolate firm, and of Leverhulme's, had suburbs designed by benevolent owners. As to the astonishing growth of London and its far-flung suburbs, it has been suggested that directors' wives in rising industries pressured their husbands into finding central offices in the capital, which was the heart of social intercourse and public entertainment.[6]

During the nineteen-twenties the coal mines became the industrial Cinderella. In 1925 the gold standard, suspended during the war, was restored, which had the result of overvaluing the pound sterling and therefore handicapping exports. Apart from this disadvantage, the output of coal for domestic purposes remained fairly high and the industry still employed nearly a million workers; but the price of coal obtained at the pit-head started falling. So in 1925, when the agreement about wages and hours concluded in 1921 (but modified in 1924) expired, the coal owners demanded a reduction in shift pay, to be negotiated by districts, and the abolition of the minimum subsistence wage. Admittedly, miners' wages in England were then higher than in two of its competitors, Germany and Poland, but they were pretty wretched, amounting to 8 or 9 shillings a shift. To avert a crisis (since the miners had the backing of other trade unions in their demand for a decent wage) the Government intervened, granted a subsidy of £23,000,000, and appointed another commission of inquiry, this time chaired by Sir Herbert Samuel, a former Home Secretary. The Samuel Commission recommended as an immediate measure a reduction in wages by national agreement. But the miners were adamant: 'not a penny off the pay, not a minute on the day', they declared, whereupon the owners locked them out on 30 April 1926.

The trade union movement, led by the General Council of the TUC, agreed to support the miners fully in what was to become known as the 'General Strike'. It began, provoked by the Government's breaking off negotiations with the TUC, on 3 May. At first the TUC called out only members of unions, such as the railwaymen, who handled carriage of coal. Thus the strike was effectively sympathetic, though the Government insisted it was political and unconstitutional. While the rank and file of the trade unions were loyal, some of the leaders were half-hearted. For example, J.H. Thomas, the general secretary of the National Union of Railwaymen, feared that the strike might degenerate into rioting and chaos.

In fact the General Strike had no serious social consequences, except that it divided the nation more acutely in two and stressed class differences which had always existed. The middle classes regarded A.J. Cook, the general secretary of the Miners' Federation and a brilliantly outspoken orator, as a red revolutionary. They enlisted in their thousands as 'special constables' – their youth thought it rather a lark – rallied behind the Government and attempted with limited success to run the buses and trains in London. No scarcity of food occurred as it was distributed by lorries, sometimes with permits from the TUC. The Government had the overwhelming advantage in propaganda because hardly any newspapers were published, while a British Gazette, officially sponsored and attaining a circulation of two million, reiterated the point of view that the strike was illegal. Although the British Broadcasting Company was not commandeered, as it could have been, it accepted the view that the strike was unconstitutional, allowed the Prime Minister and the Archbishop of Canterbury to broadcast, but denied the right to leaders of trade unions or Labour MPs who wished to address the public over the air.

On 12 May, the very day when the TUC called out its 'second line', which included shipyard workers and engineers, it seized on a transparent excuse, an unofficial compromise plan drawn up by Sir Herbert Samuel which the miners themselves refused to accept, to call off the strike unconditionally. Before the end of the year the miners were forced to consent to lower earnings, negotiated by districts, and the introduction of an eight-hour day, made legal by a hurriedly-passed act of parliament, though in 1930 a Labour Government reduced it to seven and a half. A Trade

Disputes Act also outlawed general and sympathetic strikes, thus trying to shut the door after the horse had bolted.

It was not until seven years after the General Strike that the coalmining industry gradually regained vigour. By 1939 a considerable number of amalgamations or mergers had taken place voluntarily, and much coal was being cut by machinery and moved mechanically in the mines. But the bitterness understandably felt by miners over their treatment by society as a whole in 1926 has endured until the present day.

Between 1926 and 1929 England experienced a mild boom; output rose and so did exports, yet the number of unemployed remained at nearly a million, a fact which deeply disturbed the consciences of those at work. Unemployment was worst, as has been noticed, in the so-called staple industries, particularly in coal, iron and steel, and cotton.

It was in an atmosphere of mixed unhappiness and hope, felt strongly by the young, that a second Labour Government took office in 1929. While it was trying to make up its mind about how to solve the unemployment problem, the New York Stock Exchange collapsed in October 1929. This damaged international finance and business and undermined confidence everywhere. The result was that the value of British exports fell from £729,300,000 in 1929 to £390,600,000 in 1931, and unemployment rose to 1,900,000 in 1930 and to 2,700,000 in June 1931. The minority Labour Government panicked and fell. The nation was wrapped in gloom. Even those with high qualifications were hard pressed to find work. When, for instance, the ill-paid post of assistant lecturer in modern history at Reading University fell vacant, well over a hundred applied for it.[7] In spite of the Bank of England raising its interest rate and borrowing abroad, trust in the pound sterling was shaken.

To restore confidence a National Government was formed and a variety of desperate measures tried. The pound was devalued by abandoning the gold standard, the bank rate was raised to a modest 6 per cent, the Budget was balanced by increasing the income tax from 4s 6d to 5s in the pound, and government employees of every kind, from Cabinet Ministers to school teachers and from judges to policemen, had their pay cut. Finally, free trade was given up. With certain exceptions a Customs duty of 10 per cent was imposed on all imported goods and an Import Duties Advisory Committee was appointed to recommend higher duties to protect specific industries: these could amount to 33.3 per cent. At an imperial economic conference held in the summer of 1932 at Ottawa imperial preferences were granted; in return the Dominions gave preference to certain British manufactured exports.

At about the same time the Government made a tremendous effort to sustain agriculture. Two Agricultural Marketing Acts of 1931 and 1933 enabled marketing boards to be set up in order to improve the sales of specific commodities, of which the most successful was the Milk Marketing Board. Farmers were protected from foreign competition by quotas and import duties on most foods and subsidies were paid to growers of wheat and sugar beet. The *Manchester Guardian* and *The Economist* criticized these schemes severely as pampering farmers at the public expense. But their lone voices commending free-trade principles were backing a dying cause.

John Maynard Keynes, who was both an original and distinguished economist and a successful financier, thought the Government's deflationary policy ill-advised. He attributed the cause of the depression to a disequilibrium between savings and investment, and he strongly advocated that the Government should borrow sufficient money to pay for large-scale public works and should reduce taxation; he also approved a revenue tariff. Another economist, a colleague of Keynes, stressed the manner in which an increase of investment added to output by means of a 'multiplier' – for example, because men in employment bought more goods than men unemployed. Keynes's solution was put forward politically during the general election of 1929, when the former Liberal Prime Minister, David Lloyd George, published a pamphlet entitled *We Can Conquer Unemployment*. Although the argument made little impression at the time and 'the Treasury view' of the need for economy prevailed, later the conviction spread that full employment might be achieved by such unorthodox methods.

In fact the economic depression of 1929–32 in England was moderate compared with that in other countries, especially the United States of America.[8] Its chief characteristic was the falling off in exports, largely owing to a reduction in demand from countries dependent on primary products, such as Argentina. Unemployment was highest in iron and steel, engineering, cotton and coal. By 1932 2,829,000 men and women were out of work, which was over 22 per cent of the number registered. On the other hand, the level of consumption was maintained; the real wages of those in employment fell only slightly or even rose; the deficit in the balance of payments in 1931 was not unduly serious and exports soon picked up. An attempt by the Government to single out the worst-hit areas – named 'special areas' – for assistance was not a success, but some new housing estates, such as Welwyn Garden City near London and Wythenshawe near Manchester, were destined to flourish. In 1932 the bank rate was down to 2 per cent, though it was confidence that was needed to promote new investment.

For those who were young in the early nineteen-thirties unemployment was a personal dread, and anxiety to find congenial work outweighed everything else. But the unemployment of tens of thousands and the low wages paid to essential workers smote the public conscience. By the mid thirties, however, one's thoughts were distracted by the rise of Fascism in Italy and National Socialism in Germany. Modern research has proved that the 'great depression' of 1929-32, though no myth, was less severe than imagined at the time and that the panic that led to such measures as cutting the relief of the unemployed was unnecessary.[9] Soon rearmament, brought about by fear of Hitler's Germany, contributed to industrial recovery. Admittedly, while exports increased somewhat, they no longer contributed so much to the total national income as they had done in the past; but home consumption rose, money wages in unionized industries remained steady, and an improvement in the terms of trade (because imports were cheaper) meant that most people had more to spend. A resilient economy- so it has been argued - proved to be compatible with some unemployment.

However moderate the depression may be made to look by economic historians who did not themselves live through it, the fact remains that at the time the dismal impression received of life in the areas that suffered the worst distress, where men out of work hung about the streets merely to pass the time, coupled with the consciousness that the Government had not only failed to find any long-term solution to the problem of unemployment but had bungled the question of relief, could hardly be avoided.

It was at first assumed that unemployment insurance payments would suffice to meet the needs of men and women out of work. Acts passed in 1920 and 1927 had extended the scope of insurance to cover most of the wage-earning population (except agricultural labourers). But as the Prime Minister confessed, the benefits received were nothing like a living wage. Moreover in the crisis of 1931 they were cut by 10 per cent. During the depression 'transitional payments' were given by the Treasury to those who had exhausted their claims to draw insurance benefit, or else assistance was provided by local authorities out of the rates (the elected Boards of Guardians were abolished in 1929). From 1931 the recipients of outdoor relief, nicknamed 'the dole', were subjected to a household means test (administered by local public assistance committees), which was deeply resented. Those who suffered long periods of unemployment claimed it

173

was not their fault that they could find no work, and saw no reason why the amount they received as 'dole' should be determined by whether members of their family were earning a living or had savings.

It was not until 1935 that the Government created an Unemployment Assistance Board and the transitional payments provided by the Treasury were renamed public assistance. Thus the new board became responsible for the relief of poverty and the local authorities were only required to care for the sick and aged. The board, however, blundered by promulgating standards of relief which in many cases were lower than those that had been given by the local authorities. A public outcry and 'hunger marches' forced the board to revise its rates, but the means test remained. Society had nonetheless at last recognized its obligations. By 1938 expenditure on social services, including unemployment assistance, amounted to some 11 to 12 per cent of the gross national product. Despite the numbers receiving the dole – there were still 1,800,000 registered unemployed by then – the rest of the population was better off and could afford to foot the bill. 'No one can seriously doubt', writes one expert on the cost of living, 'that the working classes on the eve of the second world war were better fed, better clothed and better housed than their parents had been a generation earlier.'[10]

The war that began in 1939 wiped out unemployment. By then it had become widely believed, at least by the intelligentsia, that an enlightened government willing to invest in public works (such as road-building) could create full employment for all time. Meanwhile, when by the spring of 1940 the United Kingdom was left alone to fight the German and Italian war machines, everyone had plenty of work to do. Not that there was the same enthusiasm to enlist in the forces as had been shown in 1914. Once the German air attacks started people were excited and drawn together by the common danger. And when, as in 1918, the war ended in victory, the future of the English people looked rosy.

Before and after the two world wars in the first half of the twentieth century many social restraints were lifted. Moreover, at the beginning of the century the defeat of the Boers and the generous peace settlement confirmed beliefs in the virtues and values of an enlightened imperialism and also gave hope of profiting from the gold in South Africa.

Edward VII, who became King in 1901, was not very interested in the Empire: his reign symbolized the exit from Victorian pride and respectability. His love of women and horses, champagne and gambling, set an open example to English 'society'. He was even said to have invented the 'English week-end'.

For the rest of the population amusements were fewer and less expensive. They consisted largely of drinking beer and reading newspapers. Alfred Harmsworth (later Lord Northcliffe), a journalist of genius who left school at fifteen, launched periodicals and newspapers calculated to appeal if not to the masses at least to the lower middle classes, starting with *Answers* and following with the London *Evening News*, the *Daily Mail* and the *Daily Mirror*. Professional football was particularly popular in the north and attracted gambling, though not yet in the form of 'pools'. The cinema was a fairly primitive form of entertainment (though superior to the magic lantern) until Charlie Chaplin, an Englishman by birth and originally a music-hall comedian, justly became internationally famous. Posterity has recognized his genius by erecting his statue in the heart of London. The 'picture palace' did not successfully rival the music hall until the nineteen-twenties. It was then that younger people were seeking and finding liberation from customary restraints, though their elders condemned them for frivolity and cynicism. Dance halls sprang up all over the country and the drinking of 'cocktails' (an American invention) became popular, though less alcohol was consumed than in Edwardian days. During the war of 1914-18 the hours at which public houses could stay open were reduced and the notorious afternoon gap introduced. It was then that King George V (1910-36) had been persuaded to take the pledge of abstinence to set a good example to munition workers. Sex was no longer an unmentionable topic in mixed company.

After the First World War women gave up wearing whalebone corsets and tight-laced stays. Young women wore short skirts, flesh-coloured stockings and aimed to look slim and boyish with their hair cut short and their hats close-fitting. The Matrimonial Causes Act of 1923 gave women the right to sue for divorce on grounds of adultery, but it was not until 1937 that desertion, cruelty and insanity were added as grounds for both parties. But in the case of desertion the aggrieved party had to undergo five years of separation before a divorce was granted.

Tastes in middle-class reading reflected the growing emancipation of women, though what were regarded as daring novels – James Joyce's *Ulysses* (1922) and D.H. Lawrence's *Lady Chatterley's Lover* (1928) – were sold only under the counter. Poets became more audacious, not only in their subject matter but also in their rhythm. An act passed in April 1928 at last gave women the vote on the same terms as men, an act which can be interpreted as recognizing sexual equality, although the decision that women should be employed and paid on the same terms as men awaited the nineteen-seventies.

The year 1928 may be taken as the dividing line in the social history of the time. The country then seemed prosperous enough as new businesses developed, even though unemployment and distress in the coal and cotton industries endured. The cinema was a cheap and congenial form of entertainment as the 'talkies' came in. Even hard-working, ambitious young men went to the cinema three or four times a week; one of the author's landladies and her husband visited the same cinema every Saturday regardless of what was showing there. 'Super cinemas' were erected in all big towns. At the same time radio programmes could be heard on loudspeakers and one could listen to invisible music-hall entertainment and jazz bands for practically nothing.

One significant social change that has been assigned to the twentieth century is a decline in the prestige of the land. Whereas in Victorian times the majority of Cabinet Ministers were hereditary landowners, by the first half of the next century the House of Commons, if not the Lords, consisted mainly of professional and business men, of whom Stanley Baldwin and Neville Chamberlain were typical examples. But love of the countryside was still strong. Nearly every town had its public parks. The cheap motor car (in the days when petrol too was cheap) enabled fathers to take their wives and children to the countryside or seaside at week-ends, or to live in dormitory villages and commute to work. Ministers and others discovered that buying themselves farms, whether they made profits or losses, was a wise means of investing their savings. Those who could not afford to do that kept small yachts or at least subscribed to the National Trust, formed in 1895, which bought up many beautiful stretches of English countryside to preserve them from developers.

Leisure was valued more than ever before. The middle classes began taking holidays abroad in large numbers. French and Belgian seaside resorts were almost as popular as English ones. By 1939 a quarter of the population obtained holidays with pay, though usually for only one week. Billy Butlin opened his first holiday camp at Skegness in 1937, but it was only a minority of the working classes who could afford a holiday away from home. Hours of work were still long; a forty-eight-hour week was commonplace, but it was made a maximum for women and youths in a Factory Act of 1937. The commuter trains were as full on Saturday mornings as on any other weekday. Even Civil Servants worked on Saturday, though they had long holidays. The Bank holiday, determined by religious occasions, was valued; it had not yet become an anachronism.

A feature of this period of English social history was the arrival of the motor car. Before the First World War only the rich possessed motor cars. The author's maternal grandfather, a city merchant, had a Daimler driven by a chauffeur, although when we visited him as children we went on omnibuses driven by horses. By 1928 Morris motor cars were rivalling American Fords. Motor coaches began competing with the railways for passenger traffic. The motor car and the motor bus brought rural life much closer to towns.

Because unemployment, unaccompanied by inflation, kept down wages and imported food was untaxed, prices were low and salaries could be made to stretch a long way. The nineteen-thirties can be described as the prosperous age of the middle classes even more emphatically than the mid Victorian period. My father was an Assistant Secretary at the Board of Trade. My mother did no housework except shopping. She had two servants, a cook and a housemaid, who lived in and were never out together except on Sunday evenings, when a cold meal was left for us. A woman came to do the sewing and another to clean the silver; a gardener also came once a week. The postman called four times on weekdays and once on Sundays. It is true that we never drank wine or spirits except on special occasions, and once my father gave up *The Times* and took the *Daily Telegraph* instead because it was cheaper. That was when I was at a public school. My father then told me that he could not afford to send me to a university – he meant Oxford or Cambridge – unless I won a scholarship, but he could certainly have afforded to send me to the London School of Economics, where he had once been a lecturer.

Undoubtedly English society has become more egalitarian in the second half of the twentieth century, though less so than in the United States. On the whole, equality of opportunity is a reality, although modern research indicates that heredity is a more important factor in promoting ability than it was believed to be 150 years ago, when socialists like Robert Owen laid most stress on environment. But as to middle-class life, modern gadgets such as deep-freezers and dishwashers, though they are conveniences, are perhaps less helpful than a domestic staff at one's beck and call. And of course nearly everyone today owns a car, which makes shopping somewhat easier. But it needs to be remembered that in the twenties and thirties tradesmen delivered goods (and even library books) at the door and frequently called for orders, while privately owned shops gave personal attention to the needs of their customers. So it can be argued that the era of supreme comfort for the middle classes faded away in 1939.

Notes

1 Randolph Churchill, *Winston S. Churchill*, II (1967), p. 284
2 William Ashworth, *An Economic History of England 1870–1939* (1972), pp. 252–3
3 Cit. from *Industrial Efficiency, A Comparative Study of Industrial Life in England, Germany and America* (1905) by Donald Read in *Edwardian England* (1972), p. 9
4 Churchill, op. cit., p. 278
5 Suzanne Buckley, 'The Family and the Role of Women', in *The Edwardian Age: Conflict and Stability 1900–1914* (1979), p. 140
6 This was suggested by my friend, Colin Clark
7 I was one of them. Professor A. Aspinall, as he became, was wisely selected.
8 Denis H. Aldcraft, *The Inter-War Economy: Britain 1919–1939* (1970), p. 41; H.W. Richardson, *Economic Recovery of Britain* (1967), p. 15
9 Aldcraft, op. cit., chapter 9; Ashworth, op. cit., pp. 398–9; R.F. Harrod, *The Life of John Maynard Keynes* (1951), p. 438
10 J. Burnett, *Plenty and Want* (1968), p. 319

TEN

The Last War and After

It is often denied that any practical lessons are to be learnt from history: Philip Guedalla, for example, wrote that 'history repeats itself with differences and it is the differences that make all the difference'. But at least so far as social and economic affairs were concerned the Conservative Government of 1939 based most of its plans on experiences acquired during the war of 1914-18. Two Emergency Powers Acts were passed in 1939 and 1940 giving the Government almost unlimited authority. Ministries of Home Security, National Service, Economic Warfare, Food, Shipping and Information were all set up at once. Petrol rationing was introduced. Local agricultural committees were appointed. Conscription was imposed up to the age of forty-one and lists of persons who could be employed in the vast amount of additional administrative and intelligence duties required in war time had been drawn up. The Government was fully aware that once again the island, in which over forty-six million people now dwelt, needed to be safeguarded against starvation. Among other things it was hoped that the invention of Asdic, an apparatus for detecting the position of submarines under water, would enable merchant shipping to be adequately protected by destroyers. Escorts for convoys were instituted from the outset.

But of course the differences since 1918 were marked. It was generally believed that once war was declared London and other cities would immediately be attacked by German bomber aircraft. The bombers, it was thought, could not be stopped from reaching their targets, even though radar could give sufficient warning to fighter command and the troops manning the aircraft batteries. As one walked along Whitehall in September 1939, one asked oneself how many buildings, from the Admiralty to the Treasury, would be left standing in a few weeks' time. Beds were prepared in hospitals to receive huge numbers of casualties. Arrangements

179

had been made for the evacuation from towns believed to be in most danger of four million schoolchildren with their teachers and children under five with their mothers, though in fact only a million and a half went, which helped the operation to be completed smoothly. Air raid shelters and gas masks were made available. Wealthy parents packed their children off to friends or relatives in the United States and Canada. A previous decision to evacuate whole Ministries from London was counter-manded.[1] Deep shelters were ready to provide protection for meetings of Cabinet Ministers.

The second main difference from what happened at the beginning of the previous world war was that for the first ten months nothing happened at all. There were no air raids on England and no fighting on the western front. A number of merchant ships were sunk by U-boats, as well as a battleship thought to be safely anchored at Scapa Flow in Scotland. The period of phoney war, as it came to be called, had some curious consequences. Because of the continuing fear of air raids a 'blackout' was imposed at night, which brought increased deaths and injuries on the roads. It also resulted in high-minded citizens badgering such of their neighbours as allowed shafts of electric light to penetrate their windows. A million of the women and children evacuated from the towns returned home after taking a dislike to the country, while their hosts and hostesses often failed to welcome children from the slums, who were sometimes dirty and misbehaved. One or two theatres, which were shut at the start of the war, bravely reopened. The army rejected volunteers on the grounds that the regiments were at full strength and, as in 1914, rifles and ammunition were scarce.[2] A few men who wanted to get away from their wives or were unemployed enlisted. During 1939-40 unemployment remained at a figure of around a million.

The Government, which had at first made itself unpopular by appeasing the German dictator, Hitler, and then turned round and pledged itself to lend all support in its power to protect the independence of Poland, Romania and Greece (which in fact it had no means of doing), became understandably even more unpopular. Thus it was not until 10 May 1940, when the German army, after violating the neutrality of Holland and Belgium, invaded France and cut off the British army stationed to the left of the French line, that the patriotic spirit engendered at the outset of the previous war was aroused and the English people braced themselves for sacrifices.

The Government did its utmost to keep down the cost of living.

Immediately after the outbreak of war it extended rent control to about 90 per cent of unfurnished houses. Food subsidies were introduced in December 1939. 'Utility clothing' became available at modest prices from the spring of 1942. 'Points rationing', which gave consumers a choice of how to use their rations, was applied to clothing and certain foods. That these measures succeeded in their aim was shown by the fact that whereas between the beginning of the war and December 1945 wages increased in value by over 50 per cent, the cost of living during the same period rose by only just over 30 per cent.

Churchill as Prime Minister from May 1940 made a brilliant choice when he persuaded Ernest Bevin, the general secretary of the Transport and General Workers' Union, to accept the post of Minister of Labour and National Service. Already a list of 'reserved occupations' had been issued to preclude skilled workmen essential to the production of munitions from being called up by the armed services. In spite of the large number of men who were enlisted, by the middle of 1940 the number employed in industry had fallen by only half a million. This was partly because the population was still growing, partly because more women and youngsters took jobs, and partly because immigrants were still arriving to offer their help in the war effort. After 1941 the age at which men could be conscripted for military service was raised from forty one to fifty, and the Minister of Labour and National Service was empowered to call up women between the ages of twenty and thirty to do war work. The War Cabinet had been reluctant to agree to the conscription of women because it feared that servicemen might resent such treatment of their wives: in fact this power was cautiously exercised and caused little umbrage.

The problem of finding the resources with which to wage the war after the fall of France was met in various ways. Domestic consumption was reduced by rationing, by imposing income tax at 10 shillings in the pound, by the imposition of Pay As You Earn (PAYE), which deducted tax immediately from salaries and wages, and by the device of levying further deductions through a scheme of post-war credits invented by J.M. Keynes. The consequence was that some 55 per cent of the cost of the war was met out of taxation and personal expenditure on consumer goods fell from £4,309,000,000 in 1939 to £3,706,000,000 in 1944.

Such savings in public expenditure only assisted the purchase of food and raw materials from countries belonging to the 'sterling area'. Imports from the United States, Canada and other countries outside the sterling area had to be paid for in gold or dollars. At the outset of the war Treasury regulations required that all holdings of foreign currencies and gold had to be offered for sale to the Government. Though foreign investments amounted to some £3,000,000,000, only about £700,000,000 was actually available for spending abroad. Out of US $335,000,000 the Government paid in cash for all imports bought up to November 1940. By the following year it was expected that dollar credits would be exhausted. However, in March 1941 the United States Congress passed the Lend-Lease Act, which empowered the American President to supply arms to other countries on any terms. So far as Great Britain was concerned, no provision was made for repayment and 'no formal account kept in dollars or sterling'.[3] Lend-Lease ended on 2 September 1945 on the rapid conclusion of the war against Japan. By the final settlement with the United States the Government had to repay only $650,000,000.

Unquestionably the war created a spirit of comradeship and altruism. No doubt a black market came into being and instances of profiteering, especially among farmers, were to be found. But the presence of Ernest Bevin and other Labour representatives in the National Government ensured that little scope for inequalities was allowed. Excess profits were taxed; rationing was strict; in the army promotion from the ranks was commonplace. Any skilful man could be trained as an officer. In the London underground stations, where families without shelters slept during the German bombing of the capital, in the fire stations, largely manned by elderly auxiliaries, among the air raid wardens and Home Guards a camaraderie inconceivable in peace time developed rapidly. The American soldiers and airmen who flooded the country between 1942 and 1944 introduced the 'Jack is as good as his master' attitude characteristic of the United States. The contrast with the class society that prevailed in pre-war England was obvious. Men and women grew to understand how the 'other half' lived. A story told of Winston Churchill as Prime Minister is symptomatic. Driving through London one day he stopped his car to find out why a long queue of men and women was assembled outside a shop: he learned they were queuing for bird seed.

Many were convinced that 'war socialism', that is to say, the taking over of industries such as coalmining by the State, worked satisfactorily. Moreover, most of the fighting men doubted whether a Conservative Government, which had been in office for fifteen years between the two wars, was likely to establish full employment and a Welfare State. When a general election was held in July 1945 their wives told canvassers that they could not say how they would vote until they heard from their husbands.

Because of these reactions the Labour Party, founded in 1900, for the first time won a victory that gave it complete power.

The five years after the war were a period of difficulty mingled with hope. While fewer than half the men perished in the fighting than did in the 1914-18 war, over 60,000 civilians had been killed in air attacks and 240,000 injured. Factories and houses had been destroyed or damaged and needed to be rebuilt. Foreign investments worth £1,118,000,000 had been sold and the value of exports had fallen from a quarterly average of £3,117,000,000 in 1939 to £821,000,000 in 1944. Shipping needed replacing, railway equipment required renewing, huge debts had to be repaid and military commitments, particularly in the occupation of Germany, were costly. One bright spot was that farming had been so intensively mechanized during the war that British agriculture became the most efficient in Europe.

The financial situation was remedied partly by borrowing £1,100,000,000 (3.75 billion dollars) from the United States Government free of interest for six years and then at the low rate of 2 per cent, partly by joining the International Monetary Fund, which undertook to lend to member countries in difficulties, and partly by the institution of an 'export drive' aimed at increasing the total value of sales abroad by 175 per cent. Exchange controls were retained; so was rationing. Indeed, bread was also rationed for the first time in July 1946. Restaurants, which had previously substituted bread for potatoes, now substituted potatoes for bread. But no one was allowed to spend more than 5 shillings (25p) on a meal out. The Chancellor of the Exchequer appointed in 1947, Sir Stafford Cripps, was an austere figure himself and preached the virtues of austerity with puritanical fervour. From the beginning of 1948 he enjoyed fresh financial assistance from the United States: the American Secretary of State, General George Marshall, was afraid of Russian intentions towards Europe after the Soviet Union had become supreme behind the Iron Curtain, and he was able to persuade Congress to vote money to aid recovery in western Europe. The British share came to £700,000,000, without any obligation to repay.

In spite of all this help - and the target of a 175 per cent rise in the value of exports was exceeded by 1950 - the balance of payments remained adverse, with the consequence that in 1949 the pound had to be devalued from $4.05 to $2.80. One reason for the devaluation was the higher cost of imports owing to the natural growth in demand for materials essential to post-war reconstruction. The transcendence of the almighty dollar had to be recognized: the idea of maintaining anything like the pre-war value of sterling in terms of the dollar was abandoned. For the time being devaluation stimulated exports and thus enabled the price of imports to be paid more easily.

As in 1918, during the years immediately after the war ended young men and women trusted that they had fought for a better world, not merely 'homes for heroes to live in' - though these were badly needed - but relief from the unemployment that had pulverized the country until 1940, and escape from poverty, the kind of poverty below a minimum subsistence level that philanthropists and social reformers had unveiled in English towns in the nineteen-twenties and thirties.

In planning for reconstruction Sir William Beveridge, an able and experienced administrator who had been concerned with social welfare thirty years earlier, had been invited to draw up an insurance scheme which, as he expressed it, would ensure freedom from want, disease, ignorance, squalor and idleness. What he advocated in his report, published in 1942, was an all-embracing scheme of national insurance, covering not only unemployment, but illness, destitution and the needs of old age. Everyone, including the self-employed, was to be required to buy weekly insurance stamps. Out of the proceeds the unemployed were to receive benefits and, if needed, supplementary assistance, the retired were to obtain higher pensions, and large families were to be helped with money grants. The Government also decided to establish a free State medical service open to all and paid for by taxation. The means test, the workhouse and, in theory at least, the stigma attached to seeking public assistance were all to be abolished. Instead of the dismal workhouses of pre-war England local authorities were empowered to find decent residential accommodation where the old, the sick and the infirm could live in some degree of comfort. The Poor Law was to be killed stone-dead.

All the political parties accepted the Beveridge plan. In June 1945 family allowances were introduced and school meals were provided for nothing. The National Insurance Bill was passed in August. After complicated arguments with the doctors a State medical service, which included consultants, physicians and surgeons, was established in November 1946. Private hospitals were taken over by local authorities or run as charities. Pills and medicines sold in chemists' shops on prescription were paid for by the Ministry of Health. The sick (and the hypochondriacs) could confidently go to a surgery and obtain prescriptions.

So the Welfare State came into being. But two serious difficulties arose, unexpected by idealists. The first was that the health scheme proved enormously expensive. In the years to come governments both of the right and left were obliged to introduce charges for dentistry, spectacles and prescriptions. Secondly, the original intention had been to set up clinics where some measure of specialization could be arranged among doctors. Few such clinics came into existence. Doctors in cities were often overloaded with work, though country physicians were not. Gradually group practices were increased to the mutual benefit of doctors and patients.

With the return of large-scale unemployment in the late nineteen-sixties the cost of the health service rose substantially. The discovery of new and costly medicines and two devaluations of the pound, which raised the price of imported drugs, magnified the total bill. Another major difficulty in the evolution of the Welfare State was that the assumption made in a White Paper published by the Churchill Government and adopted in Beveridge's book, *Full Employment in a Free Society*, that unemployment could be conquered, was not realized. After the war informed people besides Beveridge believed that an unemployment rate of 8 to 10 per cent could be tolerated because it simply meant that workmen were changing jobs, that for family reasons a number of men and women were temporarily out of work, and that school leavers (the leaving age was raised to fifteen in 1947 and sixteen in 1972) were not yet absorbed. During the period of reconstruction and for some years afterwards full employment was attained; but by 1981 it was higher than during the depression of the thirties.

Besides inaugurating the Welfare State, the second (and on the whole less successful) achievement of the Labour Government was the nationalization of much of the country's industry and finance, long regarded by convinced socialists as a cure-all for the ills of capitalism. The first industry to be nationalized in 1946 was coal. Except for the owners, who were generously compensated, few doubted the wisdom of this step. Indeed, it had been recommended by Lord Sankey twenty-six years earlier. In the same year an act nationalizing the Bank of England and the Cable and Wireless Acts were passed. A Civil Aviation Act, also passed in the same year, gave a monopoly to British European Airways and British Overseas Airways, covering the rest of the world; this was operative from 1949. The two lines, though heavily subsidized by the government, were never a financial success, for they had to meet competition from the airlines of other countries; and in 1960 their monopoly was broken. By 1981 they had been amalgamated, but their condition was parlous. In 1947 a Transport Act not only nationalized the railways but also road haulage and the canals. Later long-distance haulage was returned to private enterprise. In the same year the Electricity Act and in the following year a Gas Act were passed. Iron and steel nationalization did not become effective until October 1950.

The organization of these industries varied somewhat, but a considerable degree of uniformity was to be found in the nationalization of coal, transport, electricity, gas, and iron and steel. Other monopolies, some of which – broadcasting, for example – were established before the war, were corporations. The power of Ministers, who had to answer for them in the House of Commons, consisted chiefly in making appointments, usually of chairmen and boards of governors or directors. In theory it was not a ministerial duty to answer detailed questions about the working of the nationalized industries in Parliament, but in practice Ministers often had to do so.

The case for nationalization sprang partly from the conviction that public ownership, which eliminated wasteful competition, was to the interest of the whole community, and partly from the belief that effective economic planning was impossible without control over the basic industries of the country. Nationalization was thought of by its prophets as a means to full employment, high productivity and social justice. Few of the nationalized industries succeeded in doing all this, or did so only by taking advantage of their monopoly positions to put up prices. Ten years after their inception the National Coal Board's deficit was £32.6 millions, the British Transport Commission's was £90.2 millions and that of the two Airway Boards was £28 millions.

It has been cynically argued that it would have been wiser for the Government to take over industries already making a profit, such as life insurance or chemicals, instead of staple industries that had been struggling to survive for years. Apart from this the case against nationalization could be put together from a number of generalized criticisms. First, it has been considered a misfortune that industries should be made the plaything of political parties. Iron and steel, for example, was first nationalized, then denationalized and after that largely renationalized again. Road haulage was denationalized so as to challenge the railways in their freight business. British Airways gradually lost their monopolies, as did the BBC. On the other hand, all parties accepted the nationalization of coal and the railways, gas and electricity, and in 1954 a Conservative Government established an Atomic Energy Authority.

Another criticism was that big industries were insufficiently decentralized. It was also argued that despite the existence of various tribunals and advisory bodies the interests of consumers were not adequately catered for: these monopolies, it was asserted, were run for the benefit of the work force rather than the community at large. A contradictory argument was that all these organizations were undemocratic because representatives of the workers took no direct part in their management. The ideals of what was called in the twenties 'guild socialism' were ignored. In fact it is broadly true that the trade unions did not want to participate in the running of large industries, for they regarded it as their primary duty to secure good wages and conditions for their members by fighting the management, not by co-operating with it. They were able to do this more easily because they now had to deal with one centralized body of management, which, if it was compelled to grant concessions it could not really afford, was able in the last resort to appeal to the government for financial aid.

Although in due course many railway lines and stations were closed, unprofitable coal mines were shut down and air routes were abandoned to private enterprise, it could be contended that had these concerns not been publicly owned, the existence of the profit motive might have forced them to cut their coat according to their cloth more drastically and rapidly. Even the Labour Party, which was responsible for the nationalization of industries, was split asunder in the nineteen-fifties when its leader, Hugh Gaitskell, expressed his belief that the moral and economic case for nationalization had ceased to be acceptable and advocated its excision from the Party's programme.

In 1951 the Labour Government that had presided over the inception of the Welfare State and the revolutionary spread of nationalization had come to an end, and a Festival of Britain, held on the south bank of the river Thames in London, commemorating the hundredth anniversary of Prince Albert's Great Exhibition, was hopefully regarded as pointing the way to another era of progress nurtured by private enterprise. Marshall Aid was suspended at the beginning of the year, a deficit in the balance of payments persisted and the loss of gold and dollars was described as the worst on record. To cope with the situation income tax was increased by 6d to 9s 6d in the pound, the amount allowed for foreign travel was reduced to a ludicrous £25, a charge for medical prescriptions was imposed for the first time and food subsidies were reduced from £410,000,000 to £250,000,000.

In 1952, however, the outlook brightened. At last the restrictions introduced during the war were lifted. Most food was derationed and in 1954
the Ministry of Food was itself abolished. Industrial production rose, the
terms of trade improved, exchange controls were relaxed and the Bank
rate was lowered first to 3.5 per cent and then to 3 per cent. Wage rates,
notably those of coal miners and engineers, were raised and the Government celebrated by increasing the salaries of Members of Parliament from
£1,000 to £1,500 a year. By the summer of 1955 unemployment had
fallen to less than 1 per cent of the insured population. Two years later the
Prime Minister, Harold Macmillan, was able to proclaim that the British
people 'had never had it so good'.

After a mild recession in 1957-8, which necessitated a credit squeeze,
recovery fully set in at the end of the nineteen-fifties: wage rates were
higher, exports rose, unemployment fell and even the cotton industry,
which was being reorganized with government help, claimed to be 'in
better shape and heart than for years'.[4] The rate of industrial growth,
though less dramatic than in other industrial countries, 'was faster than in
any previous period of equal length in British history' in the twenty-five
years from 1948 onwards.[5] The community benefited from the expansion
in world economic activity and a policy of cheap money was conducive to
capital investment.

During this happy era of full employment and economic growth the
British Empire was gradually disappearing. Although Winston Churchill,
who had declared during the war that it was not his intention to preside
over the dissolution of the Empire, was again Prime Minister from 1951 to
1955, he had already acquiesced in the independence of India, which after
an initial blood-bath was divided into the Dominions of India and Pakistan.
Years before Lord Curzon had prophesied that so long as the British ruled
India they would remain a great power, but that once it was lost it would
be a third-rate power; while Gandhi in 1942 had assured President Franklin
Roosevelt, who disliked 'British imperialism', that as soon as India was
free, the rest of the Empire would be dismantled.[6] So it proved. After
Anthony Eden, who replaced Churchill as Prime Minister, had vainly
waved the imperial flag by fighting the Egyptians when they nationalized
the Suez Canal, his successor, Macmillan, recognized 'the winds of change'
in Africa. In 1957 the Gold Coast led the way by becoming the independent
republic of Ghana. In quick succession Nigeria, Tanganyika, Uganda and
Kenya followed, and in 1965 the white rulers of Southern Rhodesia made
a unilateral declaration of independence. The expense involved in liqui-

dating the Empire, sustaining the 'sterling area', which for a time replaced it, and jeopardizing markets has not yet been analysed, but it was certainly burdensome. In 1966 the Colonial Office was abolished. As to the Empire, after it had first been rechristened the British Commonwealth and then the Commonwealth of Nations, it dissolved into an amicable periodic meeting of English-speaking heads of state, as at Melbourne in 1981.

The transformation of the British Empire into the Commonwealth in the course of a generation had an immense effect on the social and economic life of England, for it helped to change it into a multiracial society. To start with, it was the law of the land that anyone with a British passport might settle in England. Poverty in the erstwhile imperial components of the West Indies, India, Pakistan, Malta and Cyprus drove many to emigrate to a country enjoying prosperity and a generous standard of social welfare. By 1962 it was realized that what had become a flood of immigrants had to be checked and a Commonwealth Immigration Act was passed which came into force on 1 July: this made provision for the control of immigration and for the deportation of criminals. A scheme was introduced dividing immigrants into three categories, those with definite offers of employment, those with special skills such as doctors, dentists, nurses and teachers, and lastly those looking for work. The third category was abolished in 1965, when a limit of 8,000 was imposed.

By 1968 long waiting lists existed. Every immigrant who settled was allowed to bring over his family or 'dependants', who were on average 2.7 persons. The dependants had to obtain certificates from British consuls in the countries from which they came. About half the immigrants who had offers of employment came from the West Indies and Malta and a quarter from India and Pakistan. Half of the total number of immigrants found work in manufacturing industries, chiefly in the Midlands, about a quarter secured work in catering as waiters and waitresses or on kitchen staffs, mainly in London and south-east England, and 12 per cent were employed in transport.[7] The question has often been asked whether the London transport system could function without them. The Indians and Pakistanis proved themselves first-class workers, willing to accept longer hours than Englishmen.

Although immigrants were protected by a Race Relations Act in 1968 employers tended to prefer white people for the better-paid jobs, and the same pattern emerged as could be seen in the United States, with coloured people doing most of the dirty work. An independent inquiry conducted by Lord Scarman in 1981 suggested that they should be given wider

189

opportunities of employment. However, no deliberate segregation in schools and in clubs took place. Such segregation as existed was voluntary, because the coloured people tended to congregate in specific areas such as Notting Hill in London and Nottingham in the Midlands. At times riots were sparked off; at times coloured communities have been antagonized by the actions of the police; and in the nineteen-seventies rising unemployment created animosity among immigrants willing to work, even though another Act passed in December 1971 further restricted immigration by requiring would-be settlers to show that one of their parents or grandparents had been born in the United Kingdom or that they themselves had been settled there for five years. By 1981 the number of such immigrants was estimated to be about 2,500,000. On the whole, multiracialism has been accepted as a new and tolerable fact of life. Many Englishmen cannot fail to admire the contribution made by immigrant settlers, whether railwaymen or bus conductors, doctors or nurses, professional cricketers or footballers, to the fabric of society.

A factor which influenced the break-up of the Commonwealth was the decision taken by a Conservative Government in 1961 to apply for membership of the European Economic Community. This Community had been formed in 1958 after the signature in the previous year of the Treaty of Rome by Italy, France, West Germany, Belgium, Holland and Luxembourg, the aim being to stimulate international trade by the creation of a duty-free Common Market. In 1959 the British Government had retorted by organizing and joining a European Free Trade Association, a Customs union consisting of seven other countries, most of them more modest than those in 'the inner circle'.

In spite of the establishment of EFTA and the existence of imperial preferences, which survived from the Ottawa conference of 1932, and in spite of the opposition of the Labour Party, the decision was taken three years later to apply for admission to the Common Market. Surprisingly, the application was rejected, but as exports remained steady and unemployment was negligible the snub was not at first considered significant. When in 1964 a Labour Government came to power and set up a Ministry of Economic Affairs, dedicated to planning an export drive to put right the balance of payments (in deficit by £356,000,000), for a short time exports to the sterling area or Commonwealth countries increased.

But then the position began to deteriorate. By 1967 the deficit increased to £500,000,000 and the pound had to be devalued. Five years later a floating exchange rate was introduced, which meant that the pound sterling was allowed to find its own level, protected merely by high interest rates and the ability to draw on the International Bank. Thus the sterling area in effect came to an end. In June 1972 the unemployment total reached a million for the first time since before the Second World War. A Conservative Government, which had been elected in June 1970, faced with unemployment, inflation and numerous strikes, resolved to make a fresh application for membership of the Common Market (a decimal coinage had been established on 15 February 1971, abolishing the old half-crowns, shillings, pennies and farthings). This time the application was accepted by the Six and on 1 January 1973 Great Britain became a member of the European Economic Community. A Labour Government elected in March 1974, after renegotiating the terms of membership, held a referendum asking the electorate whether it approved of joining the EEC; a majority of two to one said 'yes'. But it proved to be no magical panacea.

In the very year that Great Britain joined the EEC there was a staggering increase in world commodity prices, and the price of petrol, vital to the whole economic and social life of the community, multiplied fivefold. The deficit on the balance of payments was over £900,000,000. Inflation set in. Workmen were laid off by private industry. State-run industries had to thin down with redundancies and the level of unemployment was higher than in the depression of the early nineteen-thirties. But one difference between the situation in the seventies and that in the thirties was that unemployment was now accompanied by rising prices. Consequently, despite the high level of unemployment many strikes shattered the public. During the seventies even nurses, ambulance men, hospital workers, firemen and Civil Servants went on strike, always for more pay to offset higher prices.

By 1975 the value of money to the consumer was not much more than one-fifth of what it had been thirty years earlier. Ministers and Members of Parliament, who voted themselves bigger salaries (£13,150 a year in the Commons and an allowance of £36 a day in the Lords), and chairmen of nationalized industries with salaries soaring towards £100,000 a year found an understandable difficulty in preaching wage restraint. Each month the rate of inflation rose and the Government congratulated itself if it was less than 10 per cent. The prices of coal, gas, electricity, postage, telephones and petrol went up; and it was small consolation to drivers to be told that owing to the discovery of oil in the North Sea Great Britain was in the process of becoming self-sufficient, for the price was not reduced, though after a panic in the nineteen-fifties, owing to restrictions by the Arab countries, a glut had prevailed.

During the nineteen-seventies prices rose steadily throughout the world. The government in England, whatever its political complexion, tended to argue that this was owing to excessive demand, so that wage freezes, credit squeezes, prices and incomes boards monitoring changes and desperate attempts to cut State expenditure were all tried in an effort to keep inflation under control. But because England is dependent on buying half its food and much of its raw materials abroad, the increase in import prices was a dominant factor; and rises in prices in turn stimulated demands for higher wages, which in general were met in spite of the huge pool of unemployed (amounting to over three million at the outset of 1982).

Thus the economic history of England over the last thirty-five years can be summarized as consisting of gradual recovery from the war at first, then a period of affluence and full employment lasting for more than fifteen years, and finally in the seventies a catastrophic phase of inflation and rising unemployment.

An outstanding social change in post-war England was in the attitude to sex. An act was passed allowing homosexual activity between consenting males who had reached the age of twenty-one. The law concerning prostitution was altered. As medical discoveries had made the two principal venereal diseases, syphilis and gonorrhea, easily curable, irregular inter-course became safer, although professional prostitutes (who were well organized) complained that there were too many amateurs about. A movement was started to legalize brothels. In 1960 a test case in the courts won the right to print *Lady Chatterley's Lover*, banned in the twenties, as a paperback. Nude bathing was allowed at a marina in Brighton. Three national newspapers with large circulations, the *Sun*, the *Daily Mirror* and the *News of the World*, all relied on sex stories and illustrations to titillate their readers; but this was hardly new, only a little more blatant.

Nevertheless many people thought that the permissive society that was emerging had gone too far. The West End of London was now filled with blue cinemas and pornographic bookshops; and in any case commercial films such as *Last Tango in Paris* and *A Clockwork Orange*, which were frank enough, could be shown in ordinary cinemas so long as they carried an X certificate banning the attendance of children. The exploitation of children for pornographic purposes was actually prohibited by a Protection of Children Act passed in 1978.

Another great social change was the progress of sexual equality. Women, who had played a full part in two world wars and had after a long struggle at last achieved political equality, were no longer treated as the weaker sex entitled to courtesies from, but not equal opportunities with, men. In 1967 abortion was legalized; in 1971 a Divorce Reform Act permitted a divorce to be obtained after three years' wait if a marriage had irretrievably broken down; a pill invented as a contraceptive could be obtained on the National Health to allow family planning.

What was more important to women even than the right they acquired to determine whether they wanted children or not was the recognition that they were accorded as the equals of men in work and pay. The Equal Opportunities Act of 1975 required that with certain exceptions vacant posts must be thrown open to either sex. Avoiding any specification of their marital status, women could call themselves 'Ms' instead of 'Mrs' or 'Miss'. The election in 1979 of Margaret Thatcher as Prime Minister was a unique triumph for her sex, though women had been Ministers of State before the last war. The Sex Disqualification Removal Act of 1919 had enabled women to become judges or enter such professions as accountancy and banking. Policewomen had become a familiar sight, and by the 1960s the working wife was quite usual, not only because she was able to increase the family income but because she valued her independence.

One way in which the egalitarian movement was most clearly demonstrated was in hairstyles and clothing. Previously the wearing of trousers had been a symbol of masculine superiority. By the sixties women were wearing trousers, and blouses were rechristened as shirts. Young men then began to wear their hair long and in the seventies the growing of beards became popular. The new fashions, though they might be characteristic of sexual equality, also had the advantage of being cheap. Trousers made of denim or 'jeans' were inexpensive; hair worn long needed only an occasional visit to a professional hairdresser, especially as 'perms' went out of fashion with the young. On the whole, in the 'permissive society' it was fashionable to be dowdy.

Another great equalizer was television. The British Broadcasting Corporation began putting out regular programmes in November 1936, but the service was suspended during the war. It was resumed soon afterwards and by 1951 commanded a million viewers. In 1954 the BBC's monopoly was broken and a rival organization, the Independent Television Authority, was set up to issue franchises to selected commercial companies, which paid for their programmes out of advertising; their licences proved so profitable that they were called licences to print money. By the sixties television programmes could be received everywhere. As the price of sets fell and sets could be hired by the payment of monthly fees, millions of people watched the rival offerings. At one stage the BBC programmes were generally regarded as being for 'them' while the commercial programmes were for 'us' and won larger audiences. However, when the BBC was allowed to start a second programme in 1964 a very direct competition developed between the independent companies and BBC 1: at times 60 per cent of the viewers favoured independent television; sometimes it was 50 per cent, and for a period in the late seventies the BBC went ahead. Since television was fabulously expensive to run the cost of television licences required by owners of sets, which had originally been £3 after the war, rose to £46 in 1981. The BBC felt it must prove its popularity so as to justify its claim to be given more licence money, naturally put forward during an era of galloping inflation

The programmes put out on three different channels became the subject of conversation almost as much as the weather. They made all men equal, just as Sir Robert Walpole is supposed to have justified his telling dirty stories because then anyone could join in the conversation. Did you see this or that was the question asked in clubs, shops and public houses. Thus television was an egalitarian and democratic institution. It was also educative. An 'Open University' was established which anyone could join and through which they could learn a variety of subjects from lectures and demonstrations given on BBC 2. But young people regarded television as a tyranny, because they found – since few families had more than one set – that it tied them too closely to the home circle. To get away from the old folks at home they preferred to go to the cinema or the public house. The film producers of the television age soon realized that the bulk of their audiences consisted of people between the ages of adolescence and marriage. Very few films induced the middle-aged to desert their television sets for an evening out. So the whole film industry, if not engaged in making films for television, had to adapt itself to a new and diminishing audience. 'Super cinemas', which had mushroomed during the inter-war period, disappeared and were replaced by small intimate theatres which gave their patrons only one film for their money.

The all-pervasiveness of television also transformed the Press. News was no longer of prime importance: no newspaper proprietor would have dreamt of bringing out a special edition on a Sunday to describe an air accident, as happened in the past, for television or radio could broadcast the story of any event of public interest hours before it could be recorded in print and distributed. So newspapers began to be filled with background stories, the lucubrations of columnists, interviews with public figures (often television stars), or investigations 'in depth'. This broadening of newspapers hit general magazines of the kind relished by middle-class Victorians, which, unless they were heavily subsidized, disappeared. Few newspapers made much of a profit. If they failed to appear because of strikes by their employees, they were barely missed. (When it was suggested to Winston Churchill in the spring of 1955 that he should postpone the announcement of his resignation as Prime Minister because a newspaper strike was in progress, he rejected the idea out of hand. Everyone learned about it from broadcasts.) Even investigations in depth could be found in television documentaries.

Gambling was one of the substitutes for cinema-going from which newspapers obtained a little help. Many local cinemas were converted into bingo halls and in 1981 popular newspapers ran bingo competitions to sustain their circulation. Football pools, which sometimes produced huge prizes, as well as betting on horse and greyhound races, offered opportunities for newspapers to publish statistics for the guidance of their readers or to print the opinions of tipsters. A Betting and Gaming Act, passed in 1960, the principal aim of which was said to be to 'enable innocent housewives to play whist for sixpence with their friends and no less innocent vicars to hold raffles and devote the proceeds to the restoration of their churches',[8] permitted the opening of betting shops all over the country, as well as casinos for the fleecing of the foolish rich. It was estimated that the turnover in betting and gambling of all sorts was about £300,000,000 a year. Although gambling had been popular enough before this, never did so many legal establishments exist to promote it. Even the government got into the act when in 1956 it started issuing premium bonds, which carried no interest but gave their holders the hope that they might win substantial prizes in monthly draws. If they bought enough of them they were more or less assured of some sort of prize one sunny day.

In the seventies many people thought – admittedly they thought this in every generation – that the quality of social life was deteriorating. Attacks on elderly men and women or 'muggings', frequent enough in New York or Washington, spread to London. Vandalism was increasingly commonplace. Burglaries were so usual, not only when high unemployment prevailed but also during the affluent fifties and sixties, that the police admitted that they could do little to prevent them or discover their perpetrators: this was equally true of vandalism. Yet among the young were many idealists. Voluntary service in developing countries was often undertaken by young married couples. Organizations like Oxfam and the Save the

Children Fund had no difficulty in finding young helpers. Blood sports and nuclear warfare establishments were targets for many demonstrators.

Above all, unemployment was the real curse of society during the seventies, as it had been in the thirties, though it was tempered now by a more generous system of social security. Here, however, was a paradox. While in some areas, like Wales or north-east England, unemployment affected most trades, in London and the south-east it was selective. There plumbers, electricians, gardeners and other skilled workers were in short supply. A large number of commercial agencies sprang up to profit from the scarcity of nurses, secretaries, typists and clerks. Even relatively attractive work, such as that offered by the BBC, was frequently done by secretaries hired through agencies.

In holiday times London Transport would announce that trains and buses had to be cancelled because of 'staff shortages'. If the question was asked why this was so, with hundreds of thousands unemployed, the answer was given that no one wanted to work 'unsocial hours', though many did. Also in London a vast amount of 'moonlighting' took place, that is to say, work done by men who had regular employment with relatively short hours and were anxious to add to their earnings by doing jobs in their spare time, both on weekdays and at week-ends. For such work they would normally be paid in cash and thus evaded taxes. The shorter hours worked, as compared with earlier times, also resulted in a lot of overtime being undertaken, not merely in an emergency but as a regular practice. According to the Ministry of Employment, the amount of overtime worked in Great Britain in the autumn of 1981 was equivalent to 880,000 full-time jobs.[9] In the capital middle-class people could earn bonuses or receive special London rates.

But it has to be recognized that bigger salaries and wages and the proceeds of higher taxes had been wisely invested, for example, in providing higher education at all levels: twenty-one new universities were founded in the nineteen-sixties and seventies, and over half a million students now received full-time education at schools and technical colleges. Furthermore the leisure created by shorter working hours has resulted in much part-time education, particularly that provided by the Open University and by books made available through public libraries. Whether we have aimed at too high a standard of life, which we cannot really afford, is a difficult question to answer. But if it is a fault, it can be argued it is a fault on the right side.

Whereas historians writing about a past they have never known can reach judicious conclusions that can, they believe, be fully substantiated by statistical evidence – though, since history is not an exact science, they do not always agree with one another – in contemplating what has happened during one's own brief time on earth, it is easy to be sunk in gloom and express moral disapprobation about the changes that are taking place. One can ask such questions as whether the institution of marriage is in peril, since one-third of present-day marriages end in divorce and one child in eight lives in a one-parent home. Will churches, lecture halls, theatres and cinemas become even emptier as more information is on tap from television and more entertainment from cassettes? Is there no solution to unemployment as microcomputers take over more and more of the work of calculation and mechanical processes, or can men and women derive benefits from the advance of technology so as to enjoy even greater leisure to pursue creative activities? In every age mankind looks back to a golden past; few trust in a golden future.

Looking back on the twentieth century and comparing it with the 2,500 years of our known history, one is wiser to count one's blessings and in analysing the social and economic life of our times reflect that what has changed has generally been for the better. Different people will select different events that have transformed modern society. Some may think that air travel has been the most revolutionary event. It is now easy to cross the world quickly and visit one's friends and relations wherever they may be or do first-hand business. This can or should kill narrow-mindedness. Others may plump for the cheap motor car, which has also broadened society, bringing town and country closer together. Then there is always television, the unforgettable discovery of the mid twentieth century, although no one agrees about the depth of its influence. Has it indeed stimulated violence and crime? Or has it enlivened people's minds by bringing into their homes a fuller realization of the problems of society, as well as of the triumphs of literature and art? The ever increasing number of new book titles published every year suggests that television has not killed reading.

To one historian it seems that the outstanding social fact of his lifetime is the advance in medicine. One can of course be cynical about this. Is society burdened with too many geriatrics who would not exist had it not been for medical discoveries? Today about one-eighth of the population is over the age of sixty-five. Pneumonia, once the old man's friend, can now generally be overcome with antibiotics. Tuberculosis, which was still regarded as a nearly fatal disease in the nineteen-thirties, can be dealt with so efficiently that the hospitals exclusively devoted to its treatment have been closed down. Deaths from typhoid and diphtheria have fallen enormously because of immunization, vaccination, better sanitation and new drugs. Diseases as varied as pernicious anaemia and malaria can be effectively treated. Certain kinds of cancer and deafness are now curable. One is as likely to be killed in a motor accident as to die of a specific illness. Moreover, less alcohol is consumed than in the prosperous days of Queen Victoria and King Edward VII.[10] Campaigns against cigarette smoking have made their impact. 'The advances of medicine', says a distinguished authority, 'have affected general practice more than hospital practice',[11] so that a visit to a doctor's surgery is often the pathway to a happier life. Only mental diseases appear to have increased in modern times. No one can gauge how successful psychiatry has become or whether enough mental hospitals exist. Otherwise medicine has helped to transform English society out of all recognition as compared with the position, say a mere 250 years ago, when 'hacking coughs, violent fevers, bloody remedies and desperate deaths' afflicted all mankind and made life not a measured course but a terrible gamble.

Notes

1 In 1936 a plan had been prepared to evacuate half the population of London if war came. Martin Gilbert, *Winston S. Churchill*, IV (1976), p. 777

2 The author went to a recruiting office near the War Office early in May 1940 and was told there were no vacancies in the army except for clerks. When later he enlisted in the Grenadier Guards, in which vacancies had occurred in France, he found that the rest of the squad had joined because they were out of work. When Anthony Eden, Secretary of State for War, made a patriotic appeal on the radio, they could not be bothered to listen

3 Winston Churchill, *World War II* (1949), p. 503

4 This was stated by the Chairman of the Cotton Board set up under the Cotton Industry Act of 1959. *Annual Register* (1960), p. 521

5 Sir Alec Cairncross, 'The post-war years 1945-1977', in *The Economic History of Britain since 1700*, II, R.C. Floud and D.N. McCloskey (eds) (1981), p. 376

6 James Morris, *Farewell the Trumpets* (1978), p. 405

7 A. Bottomley and Sir George Sinclair, *Control of Commonwealth Immigration* (1970)

8 Bernard Levin, *The Pendulum Years* (1970), p. 13
9 The *Observer*, 8 November 1981
10 Many fewer on-licences are taken out and fewer convictions for drunkenness per head of population are recorded than during those reigns
11 Sir George Godber, *Medical Care: the Changing Needs and Pattern* (1970)

ELEVEN

Conclusions

Looking back on the economic history of England, the first impression that strikes one is how changes in the size of the population have influenced national welfare. Before the number of people living and working in England began to mount rapidly in the nineteenth and twentieth centuries, an essay on the principle of population was published in which it was argued that the growth of population was necessarily limited by the means of subsistence; and since historically the constant trend was for the number of people to increase before the amount of food needed to sustain it did so, the standard of living for the bulk of the population had been and always must be on a mere subsistence level. For if the means of subsistence increased, it stimulated the birth of more children and thus the minimum subsistence level was re-established. The book in which this theory was put forward was anonymous, since it was in fact written by a clergyman, the Reverend T. Robert Malthus, and the publishers feared that the public would be shocked if it discovered that a scholar in holy orders was pontificating on such a theme. The world, it was explained humorously in a novel written by Thomas Love Peacock, was 'overstocked with feather-less bipeds' and the only way this could be checked was by vice or misery or 'moral restraint'.

Malthus's arguments are not so easily dismissed today as they were when the population of England rose dramatically after his death in 1834, since in countries like India and Sri Lanka, where birth control is little practised and mortality rates have declined, immense poverty is to be found. Moreover, the history of England tends to show that its people as a whole were better off when the population was falling, at least before industrialization. It is true that a fertile soil and a temperate climate promoted the output of food, while the possession of minerals like coal, metals like tin and an ample pasturage for sheep has always made a reasonable standard of subsistence possible.

Caesar, as has been noted, thought the population 'exceedingly large' and the ground 'thickly covered with homesteads'. Modern archaeological research has confirmed Caesar's opinion and a population as high as five or six million has been considered likely during the Roman occupation. Massive settlements have been detected by air photography. Yet it was after the Romans evacuated and the size of the population fell owing to the ravages of barbarian invaders, plagues and some emigration across the Channel that Gildas could write of the country as abounding 'with such plenty of grain as no previous age remembered'; a modern historian has observed that the collapse of the Roman government in Britain 'made possible an economic exploitation of our natural resources on a scale never attempted in prehistoric or Roman times'.[1]

Again, after the Anglo-Saxon and Danish invasions, the butchery of natives and internecine warfare, the Father of English history, the Venerable Bede, could write in the eighth century of 'the peace and prosperity that prevailed'. No medieval historian has ventured to put the size of the population of England at more than two and a half million when the Normans thought it worth their while to take over this affluent land. Indeed, one expert on the period has claimed that 'the primitive means of exploiting natural resources prevented the population from rising much above a million'.[2] By the end of the thirteenth century, however, the population had doubled or trebled, and it was then that the condition of the peasantry worsened, real wages fell, poverty and distress were widespread and the villages were so full of people that some of them starved.[3] But after the Black Death, when the population declined from some four million to two and a half million, the mass of the people enjoyed a golden age which lasted through much of the fifteenth century.

The latest estimate of the size of the population of England when Queen Elizabeth I came to the throne in 1558 is about three million, but after that it exploded, particularly among the gentry and yeomanry. It is now generally accepted that the growing imbalance between the size of the population and that of agricultural output offers the most satisfactory explanation of the inflation of that age. During the sixteenth century the population is thought to have increased at the rate of almost 1 per cent a year, and the value of real wages fell drastically. By the time the civil wars began in 1642 the population of England had again reached five million, and afterwards prices rose to the highest level recorded in the seventeenth century.[4] After the restoration of Charles II to the throne in 1660 the population declined, prices fell and real wages improved. By 1701 the population was still only about five million (or just under six million including Wales), but with the industrialization of the country in the second half of the eighteenth century it shot up to over nine million and continued to rise fast in the nineteenth and twentieth centuries. By 1931 the population of England and Wales was nearly forty million; fifty years later it stood at over forty-nine million. In each case it included two to three million unemployed.

The claim has been made that on the whole Malthus's correlation between the growth of population and the rise in prices of food can be proved statistically up to the time he was writing.[5] In the Middle Ages, when England was predominantly an agricultural country, the cost of living remained pretty steady except in years when harvests were poor; but in early modern England rising prices were the rule. It was not until the nineteenth century that prices fell when the population rose: this was the biggest economic and social revolution in English history until modern times. Without the increase in the size of the population before and after the Napoleonic wars the new industrial technology, which gave England a head start or what has been called a rapid take-off, would have been retarded. Nevertheless between 1754 and 1954 prices multiplied six times and between 1956 and 1976 prices trebled. By then the value to the consumer was about one-fifth of what it had been at the close of the 1939-45 war. The idea that economic stability is the characteristic of long periods of English history is completely mistaken, especially since industrialization. Trade cycles can be shown to have taken place every seven or ten years.[6] To the modern economic historian it looks as if price inflation is the normal lot of mankind.

Because it is essential today to export manufactured goods to pay for half our food and much of our raw materials, economic historians have been inclined to lay too much stress on the importance of foreign trade to the national economy in earlier times. More than 200 years ago Adam Smith wrote: 'that foreign trade enriched the country experience demonstrated to the noble and country gentlemen as well as to the merchants; but how, or in what manner, none of them well knew'. In 1981 a distinguished British economist could write: 'The link between exports and [economic] growth is not self-evident.'[7]

In fact through much of known economic history English exports consisted predominantly of wool. This largely paid for luxury imports like wines and silks, not for grain or raw materials, which, when a surplus was available, were exported. It was not until the fifteenth century that cloth replaced wool as England's principal export, and then at least half of the export trade was handled by foreigners. During the reign of Elizabeth I four-fifths of English exports consisted of cloth. At the opening of the seventeenth century the total value of English exports was only one million pounds.

The beginnings of a more varied export trade are recorded in the second half of the seventeenth century and are associated with the development of the first British Empire, such as the colonization of Virginia and Maryland and the conquest of Jamaica. Tobacco and sugar were valuable re-exports; so were slaves. Nevertheless, it has been estimated that at the end of that century exports only represented 10 per cent of the gross national product and that the bulk of manufactured goods were destined for the home market. The value in sterling of re-exports continued to grow fast until the middle of the eighteenth century. Commerce was interrupted by the American War of Independence, but because of England's island position, its large fleet and its command of the sea foreign trade as a whole did not decline. However, it was only in the middle of the nineteenth century that the speedy growth in the export of cotton textiles, outstripping woollen textiles, particularly to Europe and the United States of America, plus 'invisible exports' promoted a favourable balance of payments and substantial investments abroad.

The peak of British success as an exporter was reached in the period between 1850 and 1875, when British exports amounted to about a fifth of all international trade; this accounted for the marvellous air of prosperity in mid Victorian England, but the population was increasing fast and long hours were being worked. After that exports grew more slowly, but this was offset by improvements in the terms of trade, that is to say, the price of imported food and raw materials fell. When the first census of production was taken in 1907 it was estimated that one-quarter of the goods produced in the United Kingdom were for export and one-fifth of the goods at home came from imports, which revealed how much the country then depended on foreign trade. In 1913 exports constituted nearly one-fifth of the net total income, but by 1929 they fell to 17 per cent and by 1938 to 9.8 per cent. After the temporary spurt in exports following the war of 1939–45 they became sluggish.

Balance of payments difficulties induced governments to pursue stop-go policies so as to cut down excessive demand at home, to which these difficulties were attributed. But the conclusion could be reached, as Sir Alec Cairncross has observed, that exports had been held back by the same

203

forces and to roughly the same extent as output itself, in other words by the failure of the English people as a whole to increase their industrial productivity. Thus in recent years in practically every branch of the economy, from the coal mines to the railways, managements have insisted that wage increases should be linked to productivity. Export drives are only necessary if it is essential to enlarge the volume of imports, particularly of consumption goods. Arguably the standard of living of the people of England could be improved by manufacturing more goods for domestic consumption and fewer for export.

The people of England have been fortunate in their natural resources, such as coal and North Sea oil, and in the skills of their inventors. Only in war time have they needed to respond to challenges, as the Dutch did in the sixteenth and seventeenth centuries and as the Japanese and Germans did after defeat in the twentieth century. Some foreign visitors in the pre-industrial age inclined to the opinion that the English were a lazy people. When the Tudors reigned an Italian declared that 'the farmers are so lazy and slow that they do not bother to sow more wheat than is necessary for their own consumption', and Polydore Vergil, who lived in England for a long time, wrote that 'men do not over-exert themselves and live to a great age'. As has already been observed, an English pamphleteer writing in 1675 said: 'it is our own negligence and idleness that brings poverty upon us'. That such lack of enterprise continued in the industrial era was suggested by the Macmillan report of 1931 on finance and industry, which noted: 'the feeling is that the former easy-going ways will no longer ensure our prosperity in a crowded and increasingly capitalist world'.

It is true that exports fell off between 1919 and 1939 as compared with the increase earlier, but output per man hour was higher and compared favourably with that of other countries, at any rate after the 'great depression'. But following the war of 1939-45 industrial growth 'was less dramatic than in other industrial countries'.[8] It has been suggested that because productivity was relatively high when a three-day week was established during the coal strike of 1973, it should have been higher during a five-day week. But equally the thesis has been put forward that British governments demanded too high a rate of growth in the post-war years. In fact modern research does not substantiate the belief that the English are a lazy and idle people, resistant to inventions and incapable of making discoveries. Nevertheless, economic change is usually troublesome.

Even before industrialization, enclosures understandably dismayed farmers and contributed to riots and revolts. The earliest large English export industry, woollen cloth, was disrupted by opposition first to the introduction of fulling mills, then to gig mills, described as 'a nefarious means of stretching cloth', and finally in the eighteenth century to power looms. The invention towards the end of the sixteenth century of a knitting frame, which made the output of silk and worsted stockings much faster and cheaper than hand knitting, provoked resistance, and for various reasons the smashing of hosiery frames continued into the eighteenth century. In general the transformation of the domestic system of industry into the factory system was a painful process.

In the twentieth century we have seen the prolonged resistance of print workers to photographic typesetting, computerization and other labour-saving devices, with the result that newspaper offices have been grossly overmanned and some newspapers forced to close. This has been contrasted with the attitude of trade unions in the United States of America, which have welcomed reduced hours and higher wages rather than clinging to outmoded industrial methods. The Luddites, who started breaking up machinery during the Napoleonic wars, were by no means unique. 'The protest against the power of machinery over man', noted a Russian journalist who worked in England for five years as correspondent of *Pravda*, 'so naïvely expressed by the Luddites in their day is typical of their fellow countrymen even now.'[9] They had precedents in the past and imitators in the future. Their indignation should be treated sympathetically.

The Luddites and their predecessors smashed up machinery or pulled down fences because they feared their livelihoods were being taken from them. At the same time an enduring habit among the people of England has been to gaze back wistfully to a golden past. Gildas, the Welsh historian, looked back 'with bitter nostalgia to the vanished glories of the civilized past'.[10] The first great Anglo-Saxon historian, Bede, admired the Romans and wrote of an age when 'everywhere the Faith advanced victoriously, the shrines of the martyrs were built and endowed, the festivals of the Church were observed ... and the Church in Britain remained in peace'. Nineteenth-century historians like Bishop William Stubbs were endeared to an Anglo-Saxon society in which, they believed, egalitarianism existed. The two brilliant Roman Catholic authors Hilaire Belloc and G.K. Chesterton pictured a merry England in the Middle Ages before Henry VIII established the Church of England and destroyed the monasteries. Earlier Carlyle and Ruskin had also regarded the Middle Ages as a more congenial era than that of Victorian industrialism, which they disliked, and pictured a past with jovial yokels sporting on village greens.

In the early twentieth century, however, the Victorian age, if not admired for its arts, was thought of as a prosperous and happy time when family life was a contented reality and so was the British Empire. On 19 January 1909 *The Times* wrote of contemporaries: 'They place the golden age behind them, and assume that no generation ever had to deal with evils so great and perplexing as those of the present day.' After the Second World War the old and the middle-aged sighed for the grand old days of the middle classes, when food was cheap, shopkeepers were deferential and servants could be found who were prepared to live in. In the early nineteen-eighties the people of England for the most part have been thinking with nostalgia of the early seventies, when they rejoiced in full employment, high real wages, and inexpensive petrol. They also appear to have longed to return to the times when England was above all rural. Between 1971 and 1981 the population of rural areas rose by over a million and that of inner cities declined.

Of course exceptions can be discovered to the propensity to yearn for the past: Charles Dickens had few illusions about it, while Sir Robert Peel's 'first lieutenant', Sir John Graham, said bluntly: 'the lot of eating, drinking, working and dying must ever be the sum of life among the masses of the human family'. Only a few authors of genius, such as George Bernard Shaw (and he was an Irishman), have looked forward with any conviction to halcyon days in the future. The socialist and communist millennia which young men and women hoped for fifty years ago are still a long way off. By and large, it is remarkable how often the people of England have regretted a golden past and how seldom they have dreamt of a golden future. That explains the popularity of history books.

Most history books are written by members of an educated middle class, but in surveying the course of English social history it needs to be remembered that no such class existed until fairly recent times. Nor did the lower middle class of clerks, commercial travellers, small shopkeepers, managers of public houses and minor Civil Servants and the like, a class that surfaced during the eighteenth century and is now largely disappearing.

In the early Middle Ages society consisted of the baronage, their retainers and the mass of common people, peasants and labourers. During the later Middle Ages the gentry rose and made their presence felt in the House of

Commons, as did also such members of the professional classes as lawyers, merchants and later soldiers and sailors. By the Tudor age society was becoming more fluid. Writing in 1565 Sir Thomas Smith divided the community into monarchy, aristocracy, gentry, yeomen and the common people (*proletarii*), who 'had no voice or authority in the Commonwealth', while William Harrison, writing in 1587, observed: 'we divide the people of England commonly into four sorts, as gentlemen, citizens or burgesses, yeomen and artificers'. Until the eighteenth century the country continued to be dominated by the aristocracy, a few hundred wealthy landlords with huge estates and palatial mansions. The taxation levied during the wars against France damaged the squires and country gentlemen, but most of the great landowners survived.

As late as the reign of Queen Victoria the majority of the Cabinet were peers: even William Gladstone's first Cabinet contained seven out of a total of fifteen, and in the eighteen-nineties two successive Prime Ministers were noblemen. More prestige was attached to birth than to wealth. Then at last the old landed aristocracy began to crumble: it abdicated its authority and sold much of its land after the First World War. The foundations of English society, so long shouldered by this class, finally collapsed during the depression of 1929–32. Death duties (first introduced in 1889) had helped to spell their doom and they had to manage by gradually selling off their heirlooms, including great paintings and historic manuscripts. One has only to look round London and note how the great houses in which they used to reside have been replaced by office blocks or converted into museums.

That the middle classes expanded during the twentieth century is plain enough, but to define them with any degree of precision remains difficult. One estimate, based on the census of 1961, puts 32 per cent of the population into the upper, middle and lower middle class and 60 per cent into the skilled, semi-skilled and unskilled 'working class',[11] some ten million of whom were members of trade unions. Bringing up the rear, as always, were the old-age pensioners. The upper middle class can be said to consist mainly of professional people, such as chartered accountants and surveyors, barristers and solicitors, doctors, stockbrokers, high-grade Civil Servants and well-to-do farmers. But when one comes to the lower middle classes or 'white-collar workers', as they are sometimes called, it is hard to distinguish them from the skilled wage-earning class. It has been estimated that in 1970 the 'white collar workers' numbered nine million as compared with fourteen million manual workers.

Since striking for higher pay has permeated all classes – before the last war no one would have believed that Civil Servants would go on strike, as they did in 1981 – so one obvious class distinction has vanished. Nor do salaries necessarily mean higher earnings than wages. For example, printers often earn more than journalists, and scene-shifters than actors. Class consciousness has become a largely outmoded exercise. The raising of the school leaving age to sixteen in 1972, the increase in the number of universities and technical colleges in recent times and the popularity of the social sciences have all contributed to the number of educated people who interpret history in terms of class, leaving great men and women outside it: Marxist history has become extremely respectable, but it is a minority belief in England.

In fact it can be contended with equal conviction that it is interests rather than classes that determined the nature of English society. People talk about health, money and the weather, but what animates conversation is when common interests are found and discussed. Now that education is free and open to all, the hard-working and the ambitious no longer need to be self-taught to succeed in life: careers are open to talents.

In the twentieth century what has emerged is an Establishment that can be entered by merit. The 'ruling class' is not necessarily to be discovered in the two Houses of Parliament. Cabinets generally take their decisions for political reasons, but the decisions that are, or should be, reached impartially for what is thought to be the general good are made by Treasury knights, permanent secretaries, chairmen of nationalized industries, secretaries of big trade unions, editors of serious newspapers, directors-general of the British Broadcasting Corporation and the Independent Broadcasting Authority, the heads of other institutions like the National Trust or the Arts Council, and of course the secretary-general of the Trades Union Congress and the director-general of the Confederation of British Industry. For good measure one could throw in the Masters of Balliol College, Oxford and Trinity College, Cambridge. A typical Establishment figure at the time of writing is the general secretary of the National Association of Local Government Officers, who is also a member of the National Economic Council, a director of the Bank of England, a magistrate and a member of the TUC's so-called 'inner cabinet'. It is true that men and women in key positions often deny that they belong to the Establishment, but the fact remains that they shape the character of democratic society.

Social history, it has been said, satisfies the desire of people to escape into another world, not our own.[12] But it can also help us to analyse our own society and recognize how it has evolved. The people of England were once at the mercy of tribal chieftains; now they have different masters.

Notes

1 J.N.L. Myres, *Roman Britain and the Settlement of England* (1937), p. 325

2 Frank Barlow, *The Feudal Kingdom of England 1042–1216* (1974), p. 4

3 Edward Miller, 'The English Economy in the Thirteenth Century', *Past and Present*, 28 (1964); Ian Kershaw, 'The Great Famines and Agrarian Crisis in England 1315–1322', ibid., 59 (1973); M. Postan, *The Cambridge Economic History of Europe* I (1966), p. 566; M. Postan, *The Medieval Economy and Society* (1973), p. 228

4 According to the composite index in the tables compiled by Sir Henry Phelps Brown and Sheila Hopkins, the figure for 1629 when Charles I dissolved Parliament was 510; in 1642, when the civil wars began, it was 557; when Charles was beheaded in 1649 it was 770, and in 1651 during the third civil war it was 839.

5 E.A. Wrigley, *The Population History of England 1541–1871* (1981), pp. 402–3. Other population figures quoted are from this book, which is based on parish registers; they do not include Wales. See also J.D. Chambers, *Population, Economy and Society* (1972), p. 23 seq.

6 A.G. Ford, 'The trade cycle in Britain 1860–1914', in *The Economic History of Britain since 1700*, R.C. Floud and D.N. McCloskey (eds) (1981), pp. 27–30

7 Sir Alec Cairncross, ibid., p. 388

8 ibid., p. 375

9 V.V. Ovchinnikov, *Britain Observed* (1981), pp. 39–40

10 J.N.L. Myres, *Anglo-Saxon Pottery and the Settlement of England* (1969), p. 101

11 These estimates were made by Mark Abraham and published in D.C.Marsh, *The Changing Structure of England and Wales* (1965)

12 J.H. Plumb (ed.), *Studies in Social History* (1955), p. xiii

Index